The Value of Innovation

Scrivener Publishing
100 Cummings Center, Suite 541J
Beverly, MA 01915-6106

Publishers at Scrivener
Martin Scrivener (martin@scrivenerpublishing.com)
Phillip Carmical (pcarmical@scrivenerpublishing.com)

The Value of Innovation

Knowing, Proving, and Showing the Value of Innovation and Creativity

A Step By Step Guide to Impact and ROI Measurement

Jack J. Phillips and Patricia Pulliam Phillips

Scrivener
Publishing

This edition first published 2018 by John Wiley & Sons, Inc., 111 River Street, Hoboken, NJ 07030, USA and Scrivener Publishing LLC, 100 Cummings Center, Suite 541J, Beverly, MA 01915, USA
© 2018 Scrivener Publishing LLC
For more information about Scrivener publications please visit www.scrivenerpublishing.com.

Wiley Global Headquarters

111 River Street, Hoboken, NJ 07030, USA

For details of our global editorial offices, customer services, and more information about Wiley products visit us at www.wiley.com.

Limit of Liability/Disclaimer of Warranty

Library of Congress Cataloging-in-Publication Data
ISBN 9781-119-24237-6

Cover image: ID 96765469 © Andrew Derr | Dreamstime.com
Cover design by Kris Hackerott

Set in size of 11pt and Minion Pro by Exeter Premedia Services Private Ltd., Chennai, India

10 9 8 7 6 5 4 3 2 1

Contents

Preface

Innovation is everywhere, in every direction we look, in every type of organization, and in almost every part of the world. Leaders are obsessed with innovation, politicians cheer innovation and desire more of it, consumers demand innovation, investors reward innovation, and media coverage of innovation is relentless.

This visibility and popularity translates into billions of dollars being pumped into all types of innovation efforts. Visibility brings out the critics who expose glitches and concerns. Lack of success and high failure rates bring out even more critics. All of this creates the need to show more results.

Innovation Meets the ROI Methodology

For almost two decades, we have had individuals involved in innovation attend an ROI Certification program which involves a week of comprehensive learning. In this process, the participants enter the program with a project in mind that they would like to evaluate at the impact and ROI level. They learn how to do conduct an ROI evaluation in this process, and they pursue the work with virtual support until they complete their project. At the end of this process, the participants obtain the designation of Certified ROI Professional (CRP). With some prompting from our international partners about ten years ago, we hosted a dedicated group of individuals who were just involved in innovation, and had them pursue the certification. We conducted sessions in Copenhagen, Denmark, and Istanbul, Turkey. In these two situations, the results were amazing. The participants tackled all types of innovation projects, followed through to measure the success of their projects along the way, and developed amazing confidence to use this tool. Interest continued and we began to conduct studies globally with companies, governments, NGOs, nonprofits, and universities. As we continued to work, applying this process to innovation, we knew there was a need and a market.

The Need for This Book

When we write a book, we make sure there is not a current book already meeting the need. Writing a book that has already been written is not good for the publisher, and it's not good for us. As we examined potential competing books, we saw nothing that matched the approach and credibility of the ROI Methodology. We have a process that has become the most-used evaluation system in the world. It is built around three pillars: 1) It is user-friendly, not overly complicated or complex; 2) It is based on sound principles, using an enhanced logic model, and is very reliable and valid from a research perspective; 3) Finally, it is CEO- and CFO-friendly, producing data that passes the scrutiny of the CFO and provides data that top executives can support.

This book uses a results-based approach to innovation implementation, focusing on a variety of measures that are categorized into six data types:

- Reaction and Perceived Value of Innovation
- Learning and Confidence to Know How to Make Innovation Work
- Application and Implementation to Make Innovation Work
- Impact, the Consequences of the Innovation
- Return on Investment in the Innovation Project
- Intangibles Linked to the Innovation Project

Connected to it is a step-by-step process for identifying, collecting, analyzing, and reporting all six types of data in a consistent manner that leads to credible results.

Credibility is Key

The Value of Innovation focuses on building a credible process—one that will generate a balanced set of data that are believable, realistic, and accurate, particularly from the viewpoint of sponsors and key stakeholders. More specifically, the methodology presented in this book approaches credibility head-on through the use of

- Balanced categories of data
- A logical, systematic process
- Guiding principles, a conservative set of standards
- A proven methodology based on thousands of users
- An emphasis on implementing the methodology within an organization to ensure that the process is sustained

- A procedure accepted by sponsors, clients, and others who fund projects

The book explores the challenges of measuring the hard-to-measure and placing monetary values on the hard-to-value. It is a reference that clarifies much of the mystery surrounding the allocation of monetary values. Building on a tremendous amount of experience, application, practice, and research, the book draws on the work of many individuals and organizations, particularly those who have attained the ultimate levels of accountability using the ROI methodology. Developed in an easy-to-read format and fortified with examples and tips, this is an indispensable guide for audiences who seek to understand more about bottom-line accountability.

Audience

The primary audience for this book are the managers of innovation projects in an organization. These managers are concerned with the valuation of innovation projects, programs, processes, and people. Although they are strongly committed to their projects, they need to see value in terms executives can appreciate and understand—money.

This book is also intended for professionals, analysts, and practitioners who are responsible for implementing and evaluating the success of innovation projects. The book shows how the various types of data are collected, processed, analyzed, and reported.

Another audience includes consultants, researchers, and professors who are dedicated to unraveling the value mystery, trying to understand more about the difficult and demanding challenges of developing measures and values for a variety of innovation programs.

Types of Innovation Projects

The good news is the ROI Methodology will show the value of all types of projects, including the ten types of innovation as outlined by Keeley.[1] In his beautifully illustrated book, the ten types of innovation are projects that:

1. Are designed to make money
2. Connect with others to create value
3. Organize and align talent and assets
4. Are signature or superior methods to do work
5. Develop distinguishing features and personality

6. Create complementary products and services
7. Support and amplify the value of your offerings
8. Deliver your offerings to customers and users
9. Represent your offerings and businesses
10. Foster compelling interactions

Regardless of what type of innovation, whether it is internal, working with employees, an R&D Center where new products are developed, or the breakthrough innovation that is the basis of the company, this methodology will show how to know, prove, and show the value of innovation.

Flow of the Book

The Value of Innovation flows through three sections. The first section, involving three chapters, sets the stage for the book by reviewing the importance of innovation along with some of the major challenges in the field in the first chapter. Then, the current metrics involved in innovation and the shortcomings in those areas are discussed in the second chapter. Finally, chapter three outlines the necessary requirements for a measurement system for innovation, and introduces the ROI Methodology, which meets those requirements.

This sets the stage for the second section, the major part of the book, built around the ROI Methodology. This section involves thirteen chapters, detailing all parts of the process with examples, scenarios, and stories. Finally, the last chapter focuses on how to make this process work routinely and sustain it over a long period of time.

We are convinced that you will find this a valuable book. If not, we will be happy to refund your money. If you purchase this book and it doesn't add value to your innovation efforts, please drop us a note. Keep the book, and we will send you a refund. We have confidence in this book. We know this methodology has helped many others, and it will help you with your evaluation of innovation. Please enjoy.

Jack J. Phillips, Ph.D.
Patti P. Phillips, Ph.D.
Birmingham, AL - November 2017

Reference

1. Keely, Larry, Ryan Pikkel, Brian Quinn, and Helen Walters. *Ten Types of Innovation: The Discipline of Building Breakthroughs*. Hoboken, NJ: Wiley, 2013.

Acknowledgements

This book had its beginnings over a decade ago when we conducted our five-day ROI Certification workshop for two groups, one in Copenhagen and the other in Istanbul. The participants in both groups were individuals involved with innovation projects, and they wanted to show the return on investment for those projects. They used the ROI Methodology and completed their projects to obtain the designation of Certified ROI Professional (CRP). From that point, we worked with hundreds of other organizations in innovation, including nonprofits, NGOs, and governments. This work clearly revealed that this methodology applies extremely well in the innovation and creativity space. We owe a debt of gratitude to those early adopters of this process in our work with innovation, spanning all continents.

We want to thank our editor and publisher, Phil Carmical for his patience with the delivery of this book. We've worked with Phil for many years, and we are pleased to deliver another book to him at Scrivener, a Wiley Imprint. We also want to thank Hope Nicholas, director of publications at ROI Institute. Hope manages our publications and editorial projects and has done a marvelous job with this book in the midst of hectic schedules, numerous deadlines, and countless interruptions. Thank you, Hope, for another great job. We also want to thank Kylie McLeod, our Communications Coordinator, for putting the finishing touches on the book. Thanks Kylie for a job well done.

Jack would like to thank Patti. Patti is an outstanding consultant, top-notch facilitator, meticulous researcher, and above all, an outstanding writer. She makes our books and our work much more effective and enjoyable. Her books win awards, and her workshops have the highest rating. More important, she is an enthusiastic, creative, and lovely spouse.

Patti would like to thank Jack for putting ROI on the map in terms of its applicability to noncapital investments. Jack laid the foundation on which so many others have built their measurement, evaluation, and analytics practices. Over the years, he has given much more than he has received – and for that, we are all thankful!

About the Authors

Jack J. Phillips, PhD, is a world-renowned expert on accountability, measurement and evaluation, and chairman of ROI Institute. Through the Institute, Phillips provides consulting services for *Fortune* 500 companies and workshops for major conference providers throughout the world. Phillips is also the author or editor of more than 100 books and more than 300 articles.

His expertise in measurement and evaluation is based on more than 27 years of corporate experience in five industries (aerospace, textiles, metals, construction materials, and banking). Phillips has served as training and development manager at two *Fortune* 500 firms, senior HR officer at two firms, as president of a regional federal savings bank, and management professor at a major state university.

Jack has received several awards for his books and work. On three occasions, Meeting News named him one of the 25 Most Powerful People in the Meetings and Events Industry, based on his work on ROI. The Society for Human Resource Management presented him an award for one of his books and honored a Phillips ROI study with its highest award for creativity. The Association for Talent Development gave him its highest award, Distinguished Contribution to Workplace Learning and Development for his work on ROI. His work has been featured in the

Wall Street Journal, BusinessWeek, and *Fortune* magazine. He has been interviewed by several television programs, including CNN. Jack served as President of the International Society for Performance Improvement for 2012–2013. In 2017, Jack received the Brand Personality Award from Asia Pacific Brands Foundation for his work as an international consultant, author, teacher, and speaker.

Jack has undergraduate degrees in electrical engineering, physics, and mathematics; a master's degree in decision sciences from Georgia State University; and a PhD in human resource management from the University of Alabama. He has served on the boards of several private businesses – including two NASDAQ companies – and several nonprofits and associations, including the Association for Talent Development and the National Management Association. He is chairman of ROI Institute, Inc., and can be reached at (205) 678-8101, or by e-mail at jack@roiinstitute.net.

Patti P. Phillips, PhD is president and CEO of ROI Institute, Inc., the leading source of ROI competency building, implementation support, networking, and research. She helps organizations implement the ROI Methodology in over 60 countries. Patti serves as chair of the People Analytics Board at the Institute for Corporate Productivity, Principal Research Fellow for The Conference Board, board chair of the Center for Talent Reporting, and ATD CPLP Certification Institute Fellow. Patti also serves as faculty on the UN System Staff College in Turin, Italy, the Escuela Bancaria y Comercia in Mexico City, Mexico, and The University of Southern Mississippi's PhD in Human Capital Development program. Her work has been featured on CNBC, EuroNews, and over a dozen business journals.

Patti's academic background includes a B.S. in Education from Auburn University, a Masters in Public and Private Management from Birmingham-Southern College, and PhD in International Development from The University of Southern Mississippi.

She facilitates workshops, speaks at conferences, and consults with organizations worldwide. Patti is author, coauthor, or editor of over 75 books and dozens of articles on the topic of measurement, evaluation, and ROI. Patti can be reached at patti@roiinstitute.net.

1

The Importance and Challenges of Innovation

Clifton Leaf, editor-in-chief of *Fortune* magazine borrowed a stranger's silver and orange bicycle and rode it two kilometers. When he was finished riding, he leaned the bike against a street lamp at a city intersection. Clifton was benefiting from the remarkable business model of Mobike, a Beijing-based start-up whose more than 100 million registered users do much the same thing an average of 20 times a day. This is more than three times the rate of use by other types of ride-share bikes. Many cities have bike-sharing where users typically pay to release the bike from a docking station and return it to another docking station within a particular timeframe. Mobike has eliminated the cumbersome docking process entirely. A user downloads an app, finds a bike nearby, and scans a QR code to unlock it. After using the bike, the user drops off the bike wherever they would like, because GPS and other wireless technologies are built into the bike's chassis, allowing the company to track its whereabouts. A smart-locking system bolts the rear tire in place until the next user shows up [1].

The old dock-based sharing systems are like the first-generation PCs. According to Davis Wang, CEO and co-founder of Mobike, while first-generation PCs were attached to desktops, Mobikes, in contrast, are like smartphones—you can take them anywhere you would like. Today, Mobike has more users than Uber, although it has been in business only two years. While few consumers outside of China have likely even heard of this ride-sharing business, the company has already expanded to Singapore, the United Kingdom, and the United States.

Innovation Hype

Innovation is everywhere and is constantly being brought to our attention. In the media, stories, ads, interviews, chats, blogs, and references dominate. It's hard to read articles, stories, or see advertisements without the term innovation being mentioned. Everything we see is innovation and everything that is developed is innovative. We even have innovative leaders now.

Articles

Innovation articles are everywhere, dominating the print space. *Fast Company* magazine, which has been a driving force for promoting innovation, devotes a good portion of its magazine to the subject of innovation, as do other major publications such as *Harvard Business Review, Wall Street Journal, Bloomberg Businessweek* and *Forbes,* among others. There is even a *Chief Innovation Officer Magazine* dedicated to those who are leading this effort.

Books

Innovation books now dominate the business book scene. A few years back, that wasn't the case. Famed management guru Peter Drucker wrote one of the earliest books on innovation in 1985 when he authored *Innovation and Entrepreneurship: Practice and Principles.*[2] Tom Peters, legendary best-selling business book author, is another successful innovation author who jumped into the arena with his book, *The Circle of Innovation: You Can't Shrink Your Way to Greatness.* This book put innovation on the map for many readers and business people, as he complained that not enough space had been devoted to this important area. Perhaps the person who has contributed the most is Tom Kelley, a partner in IDEO, one of the world's leading innovation and design firms, who contributed *The Art of Innovation, The Ten Faces of Innovation,* and *Creative Confidence,* the latter co-authored with David Kelley. The person who has contributed the most about disruption from innovation is Clayton M. Christensen. His classic book, *The Innovators Dillema: When New Technologies Cause Great Firms to Fail*, showed not only the power of innovation but also the many outcomes of the innovation process. Even Google founder Eric Schmidt got into the innovation fray with his book, *How Google Works*. CEOs have also popped into the arena with books ranging from Phil Knight (CEO of Nike), author of *Shoe Dog*, to Steve Case (former CEO of AOL Time Warner), who wrote *The Innovation Blind Spot* and *The Third Wave*. Clearly, the subject of innovation is now one of the most documented and written about areas in the business book market. For example, at Stanford University Press, in the business book category, six of the 23 titles for 2017 were in the innovation area. Amazon now has over 100 pages of books in the innovation category.

Jobs

Job titles have emerged for those responsible for innovation as the responsibility is shifting to one or more individuals. The title of Chief Innovation Officer, VP of Innovation, Director of Business Innovation, and Chief Innovation and Engagement Officer point to a growing desire to have leaders of innovation within organizations. Further down the organizational chain, we have innovation managers, innovation directors, and even innovation champions. A website, www.cio.com, is dedicated to providing resources to these individuals in this job category.

Speeches

You would be hard pressed to see a speech from a top executive recapping the events and success of the organization without a mention of innovation. State-of-the-company addresses and end-of-year summaries are almost always laced with innovation progress, updates, and issues. Politicians from presidents to mayors have proclaimed innovation to be an important part of their campaigns and strategies and have created more innovation for the government. Dubai has made a commitment to be the most innovative city. In Malaysia, there is an appointed Minister of Innovation.

Experience

You don't have to be reading books, articles, or listening to speeches to be innovative. We all experience innovation every day. Imagine the complete

Uber experience compared to the use of a taxi, or the timeliness and efficiency of shopping with Amazon.com, or the amazing innovation that goes into Google's ability to find all the information we would need, not to mention the innovative efforts of organizations like Facebook, Netflix, and Apple. In our daily lives, we are experiencing innovation in a big way—in almost everything we do.

We love innovation because it often brings convenience. Sometimes it makes an entire process feel seamless, as in the Mobike example presented earlier in the chapter. In many cases, it reduces the cost of what we are doing or buying, such as with Amazon. Sometimes it is environmentally friendly, like the use of a ride-sharing program. At other times it makes us healthy, such as the medical devices that keep us alive. Few topics have enjoyed as much hype as innovation, and we've come to expect innovation and appreciate it.

The Realities of Innovation

Although there is much hype surrounding innovation, there are some realities of innovation that point to opportunities and concerns.

Innovation is Not New

Innovation has been around for many years with inventions traced to the ancient Chinese and Greek cultures. Innovation has been progressing for a very long time, but it has mushroomed in the last 50 years. Now, each year it seems to increase at a more rapid rate. Sometimes innovation is older than it looks. For example, Lockheed Martin developed a cargo aircraft, the C5A. At the time of its development, it was the world's largest airplane, much larger than the passenger aircraft Boeing 747. The C5A is huge, but also very versatile with the capability of tanks and large trucks driving through the front of the plane and out the rear. It has the capability to land and take off on unimproved runways. More impressively, it has the capability of taking off, flying, and landing entirely on autopilot. In 1969, over the mountains of North Georgia, the C5A made its first flight completely automated from takeoff to landing. In most of today's aircraft, autopilots are common. Still, many are surprised to know that the capability exists to take off, fly the entire plane, and land without a pilot. What makes this story interesting is that this capability was demonstrated almost 50 years ago. So innovation is not new, but the rate of change is rapidly increasing.

Innovation is Necessary for Survival

Figure 1.1 lists several companies that have had a near-death experience or have actually died, based primarily on their failure to innovate. Unfortunately, there are many familiar suspects on the list. In 1935, the expected life span of a company was 90 years. By 2005 this had fallen to 15 years. Yet at the same time, many companies have survived for over 100 years because they have constantly innovated.[3] For example, Johnson & Johnson, IBM, American Express, 3M, P&G, and Goodrich are on average about 100 years old, and they are still going strong. Innovation is essential; without it, it is almost certain that the company will not exist.

Innovation is Equated with Success

If something is successful, it must be innovative, and usually is. For example, on a recent flight on Delta Airlines, we noticed that *Sky* magazine, Delta's in-flight publication, had a feature on the founder of Delta with the title, "Spirit of Innovation." In this article, Delta was celebrating its success since its founding in 1929. Delta is now one of the largest, most admired, and most profitable airlines with 80,000 employees. They owe much of their success to what the company describes as the innovation driven by the founding CEO, C. E. Woolman. A review of any list of the most admired organizations, the most sustainable organizations, the most profitable organizations, or even the Best Places to Work have much innovation going on, making success almost synonymous with innovation.

Borders	Firestone	MCI world
Kodak	Polaroid	Sears
A&P	Deluxe printing	Philips
Smith corona	Bethlehem steel	RCA
DEC	Control data	Xerox
Westinghouse	Woolworths	Memorex
Siebel systems	Blockbuster	Syntex
Northwest airlines	Radio shack	Compaq
Circuit city	Merrill lynch	GM

Figure 1.1 What is True of All These Companies?

Adapted from: *Lead and Disrupt: How to Solve the Innovator's Dilemma* (Charles A. O'Reilly III and Michael L. Tushman)

Innovation is Truly Global

Innovation is not limited to the United States or even to pockets of creativity around the world. It shows up almost everywhere. The current geographic breakdown of the 2017 *Fortune* Global 500, the definitive list of biggest companies by revenue in the world, points out that the latest rankings are based on no fewer than 232 cities in 34 countries.[4] More than two-fifths of those companies, 109 in total, are based in China. That number is up from only 29 a decade ago. The example of Mobike shows that ideas know no borders. A good idea can permeate borders and turn into a truly global innovation within the marketplace.

Consumers and Investors Expect Innovation

Consumers expect the constant stream of innovation they have come to experience, be fascinated by, and perhaps even hooked on. Sometimes we can hardly wait for the "new and improved" version of our next project. Investors also expect innovation to continue to flow. For example, one has only to witness the constant pressure on Apple to continue its innovation of products and services. When the rate of innovation (new or improved products) declines, so does the stock price.

Innovation is Often Disruptive

Many of the businesses listed in Figure 1.1 were displaced by more innovated approaches. Two of the most visible causes of this are the impact that Amazon has had on bookstores and Netflix on video rental stores. Disruption creates problems because of the displacements that often follow the new processes. Investors in the original companies lose money and employees lose jobs. Even just the mere threat of some of these displacers can cause huge problems. For example, when Amazon recently announced the pending purchase of the Whole Foods supermarket chain, investors assumed that Amazon would transform the entire retail supermarket business, a business that Amazon was already involved in. Merely on the announcement of their interest alone, competitors' stocks took a dip in one day; Kroger's stock dipped 9.2%, Target's stock 4.1%, and Walmart's stock 4.7%.[5]

Packaged-goods companies additionally experienced a huge dip with the anticipation that Amazon may change the way in which people have their food packaged. It's helpful to remember that when Amazon took on the book-selling business, it also transformed the way in which books are published, fueling the e-book market and the Kindle as a device to read the books. This put fear into the packaging industry with General Mills stock falling 2.9%, Kraft-Heinz 2.4%, and Kelloggs 1.7%.

Innovation is Not a Single Event

It is also important to remember that a single event doesn't bring out a major innovation. Consider, for example, the mouse for our computer. The mouse was first displayed in 1968 during a research project funded by the U.S. Department of Defense.[6] The mouse was actually presented at a demonstration. From that meeting, two individuals developed the idea into Alto, the first truly personal computer at Xerox's famed Palo Alto Research Center. Later, Steve Jobs would take many elements of the Alto to create the Macintosh. Even with the invention of the personal computer, while Xerox built the first one, Apple launched the Macintosh with great fanfare in 1984. So, it's not entirely clear, when an invention seems to make commercial success, who invented it or where it was actually created.

Little Ideas Often Make a Big Difference

It's not the incremental product improvements or project improvements or huge breakthroughs that drive most innovation. Innovation doesn't fall neatly into the usual categories that we see in the business press. Most companies aren't disrupting their industry; nor are they sailing for blue oceans or acting like lean startups. Most are not revolutionizing the future of their business or simply improving its core products. The approach to innovation is unique, based on the power of little ideas.[7]

In the book, *Brick by Brick: How LEGO Rewrote the Rules of Innovation and Conquered the Global Toy Industry*, David Robertson tells the story of how LEGO adopted a similar innovation approach in 2003 to recover from its brush with bankruptcy.[8] LEGO's recovery and growth didn't come from just offering a better core product of from reinventing the future of its industry. In fact, LEGO tried both of those strategies and failed. The successful strategy for the toy maker was to go back to the company's core, the box of bricks, understand what the customer wanted from that product, and innovate around the box. When Lego mastered this approach, the company recovered quickly and spectacularly. When LEGO posted its annual results in early 2016, its eight-year average annual sales growth was 21% per year, and profit growth an equally impressive 36% per year. This approach to innovation, neither incremental improvement in current

---

New product development

Innovation through networking

Innovation and creativity workshops

Process innovations

Product performance

Product use enhancements

Channel innovations

Brand innovations

Customer engagement and innovations

Product system innovation

Innovation labs

Innovation task forces

Figure 1.2 Types of Innovation.

Adapted from: *Ten Types of Innovation: The Discipline of Building Breakthroughs* (Larry Keeley, Ryan Pikkel, Brian Quinn, Helen Walters)

products nor revolutionary disruption of those products, is what the author calls the Third Way to innovate.

Innovation Comes in Many Types and Forms

Innovation comes in many types and forms. Figure 1.2 lists the types of innovation projects that range from R&D efforts to product development to individual innovation, coming through any function or department.[9] Others categorize types of innovation by the nature of the innovation itself. For example, one approach is to think of some innovations as small, where the innovation is a part of the bigger system. These are small initiatives, built into all function processes. A second type is repeatable, where innovation is part of the day-to-day operations as much as possible, and finally, the third category of innovation is custom, where these are separate, but compatible, innovation tasks apart from the day-to-day operations.[10]

Innovation Spans Many Different Horizons

Finally, innovation sometimes spans many different horizons. Figure 1.3 shows the three different horizons where the focus is sustaining innovation and using existing capabilities already deployed in an existing market already served. The idea behind the three horizons framework is not to eliminate uncertainty, but to take the level of uncertainty into account when allocating resources. The bulk of resources are invested in capabilities

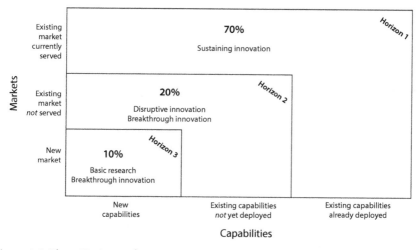

Figure 1.3 Three Horizons of Innovation.

Adapted from: *Mapping Innovation: A Playbook for Navigating a Disruptive Age* (Greg Satell)

(e.g., skills and technology) and existing markets, a much smaller portion toward adjacencies, and an even smaller proportion to future opportunities that don't even exist yet. The proportions of 70/20/10 are intended to be general guidelines and do not lend themselves to a strict accounting. The primary insight is that businesses need to pursue all three horizons at once, in different proportions.[11] While the three horizons framework may seem simplistic, it offers a simple framework with a simple language to discuss the core business, adjacencies, and long-term bets.

Trouble in Paradise: The Misconceptions

Unfortunately, not everything is as it seems. There are many misunderstandings and myths about innovation. These often lead to bad decisions, inefficiencies, lack of accountability, and lack of support. Perhaps the individual who has tackled this issue in the most thorough way is Anne Marie Knott, author of *How Innovation Really Works: Using the Trillion-Dollar R&D Fix to Drive Growth*.[12] Dr. Knott is an expert on R&D, having worked in this field for many years. She is also an outstanding researcher and a whiz at analytics. Because she saw so many misunderstandings about investments in R&D, she wanted to tackle the issue in a different way. Realizing that just investment in R&D alone doesn't necessarily translate into innovation or profitability, she developed a different measure called Research Quotient.

RQ is the efficiency of solving new problems. For any given level of R&D spending, high-RQ companies will generate more innovations. For any given innovation, high-RQ companies will invest less in developing it. Accordingly, RQ is mapped into a scale where the mean is 100 and standard deviation is 15. In Knott's research, she brings to light seven misconceptions that can confuse the support for innovation and investment in innovation.

Misconception 1: Small Companies are More Innovative

Although there has been much hype about this, larger companies seem to generate more innovation. They do so because they have more resources to develop innovation, they can spread the cost of R&D over the whole organization, and they can have systems in place to make innovation more systematic and routine within the organization.

Misconception 2: Uncontested Markets are Good for Innovation

Knott makes a strong case for the fact that most innovation is from contested markets that need improvements in efficiency, quality, or cost. This creates a competitive spirit and causes organizations to look for an advantage. An uncontested market, where there is only one active organization, might lead to innovation that is not so efficient and effective.

Misconception 3: Spending More on R&D Increases Innovation

Although it seems obvious that increasing R&D will lead to innovation, in fact, that is not necessarily the case. R&D is an input. R&D teams, especially the large ones, can become bureaucratic and efficient, not delivering on the promise. Companies want growth because it increases their market share, and the government wants economic growth because it increases the number of jobs. The best way for companies to grow and create jobs is not necessarily to invest more in R&D, but let the competitive spirit drive innovation from all processes.

Misconception 4: Companies Need More Radical Innovation

Radical innovation (or innovation that is new to the world) is very important for the economy. We see much hype paid to these inventions and innovations, from cameras to MP3, and they often take a long time to develop. For example, television took 22 years from invention to commercialization. For the personal computer, 20 years after introduction, only 50% of households had personal computers. The big hits don't necessarily pay off on a large scale, and certainly not quickly. Most innovation is coming from the incremental, systematic, and routine processes within organizations which makes it more efficient, more cost effective, of better quality, with better design.

Misconception 5: Open Innovation Turbocharges R&D

One of the biggest innovation trends over the past few years has been open innovation or open business models.[13] There is a widely held belief that open innovation increases companies' financial performance. Accordingly, open innovation has been adopted by the vast majority of companies engaged in R&D. Knott argues that, while there is some evidence that open innovation in the form of R&D outsourcing may improve companies' financial performance, the record on idea development indicates that R&D outsourcing not only fails to improve financial performance, it actually degrades it! This occurs because outsourced R&D incurs R&D expenditures without increasing revenues. Thus it decreases profits. Worse, however, it appears that outsourcing R&D is a slippery slope wherein company innovative capability decays, so the company increasingly outsources, and capability decays even further.

Misconception 6: R&D Needs to be More Relevant

The need to be relevant led to widespread decentralization of R&D. The logic of decentralized R&D is that it makes companies more responsive to the market. The view was widely held. In fact, the opposite is true, because companies with centralized R&D tend to a) do more basic research, so are more likely to create new technical possibilities, b) create technology that benefits multiple divisions, and c) derive more of their technology from internal R&D rather than through outsourcing.

Misconception 7: Wall Street Rewards Innovation

Although investors do get excited about huge R&D expenditures and announcements of improvements in R&D spending, they ultimately reward the companies with the output of the R&D spending, the innovation. Because R&D is not a good indicator of innovation, investors seek other measures, such as IP (Innovation Premium) and RQ (Research Quotient). Without a good measure, their decisions are not optimal.

These misconceptions, fully documented in Knott's work, make the process of innovation confusing to some people because some of the beliefs that have been promoted, amplified, and explored over the years are not necessarily true. This may have contributed to misguided investments in innovation.

Innovation Challenges

The path of our innovation journey brings us to the challenges of making innovation work. There is no doubt that innovation is necessary, and it must be an important part of any organization's strategy. But these challenges make us rethink our processes and the ways in which we are tackling these issues to make innovation successful, efficiently, within cost, and on time.

Innovation is Expensive

You would have to look no further than the pharmaceutical industry to see what it costs to develop new medications. A study by the Tufts Center for the Study of Drug Development suggests the road to bringing new FDA-approved medicine to patients is long, and the costs are formidable. This study revealed that the average cost to research and develop (R&D) a new medicine has doubled over the past decade to $2.6 billion. This includes the cost of failures— which tend to be more common than successes, but build on previous advances. When the costs of post-approval R&D were factored in, the estimate increased to $2.8 billion.

Researchers attribute this growth in R&D to several factors, including an increase in the complexity of clinical trials and a significant decline in clinical approval successes. According to the study, only 12% of drug candidates that enter clinical testing are eventually approved for use by patients.[14]

Basic research and development add tremendous costs to an organization. Even the processes to bring systematic and routine changes and improvements to an organization will be expensive because of the time and efforts involved. The key is to make sure that this is accomplished as efficiently as possible within the cost and time of any budget. It costs virtually nothing to communicate a vision of innovation, set goals and objectives for ideas and innovations, and ask for ideas. It costs very little to run brainstorm meetings, set up an intranet-based suggestion scheme, implement small incremental innovations, empower the team to try more initiatives in their areas, and investigate new collaborations and partnerships.[15]

Managing Innovation is Difficult

Leaders create the willingness to innovate, the ability to innovate, and they cultivate the innovation.[16] The process of leading a team, working exclusively on innovation, is a difficult challenge. The process of stimulating creativity and innovation in an organization, bringing the culture necessary to not only create and nurture new ideas, but to turn them into workable, viable products and services is also difficult. Because of this, most organizations have set up divisions, departments, and units which focus directly on innovation. One of the most interesting new roles has been the creation of the Chief Innovation Officer with the promise that this person will bring innovation to the organization.

Unfortunately, this maybe sends the wrong message and some indicate that this job should be eliminated. According to George Bradt, a *Forbes* magazine contributor, the whole premise behind the Chief Innovation Officer goes beyond useless to completely and utterly counterproductive. [17] If one person oversees innovation, then everyone else is not innovative and they must be. His point is that everyone is responsible for innovation and creativity, and leading this effort should be a part of each manager's job, and even the part of the job of most people within the organization. Everyone shares responsibility to come up with ideas, push those ideas, and help develop those ideas.

An Innovation Culture is Necessary for Success

Another challenge is that an innovation culture is necessary for success. The most innovative companies are those that seem to have a culture for innovation and creativity. Innovation is about extending what is possible. When a person develops a new idea to improve something that was perhaps difficult, now it becomes a little easier. Leading innovation is about inspiring people to see and want better futures, better work, and better processes. Getting people to do what they love the most is an effective way of inspiring creativity and commitment to that better future, and in that sense, a culture is needed.

According to Max McKeown, innovation culture is how we describe effectively or ineffectively people are working together to create and use new ideas.[18] Culture is the sum of the values, beliefs, and assumptions of human groups. Culture is about the personality and behavior of a social group, and it is all about the different factors that shape what groups are likely to do next. McKeown has an interesting way of describing different cultures ranging from *idea-toxic* cultures, where creativity is not welcomed or rewarded to *idea-wasteful* cultures, where ideas and insights are treated casually and often mismanaged. Then he describes an *idea-friendly* culture where creativity is welcomed and new ideas are valued. These new ideas may get introduced and reviewed by the hierarchy. But the best is obviously the *idea-hungry* culture, where people seek new ideas. They make the world better with improvement beyond existing limits. This is an interesting way to describe the culture in an organization with regard to improvements, new ideas, and new suggestions. Most organizations say they want innovation, but only a few work with it in an effective and an efficient way.

Dr. Amantha Imber has developed what she refers to as The Innovation Formula.[19] Dr. Imber's work identifies 14 science-based keys for creating a culture for innovation. These are based on individual-level factors, including challenge, autonomy and recognition. They also involve team-level factors of debate, team supportiveness and collaboration. They focus on leader-level factors of supervisor's support, senior leader's support, resourcing, and goal-clarity. Lastly, the focus is on organizational-level factors of risk-taking, cohesion, participation and physical environment. Dr. Imber has created an interesting Innovation Culture Audit, which involves two questions for each of these 14 factors and invites individuals to take the survey to discover where they stand in terms of their own internal culture for innovation (www.inventium.com.au).

The important point is that there is a huge challenge to create this culture. It doesn't occur quickly; it evolves over time. If the culture is not there, it will take some time to change and improve it, so it clearly becomes an innovation culture.

Innovation Requires Many Personas

Innovation requires many personas. Innovation takes on a lot of different roles and many different styles. These are often called *personas*, as described by Tom Kelley of IDEO, one of the largest organizations created to help build innovative organizations. In his early work with IDEO, Kelley discusses the ten faces of innovation. These are the personas that may already exist in large organizations, although they may be undeveloped and unrecognized.[21]

According to Kelley, there are three learning personas that help individuals and organizations gather new sources of information to expand their knowledge and grow. These roles are:

1. The *anthropologist* who brings new learning and insights into the organization by observing human behavior and developing a deep understanding of how people interact physically and emotionally with products, services. and space.
2. The *experimenter* who prototypes new ideas continuously, learning by process of enlightened trial and error.
3. The *cross-pollinator* who explores other industries and cultures, then translates those findings and revelations to fit the unique needs of the enterprise.

Also according to Kelley, there are three organizing personas, played by individuals who are savvy about the often counter-intuitive process of how organizations move ideas forward. These personas are:

4. The *hurdler* who knows the path to innovation is strewn with obstacles and develops a knack for overcoming and outsmarting those roadblocks.
5. The *collaborator* who helps bring eclectic groups together, and often leads from the middle of the pack to create new combinations and multidisciplinary solutions.
6. The *director* who not only collects a talented cast and crew, but also helps to spark creative talents.

Kelley goes on to say there is a set of building personas based on roles that apply insights from the learning roles and channels the empowerment from the organizing roles to make innovation happen. These are:

7. The *experience architect* who designs compelling experiences that go beyond functionality to connect at a deeper level with the customers latent or expressed needs.
8. The *set designer* who creates a stage on which innovation team members can do their best work transforming physical environments into powerful tools to influence behavior and attitude.
9. The *caregiver* who builds on the metaphor of the healthcare professional to deliver customer care in a manner that goes beyond mere service.
10. The *storyteller* who builds both internal morale and external awareness through compelling narratives that communicate a fundamental human value or reinforce a specific cultural trait.

These are excellent ways to think about the different roles in innovation. They are needed to bring about the innovation necessary for an organization.

Innovation Success Rates Need to Improve

The failure rate of projects is much higher than it needs to be. There has been, for example, a typical assumption that nine out of ten start-ups will fail. There have been many start-up failures which have been celebrated and almost immortalized. That seems to be changing now, and failure should not be considered the norm. Success should be considered the norm, argues Erin Griffith, a *Fortune* magazine columnist.[20]

Part of this success rate is that innovation needs to be faster, and this is no more obvious than the race to bring out new medications or find cures for diseases. Sometimes it just takes a long time for a breakthrough, but there are opportunities along the way that can speed up the mechanics. R&D sometimes falls into bureaucratic processes and may not be managed efficiently, and may not be delivering in a timely manner. Having a system in place to help manage the process in an efficient way should bring out faster innovations and faster solutions.

The Value of Innovation is Unclear

Over a decade ago, in their book on payback, authors James P. Andrew and Harold L. Sirkin summarized the situation with the value of innovation: "For almost every company, the greatest challenge of innovation is not a lack of ideas but rather, successfully managing innovation so that it delivers the required return on the company's investment of money, time, and people. Most attempts at innovation fail to deliver this return – they do not generate enough payback."[22]

About the same time, David Nichols, author of *Return on Ideas*, also expressed concern about the value of innovation:

> Innovation is the magic dust that all businesses need to thrive in today's ultra-competitive markets. It has never been more central to the CEO's agenda. But success rates are dismal and not improving despite the scrutiny heaped upon the idea development process. The culprit is the Innovation Funnel. The very process put in to make innovation more of a certainty is making it more of a dead duck; stifling it with bureaucracy, poor decision making and a focus on picking faults not building competence.

The alternative mooted by books is to be a rebel, tear up the rule book and reinvent your business from the ground up. This is fine for brilliant mavericks or bored billionaires, but won't do for core brands in core markets that need to carve out growth day in and day out. There has to be a better way.[23]

More recently, authors Madhavan Ramanujam and Georg Tacke, in their book *Monetizing Innovation*, highlighted the frustrations of still not delivering the innovation needed:

Businesses need to innovate to survive, yet the failure rate for innovation is shockingly high. Nearly three out of four new products or services miss their revenue and profit goals – or fail entirely. Companies embark on the long and costly journey of product development hoping they'll make money on their innovations, but not knowing if they will. It doesn't have to be this way."[24]

While there are many success stories and many organizations that have built fortunes on the foundation of innovation, a process of systematically evaluating innovation hasn't been put in place on a routine basis. What is needed is a method that is not built on the hope that innovation works, but is effective at *knowing* the value of innovation, *proving* the value of innovation and *showing* that value to a variety of stakeholders.

Although some previous works have attempted to do this, including the previous three references, no book provides a systematic way of providing it. This book will take a process that has worked so well in many other fields and show you how it is working now in the innovation field to *know, prove,* and *show the Value of Innovation.*

Final Thoughts

This chapter briefly summarizes the importance of innovation and how it has become a mainstream, everyday occurrence for billions of people. It also describes the realities of developing innovation and making it work. Then there is a focus on some misunderstandings and misconceptions and some detail around the challenges of innovation. The key is to make innovation more easily accepted and more richly supported, which ultimately will drive better outcomes. To do so requires a process to *know, prove,* and *show* the value of innovation. The next chapter focuses on what has been done in terms of measuring innovation to date.

2

Status and Concerns about Innovation Measurement

3M was famous for providing innovators money and then leaving them alone to create new ideas, products, and efficiencies. Just two output measures were really reported: the percentage of revenues from new products and the number of patents. The 3M culture was about the inputs to create fabulous new ideas including their famous 15% slack time (available to work on projects that scientists choose) and spending 5% of their revenue on R&D.

When a new CEO arrived, things changed. James McNerney brought along enough GE-inspired efficiency metrics to clog up the creative veins and arteries of 3M. Too much measurement increased short-term profits and reduced long-term growth.

The next two CEOs, both 3M old timers, reversed the changes. With creative independence restored, the number of new products soared back up to 40% in the next few years. All measurement and no joy makes creativity a chore. [1]

This story shows that the metrics for innovation must be carefully selected, and the process for measuring success must be perceived as a value-adding process. This creates a paradox, because as Peter Drucker comments sagely, "If you can't measure it, you can't manage it." A measurement system must walk the delicate line between measuring the right things, but not using that data in an improper way. It should be used for process improvement, not necessarily performance evaluation of the team.

Innovation: Definition, Models, and Measures

Many definitions of innovation have been developed. Almost any author of an innovation book has created a definition, and even associations and professional organizations have created definitions. Some organizations have created their own definition. The definition is important because it explains not only what comprises innovation, but something about the process to develop innovation, the sources of innovation, and the culture for innovation. The definition that we prefer is slightly modified from The Conference Board definition:

> Innovation is broadly defined as an activity or set of activities that results in the creation and use of 1) a new or significantly improved product or service; 2) a production or operating process; 3) a way of attracting customers by enhancing their experience; 4) an organization practice, work design, human capital competency; or 5) resources that add value. [2]

Along with the definition are the many models of innovation, often reported in articles and books on innovation. An examination of over 100 books that appear to be uniquely focused on innovation, including those often in the best-known categories, reveals that over half of the books present a model for producing, executing, and delivering on innovation. When the models from other sources (e.g., articles, associations, and consulting firms) are added, this means there are at least 100 models focusing on how to do it. That creates a tremendous amount of confusion. Measurement is critical to the model itself and, ideally, should be built into the model.

Measurement is more successful when it is a part of a dynamic model from insight to innovation. Measurement is valuable only to the extent that it helps to improve innovation. The process of measuring should help recognize opportunities for innovation, increase the understanding of what to improve, and shape the innovation efforts for success. According to McKeown, the innovator's measure of success are:

1. You understand the difference between measurement and improvement.
2. Learning is increased each time you cycle through the measurement loop.
3. The measurement system is custom-made for your purpose and situation.
4. Everyone, at all levels in any hierarchy, is part of the learning process.
5. Measurements adapt as needed to help your innovation succeed.
6. Unwelcome findings are used productively and not just ignored. [3]

Sources of Innovation

"I need 5,000 volunteers," declared Gerstner, the new CEO of IBM. He inherited a multimillion-dollar loss and wrote to employees asking for the guts to go above, below, around, and through internal hurdles. He wanted innovators willing to take risk in the face of conventional wisdom. As an ex-customer and outsider, he saw that new attitudes and new expectations were needed.

Inspired by this call for volunteers, two frontline network administrators decided to help IBM see and grab opportunities provided by an amazing idea (newborn and immature), the worldwide web. Working with an executive with the influence to get resources, they secretly built IBM's first website.

This new website was not the idea of the new IBM CEO. But the informality of the leader encouraged informal creativity to deliver what came to be known as e-business. The company grew together with the web. Rebel thinkers were attracted to skunkworks, under-the-radar innovation projects, and then went back into the organization to establish them as business-as-usual.

A reenergized IBM jumped ahead of others. They were first into new problems with new confidence to transform them into stunning new solutions. Since then, IBM has produced more patents than any other firm. It reinvested in Deep Blue, the chess-playing computer, and Watson, the artificial intelligence that beat the quiz show *Jeopardy*. This story underscores that the sources of innovation must be carefully selected and utilized. [4]

Innovation comes from many sources, as shown in Figure 2.1. The two most important sources are within the organization. Those are employees,

Figure 2.1 Where Innovation Comes From.

purposely illustrated to show a larger proportion, and the top leadership which provides the guidance for the innovation inside the organization. The collective energy, creative spirits, determination, and drive of the employees will make the difference. Sometimes, it is helpful to work with the customers, to find out what the customers need or want. But sometimes, that is not enough. For example, many of the Apple products were not built on what customers needed because Steve Jobs was interested in showing them a product that they had not even thought about, describing a need that they did not know they had.

Competitors would be another source. It is always helpful, as the old saying goes, to "keep your friends (clients) close and your enemies (competitors) closer." We have to find out what they are doing, and learn from them. Maybe we can do it better, or maybe we can build on what they have accomplished. If we don't do this, we may be accused of having our head in the sand.

We can also look to suppliers, from which a creative spirit comes. Honda, for example, requires that its suppliers be very creative in their work, changing and improving as they provide better quality products, with more features and innovations, and lower costs in some cases. In today's environment, good creative experiences are coming from crowdsourcing opportunities. Letting the public, or some portion of the public, offer suggestions and ideas on how things can and should be improved. Additionally, there is basic research developed from external organizations designed to help businesses in other organizations improve. Universities and research think tanks exist for this purpose. Incubators are designed to develop new products and services.

While there are many sources for innovation, most of it comes from within the organization.

Measurement Shifts

In recent years, we have witnessed a significant change in organizational accountability, especially toward investment in people, programs, projects, and processes. Project sponsors and those who have responsibility for project success have always been concerned about the value of their initiatives. Today this concern translates into financial impact—the actual monetary contribution from a project or program. Although monetary value is becoming a critical concern, it is the comparison of this value with the project costs that captures stakeholders' attention—and translates into ROI.

Measurement Shifts are Common

We've seen this situation evolve in several areas. For example, with leadership development programs, top leaders pumped billions of dollars into leadership development based on the faith that these programs would deliver results. But a lack of clear results and little accountability around these expenditures have forced leadership development directors to show the value in terms that executives can understand. And this often means impact and ROI.

The same situation is now developing with social media. Organizations spend billions on social media for their employees with the hope that they will use it for informal learning and with visions of improved productivity and higher quality of work. Unfortunately, the impact is rarely pursued and often perceived to be a mystery.

Culture is another area where executives strive to maintain the strong culture they have, change their culture to a more effective one, or regain the culture that they once had. The investment in culture is now being subjected to increased accountability with requests to show the value, including impact and ROI.

This is now occurring in the innovation area with many of the funders and supporters of innovation asking for more results. While these executives realize that failure will be an inherent part of this process, they need to see more success along the way.

Value Perception

A few years ago, the team at Rubbermaid, a well-known manufacturer of household rubber products, told us a story involving a new product. The marketing team had a theory. They believed consumers thought Rubbermaid was a manufacturer of rubber gloves for dishwashing, although they were not. The marketing team conducted a market share analysis, asking consumers who made the rubber gloves they were using in their kitchen. Surprisingly, the largest market share was given to Rubbermaid, although they were not in the business. So, Rubbermaid's reaction was to quickly get into the business. They already had the market share, but they didn't have the product.

This is an unusual situation, but it makes a great point that perception and reality must match. The consumer's perception was that Rubbermaid made the product. Rubbermaid had to start producing it, or they had to let people know that they didn't make it. The same situation happens in innovation. With innovation, there is a perceived or anticipated value and it may not be delivered. If we don't show the value, then we will lose support. Perception must match reality.

The Search for Money

"Show me the money" is the familiar response from individuals asked to invest (or continue to invest) in organizational efforts. At times, this response is appropriate. At other times, it may be misguided; measures not subject to monetary conversion are also important, if not critical, to most projects. However, excluding the monetary component from a success profile is unacceptable in this age of the "show me" generation. The monetary value is often required before a project is approved. Sometimes, it is needed as the project is being designed and developed. Other times, it is needed after project implementation.

This issue is compounded by concern that most projects today fail to live up to expectations. A systematic process is needed that can identify barriers to and enablers of success and can drive organizational improvements.

The challenge lies in doing it—developing the measures of value, including monetary value, when they are needed and presenting them in a way so that stakeholders can use them

- Before the innovation project is initiated
- During innovation development, to plan for maximum value

- During implementation, so that maximum value can be attained
- During post-analysis, to assess the delivered value against the anticipated value

The Value of Innovation is a basic guide for anyone involved in implementing innovation where significant expenditures of time and money are at stake. Strategies to assist in forecasting the value of the innovation project in advance and in collecting data during and after project implementation are presented.

Hoping, Knowing, Proving, and Showing Value

The founders of Lyft, a ride-share company that competes aggressively with Uber, recently shared some thoughts about innovation and venture capital. In a Business Radio interview powered by Wharton Business School, John Zimmer and Logan Green said that in the past you could secure venture capital for your ideas with hope that you will have success, that innovation will work and catch on. It wasn't too difficult to get funding on hope. These days, funding is usually based on proof of the concept. The funder must have proof that it will actually work, is needed and will be used by consumers.

So, essentially hoping has evolved to proving. Now, add two more phases to the process, knowing and showing. After hoping comes knowing the value from innovation, knowing where a process breaks down, and knowing what has to be altered to increase the value. Knowing allows us to tackle process improvement in a meaningful way. Proving is having a credible process that can actually withstand the scrutiny of a chief financial officer. Proving should be based on a process that is conservative, reliable, and valid while at the same time being user-friendly. Finally, from proving we need to show the value. Showing the value to all the stakeholders involved, the end user (who may be the consumer), the investors (who need to invest more), and the supporters (who need reinforcement that it is a good thing to be doing). This book is based on this concept…moving from hoping to *knowing*, *proving*, and *showing* the value of innovation. Showing the value builds respect, support, commitment, and yes, funding.

Innovation is Systematic

Recognizing that most innovation will come from within the organization, it is critical to have a systematic way of channeling that innovation into a productive process. A systematic approach is needed, and these are often defined by the various models that are presented. Here are a few examples. Eric Ries created a model to develop a new idea using a prototype. In this process, Ries suggested that the concept of measure, learn, and build is a systematic process. Measures are needed to observe or predict something and is the beginning point. Then there's learning throughout the process. Learning provides an opportunity to theorize and addresses four questions:

1. What do we need to learn?
2. What have we learned?
3. How do we validate learning?
4. What do we need to build?

This learning is fed back to the observer to make adjustments, and it moves onto building the experiment. This model is labeled as a build, measure, and learn wheel, recognizing that it's a continuous process with constant feedback in early stages. This is an absolute must for some type of system for innovation. [5]

In their book *Innovation and Scaling for Impact,* Christian Seelos and Johanna Mair suggest that the innovation process contains three basic processes: ideas, (leading to) piloting, (leading to) scaling. But along the way, to protect the investment, six danger points are identified that often prohibit success.

1. Never get started
2. Too many bad ideas
3. Stop too early
4. Stop too late
5. Insufficient expiration
6. Innovate again too soon

The important point is that these are phases that follow sequencing and have a focus on searching for the pitfalls to the process. [6]

The design school at Stanford used some principles of design thinking to suggest a systematic way to make ideas come to light. According to Figure 2.2, the process started with empathize, moving to define, ideate, prototype, and then to test, with the feedback to the starting point. Along the way, important learnings take place to make the process work.

There's much research about the individuals who constantly innovate. These serial innovators should be very critical to an organization's success with innovation. The opportunity lies in locating, identifying, and having

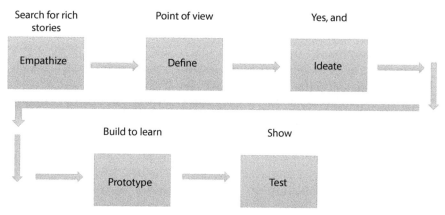

Figure 2.2
Adapted from Guido Kovalskys, the d.school, Stanford

them develop innovation in a systematic way. In a recent book on serial innovators, Abbie Griffin, Raymond, L. Price, and Bruce, A. Vojak suggest a systematic way for serial innovators, moving through a series of steps as follows:

1. Motivation to innovate
2. Find the right problem
3. Understand the problem
4. Invent and validate
5. Execute
6. Create market acceptance
7. Launch flawlessly

Along the way, there's a lot of circling back and pushing information from one part of the process to another. [7]

These are just a few examples that underscore the fact that innovation will normally occur in a systematic way following some prescribed set of steps with opportunities to make adjustments and changes on the way, but also anticipating problems and inhibitors during the process.

Macro View of Measurement

It's helpful to understand the concept of measurement from both the macro view and the micro view. The macro view is examining innovation across an entire country, or maybe measuring innovation across a group of organizations in a country (a sector, for example), or measuring innovation at the company or organizational level. This provides a view of the value of innovation at these different macro levels. The micro view is to examine measures of innovation success for a particular project. Ideally, the micro data will roll up into the macro level scorecard.

For the country level, there have been several possibilities. One is the Global Innovation Index (GII), co-published by Cornell University, INSEAD, and The World Intellectual Property Organization. This index is two subparts of innovation inputs and innovation outputs. The input involves human capital and research, infrastructure, market sophistication, and business sophistication. The output covers the creative outcomes and knowledge and technology. [8]

The European Innovation Scorecard (EIS) is constructed by the European Commission. It aims to compare the innovation performance of 27 European Union member countries. The scorecard provides a summary innovation index with an overview of innovation performance in the country. There are three building blocks: enablers, firm activities, and outputs. The enablers include human resources, finance, and support. Firm activities include firm investments, linkages, entrepreneurship, and throughputs. Outputs include innovators and economic effects. [9]

The Global Creativity Index (GCI) is constructed by Martin Prosperity Institute. This index measures creativity of 139 countries based on three pillars: technology, talent, and tolerance. [10] Technology includes R&D spending and number of patents. Talent includes educational attainment and employment in creative occupations. Tolerance is based on efforts with minorities, gays, and lesbians.

The Global Entrepreneurship Index (GEI) was constructed by the Global Entrepreneurship and Development Institute. This index attempts to measure the entrepreneurship process in 130 countries. The index is based on three pillars: entrepreneur attitudes, abilities, and aspirations. It uses both individual data and macro data from institutions. [11]

The Portfolio Innovation Index. PII is constructed by the Indiana University's Kelly School of Business and is supported by the U.S. Development Administration. The index aims to help regional practitioners identify their strengths or weaknesses of innovation performance in the United States. This index has four pillars: human capital, economic dynamics, productivity and employment, and economic well-being. [12]

These indices, while helpful, are notoriously inaccurate and incomplete. They focus on inputs and are lagging indicators. While they have critics, they do serve a useful purpose of attempting to compare innovation across countries or, in the case of the last one, within a country.

Industry Level Measures

In some cases, industry-level measures are available that focus on a very important industry and examine some of the innovation measures across a particular segment. The Service Sector Innovation index uses data from a community innovation survey and covers nine themes for 17 countries: [13]

- Human resources
- Innovation demand
- Public support for innovation
- Inputs to product and process innovation
- Outputs of product and process innovation inputs
- Inputs of non-technological innovation
- Outputs of non-technological innovation
- Outputs of commercialization
- Outputs of intellectual property

The National Endowment for Science and Technology in the Arts (NESTA) has carried out research on innovation measurement in the industry level. This index presents a relative innovation performance of each industry by three innovation stages. [14]

The Productive Innovation Index in the pharmaceutical industry focuses on a ranking of 30 pharma companies based on commercializing new products. Component variables for this index are global sales, market capitalization, regulatory efficiency, attrition rate, and value proposition. [15]

Finally, the Elastic Innovation Index of the Financial Services produced by Innotribe attempts to measure or evaluate financial service firms' ability and readiness for innovations and operating models, with a focus on digital-related operating processes. [16]

This index uses data from 60 financial service firms on five themes— content of communication, technology platform, leadership related to innovations, strategy, and externalization. Then the researchers rank firms by each theme. They identify the top five qualities of becoming a capable innovation firm.

These sector indices have some weaknesses but show that some progress is made by attempting to measure innovation at the macro level. It is a struggle to develop the data and the results are sometimes inaccurate for measuring what really matters. But it's a start for these sectors and even in the countries.

Company Level

There have been several attempts to measure innovations that can cut across companies. For example, the global surveys of McKinsey reports on company innovations each year using data from its global survey. [17] They often cover different themes each year, so the surveys cannot be compared from one year to another, necessarily.

The global surveys at Boston Consulting Group are also an attempt to measure innovation. These surveys have been conducted since 2008 and collect data on innovation priority among business strategy, innovation spending, rate of return, drivers for innovation for top management, innovation metrics, and innovation hurdles. [18]

The Technology Innovation Survey from KPMG focuses on barriers to commercialize digital innovation, business functions driving innovations, business functions identifying and nurturing innovations, innovation metrics, innovation incentives, factors enabling innovations within a company, and topics related to specific types of digital innovations. [19]

Concerns about Company Level Measures

Several concerns surface about company level measurement. The Conference Board provides an excellent summary of the concerns about these measures in these categories. [20]

1. **Overall, companies do not have a wide range of innovation measures readily available**. The McKinsey survey shows a lack of measurement—out of the 1075 respondents, 51% indicate that their organizations pursue business model innovations, but only 28% say that their organizations formally assess the innovation. The patterns are similar for process innovation (61% vs. 37%), service innovation (65% vs. 37%), and production innovation (71% vs. 54%). [21]

2. **Companies do not measure the entire life cycle of innovation**. Companies are more likely to use measures of innovation outputs than inputs. A shortcoming of output measures is that they are usually lagged and cannot provide timely information on ongoing innovation projects. As such, they could be useful for evaluation or assessment of existing efforts but they are silent on future activity without

further analysis (especially because in the world of innovation past performance is no guarantee of future success). Cordero reviews innovation measures in firms and finds that firms measure resources (for example, R&D spending) and outputs (for example, market share of new products), but tend to ignore the intermediates in the innovation process (1990). [22]

3. **Measuring innovation in a too strict manner can in fact impede the process of innovation, especially if the focus is on output measures.** Morris warns that if we define innovation as discovering the unknown, and if we try to pin down unknowns too fast, we are likely to "measure the wrong things at the wrong time," and that hurts learning, discovery and risk taking of the innovation process. [23] He uses return on investment (ROI) as an example to warn readers about the danger of innovation measurement impeding the innovation process. For example, ROI works better for short-term innovations and tends to exclude long-term innovations and breakthroughs. Premature use of ROI to measure innovation thus endangers the very thing you want to measure, and makes less likely the achievement of the end goal of the process. Researchers likely do not know the potential market value of their innovations. And if they are asked to be responsible for the future ROI, they may abandon the innovation for the sake of their performance review. The VP of Global Innovation of McCain Food, Sue Jefferson, says that companies must remove any metrics that are affecting the innovation process detrimentally. The KPIs which a company chooses are inherently linked to the way it defines progress, and its culture. Jefferson correctly points out that choosing the right set of metrics is the key in developing innovation metrics for a specific company. [24]

Some suggest that there are certain factors within a firm that should be measured, regardless of what that specific system may be in place. For example, J. Tidd, J. Bessant, and K. Bavitt suggest that the measurement should always include five points, referred to as the diamond model. They suggest that the framework should measure strategy, process, organization, linkages, and learning. [25]

Micro View of Measurement

Perhaps a more accurate and more manageable process is to examine at the micro view. The micro view is the process internally at an organization that serves as a guide to not only develop successful innovation, but to measure it along the way. This micro view provides a process to measure any particular project through this system. And, in theory, when all of the measures from the different innovations projects are rolled up into an overall company, a macro scorecard is created.

Several attempts to do this include the idea management model, which suggests that the idea of management focuses on three phases: idea generation, idea conversion, and idea diffusion as shown in Figure 2.3. Idea generation has three different components: 1) in-house creation within a unit, cross-pollination across units and external collaborations with third parties outside the firm; 2) idea conversion is screening and initial funding and moving from idea to first result; and 3) idea diffusion is the dissemination across the organization. [26]

A more popular process is the innovation funnel, which starts with inputs to the process and moves through several steps leading to the final outcome of sales. Figure 2.4 shows how this process flows.

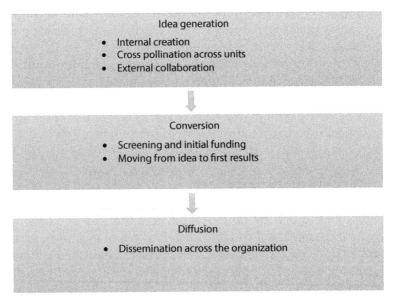

Figure 2.3 Measurement Framework for Idea Management.

Adapted from Hansen and Birkinshaw, 2007

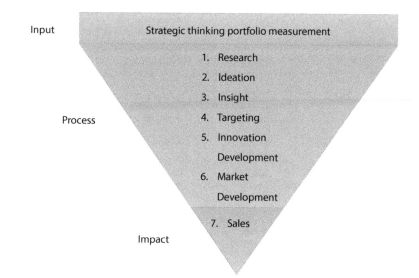

Figure 2.4 Measurement Framework for Innovation Funnel.
Adapted from Morris (2008)

Morris suggests this measurement framework allows companies to develop innovation ideas/projects, eliminate less-promising ideas/projects along the process, and bring the rest of ideas/projects into successful innovations. He recommends lists of qualitative and quantitative metrics than can be used to measure each of the innovation stages. [27]

Linear models are easier to implement than complex flow and feedback models, but we need to judge them on their merits. Linear models view innovation as a sequential process, and allow companies to manage innovation using a gate system, where a gatekeeper decides if an innovation project can move to the next phase or be terminated. The gate system tightly controls the development of an innovation project and it is relatively safe for innovation beginners, but it takes a long time for an innovation project to move from one gate to another. It is suitable for incremental innovations, but not radical innovations. It cannot sufficiently manage the complex and dynamic processes. [28]

Perhaps the most comprehensive approach to this is the conference board model for measuring innovation activities. This is an attempt to capture metrics along a value delivery chain. And this can work across different key dimensions, which are labeled signposts, as illustrated in Figure 2.5. Thus for a given signpost, there are inputs throughputs and outputs. This value chain becomes an essential part of thinking through the value of innovation in this book. Later, a process is presented by combining some

Signpost	Input	Throughput	Output
Technology	R&D	Patents	Receipts of license fees
Digitization	ICT spending	ICT access index	ICT and business model creation
Environmental & social sustainability	Investment in operational sustainability	Number if ISO 14001 environmental certificates	Environmental performance index
Customer experience & Branding	Spending on advertising	Relationship duration	Customer satisfaction
Internal innovation networks (leadership & organization, processes & tools, people & skills, and culture & values)	Spending on innovation projects	Number of new ideas created internally	Number of new products developed from new ideas
External innovation Ecosystems	Venture capital access (links with government, research & education and access to finance)	University/industry collaboration	innovators (% of SMEs)
Profit and Revenues	Innovation budget	potential of entire new product/service portfolio to meet growth targets	% of sales revenues from new products/services

Figure 2.5 Conference Board Measurement Framework.

Adapted from The Conference Board (Janet X. Hao, Bart van Ark, and Ataman Ozyildirim)

of these processes, putting more emphasis on the steps and the process to provide a systematic way of achieving innovation.

Final Thoughts

This chapter reviewed the status of measurement in the innovation field, presenting some current trends, successes, and concerns. While most all systems seem to measure input, the output measurements vary considerably. Very few systems are actually measuring the throughput, what's actually occurring to deliver the output. Several different measurement models are presented and the different views of measurement, from both the macro and micro level, were explored. Along the way, many concerns have evolved that frame the need for a systematic, proven process that can measure data ranging from inputs to outputs and all the processes in between. The specifications for this are outlined in the next chapter.

3

The Case for a New System

After speaking on the use of ROI for non-capital investments to the British Chamber of Commerce in Singapore, we were invited to visit the local offices of a European-based chemical company. The largest chemical company in the world, with customers in over 190 countries, made the decision to move much of its R&D operations from Europe to Asia. Our host was the executive responsible for R&D and he was concerned about the value of this large R&D operation, based in Asia with most of it located in India. He wanted to know how to show the ROI of all of their research and development efforts.

The next week, we received a request from a consulting firm in the United Arab Emirates (UAE) to show the ROI of innovation. As they explained, the UAE government had pumped millions of dollars into all types of innovation projects and now government leaders are asking for ROI. They see many activities, some ideas developing, and a few ideas that can be converted into useable business, but there's a sense that not enough value is being delivered. In short, they need to see the ROI on innovation efforts. They're requesting that we conduct our ROI Certification for these innovation champions and leaders so they can show the ROI of their projects.

Both of these scenarios, occurring within a week in June 2017, illustrate the concern in the organizations about the ultimate accountability, the return on investment. This is an important measure, although it can be misused and abused in the innovation field, or in any other field for that matter. There is a place for ROI, particularly when the funder is requesting it. The key is to make sure that ROI is perceived as only one measure out of a possible set of balanced measures and that the emotion around ROI be control. Many innovation projects will result in a negative ROI, and that's expected. However, as we indicated earlier, more projects need to deliver a positive ROI, and that's anticipated. What's needed is a system that will deliver ROI while at the same time, offer a set of measures that enables process improvement and consistency.

Innovation: A Cost or an Investment?

It is helpful to think about how executives view the expenses connected with innovation. Do they see this as a cost or an investment? Most would respond quickly by suggesting that innovation is an investment. We invest in innovation to reap positive returns. Most executives, in conversations, interviews, and certainly speeches, will showplace their investments in innovation, and even characterize their spending on this area as investing in innovation. This is important because if it's an investment, they will continue it, support it, enhance it, and maybe increase it, significantly in some cases. But if they see it as a cost, then it will be controlled, reduced, and sometimes even eliminated, and perhaps folded into operating processes. Since most of innovation is small improvements in all type of functions, innovation may not appear in the classic R&D budget. These could easily be cut.

We've seen examples where companies have sliced their innovation expenses because they are not seeing the value of the process, and other companies reluctant to invest more in innovation because they don't know for sure if it's making a difference. It's good to reflect on the perspective of top executives. In uncertain times, too many executives, in search of short-term profits, slice all types of costs, including innovation. And cost reductions or cost control is a way some executives see their way to profitability or even prosperity. A lean Six Sigma project in the quality section, a brainstorming program in organization development, or a design thinking workshop in learning and development could easily become victims of cost cutting.

A good example of this occurred in 2015 when two individuals purchased Kraft and Heinz, two storied brands. Warren Buffett in the United States teamed up with Carlos Alberto Sicupira in Brazil. The *Financial*

Times, in London, interviewed Carlos and asked about the value they saw with these two companies as they would be combined in a merger. Carlos replied that there are many costs that can be cut. Costs are like fingernails. You have to constantly cut them. As those two companies have come together, both have witnessed a tremendous amount of cost cutting. And many of the decisions around cost cutting involve whether the function, department, or project can show the value that they deliver. The value that they would like to see is the financial ROI. If it could not, then that budget was slashed significantly.

Figure 3.1 shows the consequences of what happens when executives see innovation as a cost. Not only will they want to control it, reduce it, or even eliminate it, but other consequences are critical such as a loss of influence, support, and even funding. On the other hand, if innovation is perceived to be an investment, then the investment may be maintained, protected, or enhanced. And the consequences are impressive. Business partnerships flourish, client relationships improve, support is increased, and funding is much easier. In short, for some major projects and processes, ROI for innovation is needed.

An ROI is calculation using a standard return on investment formula from the finance and accounting field removes any mystery about innovation as an investment. And if the ROI is very positive, innovation may attract more investments.

The challenge is to take those innovation activities or projects that have the most executive concern about their feasibility and value and push the evaluation to ROI. It's absolutely essential in today's environment. When

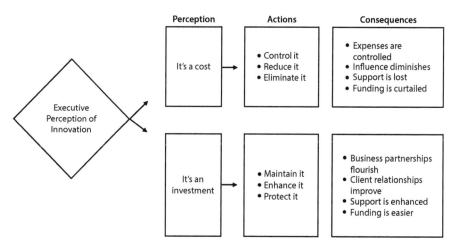

Figure 3.1 Costs Versus Investment Perception.

Figure 3.2 Use Results to Optimize and Allocate.

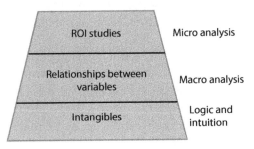

Figure 3.3 The Value of Innovation.

this is achieved, innovation can be evaluated at different steps in the process. Evaluation data are used to make changes or improvements along the way, essentially enhancing the ROI. This process is optimizing the return on investment. When this is achieved, a much better case can be made for allocating more budget. In essence, evaluation leads to optimization which leads to allocation, as shown in Figure 3.2.

The Value of Innovation: A Summary

At this point, it's helpful to summarize what's needed to demonstrate the value of innovation, which places the value being derived from three major bodies of work. As shown in Figure 3.3, the three major pillars for value are the intangibles, relationship between variables, and ROI studies.

Intangibles and the Fear of not Investing

Most investment in innovation has been made on logic and intuition. Executives know that they must have innovation. And they must invest in innovation whether it's in the R&D budget, allocating portions of a department or division's funds for innovation, or having innovation built into each unit as a systematic process. In either case, these investments are being made on the faith and hope that innovation is going to work and that it will deliver value. And all it takes is a few successes to validate this assumption.

These same executives have a fear of what happens without innovation. They see the organization going stagnant, becoming irrelevant, and ultimately dying. This fear of the consequence of not investing drives many innovation budgets, even today. These organizations want to be recognized as the most innovative organization. They want to be on the most admired list and the most sustainable list. They want to be the great place to work, the family-friendly company, or the company that protects the environment. To make these lists, investments in innovation are needed, doing things in a different way, making new products and services much better.

As mentioned previously, investments on faith and hope leave an unsettling feeling. Investing a huge amount of money based on perception is dangerous. Without any output data that's substantial, and no evidence of proof, we're funding effort and activities in the hope that it will deliver. Many executives want to move beyond this approach. As they often tell us, "We want to move out of the intangible world, move closer to the tangible proof." This leads us to our next body of knowledge.

Relationship Between Variables

As mentioned in chapter two, there are many macro levels which can show the variables that seem to be the important predictors of success, apart from just R&D spending. They include measures such as trademarks, patents, and copyrights. Which may lead to new products. While there may be a relationship between R&D spending and revenue growth, other relationships between variables may be possible. For example, is there a relationship between innovation culture and innovation outputs? Is there a relationship between the ideas generated from a suggestion system and innovation outputs? If we spend money, we should have outcomes.

Investors are always seeking a measure to predict innovation apart from R&D spending. A sophisticated approach to valuing innovation is Holt's Innovation Premium (IP). Holt is a division of Credit Suisse that develops tools for evaluating investments. Its IP measure is the basis for *Forbes's* annual innovation ranking. IP is defined as the difference between market capitalization and a net present value of cash flows from existing businesses. Figure 3.4 presents the top ten most innovative companies in 2017 based on IP.[1]

The IP is the bonus given by equity investors on the educated hunch that the company will continue to come up with profitable new growth. It is not fundamental analysis that allows you to value innovation. It is almost the opposite—it reports back to investors how much value they

Rank	Company	Industry	Country	Innovation premium
1	Salesforce	Application Software	USA	82.46
2	Tesla	Automobile manufacturers	USA	78.43
3	Amazon.com	Internet & direct marketing retail	USA	72.78
4	Shanghai raas blood products	Biotechnology	CHN	71.72
5	Netflix	Internet & direct marketing retail	USA	71.54
6	Incyte	Biotechnology	USA	70.91
7	Hindustan unilever	Household products	IND	68.59
8	Asian paints	Specialty chemicals	IND	68.28
9	Naver	Internet software & services	KOR	65.85
10	Regeneron Pharmaceuticals	Biotechnology	USA	64.40

Figure 3.4 The Top Ten Most Innovative Companies.

have already attached to a company's innovation. Accordingly, IP does not correlate with subsequent returns, as noted on the *Forbes* website: (IP) is also not a statement about expected excess returns—in fact...Knott went back through the data for the past 20 years and found that there is no correlation of IP with subsequent return to investors.[2]

Knott argues that Research Quotient (RQ) is the most intuitive measure you could construct for R&D effectiveness. It captures a company's ability to generate value from its R&D investment in a very precise way. In particular, RQ is the percentage increase in revenue a company obtains from a 1% increase in R&D, while keeping everything else the same.

These relationships are important and we expect many to come, particularly with the efforts to use analytics in the marketing, research, and development areas. Still, while these relationships are helpful, they are not always accurate and they are the macro view. It's the data across the entire organization including all innovation projects. Sometimes the data are aggregated across firms or the entire country, or even in some cases, globally. They are helpful to understand relationships, how variables are connected, and to realize that there are some important outcomes that are connected to innovation and creativity in an organization. Still, it leaves executives wanting more. If we're spending x amount of money on an innovation lab for example, what's the payoff? Or maybe we're spending on a particular new product; what's the payoff? Or we invest in a design-thinking workshop; what's the payoff? These are now micro-analysis issues and deserve attention as well.

ROI Studies

ROI studies involve evaluating the success of an innovation project with multiple levels of data, including the financial ROI. It's helpful to think about ROI for a small but significant number of innovation projects. While projects could be the different types detailed in Chapter Two, this type of analysis should be researched for projects that consume a lot of time and money, where executive expectations are high, and there is a need to understand more clearly the outcomes. The ROI analysis shows the actual value for investing in these projects. As mentioned earlier, there's a need for ROI in the innovation field. It is needed by the funders, supporters, and even for the critics. They all need to see the value at this level. This leads to the development of ROI for many innovation projects, which is the basis for this book.

Types of Data

An attempt to summarize what's needed in the innovation area brings into focus some very key issues that have been presented in the previous two chapters, as well as in this chapter. This must be considered from perspectives of principal funders of innovation, as well as the need for the various stakeholders that are involved. Add to this the need to have a systematic, logical flow of data for an evaluation and you have the data set in Figure 3.5 with inputs into the process and the six categories of data arranged in a logical chain of value, moving from inputs through five levels of outcomes, including the financial ROI.

Inputs

In any innovation project, there are inputs. These are usually the people who are involved, both in terms of number and the time they're involved in the activity, and the cost of the process. This is important because having the right people involved is critical. We have seen from some previous works that it takes a unique person to be a good innovator. The profile of the serial innovator is very impressive and clear. We want people involved who want to be involved in an engaged way. Therefore, the starting point for seeing, knowing, and proving the value is having the right people involved at the right time with the right amount of time available and on the right project. Input is important, but doesn't speak to the outcomes, the results.

Level	Measurement Focus	Typical Measures
0–Inputs	• Inputs into innovation projects including indicators representing scope, volumes, times, costs, and efficiencies	• Types of innovation • Number of projects • Number of people involved • Hours of involvement • Costs
1–Reaction and Planned Action	• Reaction to the innovation projects including their perceived value and planned action to make them successful	• Relevance • Importance • Usefulness • Appropriateness • Intent to use • Motivational • Recommended to others
2–Learning	• Knowledge gained, learning how to develop concepts and how to use skills and competencies to drive innovation	• Skills • Learning • Knowledge • Capacity • Competencies • Confidences • Contacts
3–Application and Implementation	• Application and use of knowledge, skills, and competencies, including progress made and implemention success	• Behaviors • Extent of use • Task completion • Frequency of use • Actions completed • Success with use • Barriers to use • Enablers to use • Engagement
4–Impact	• The impact of the projects and processes expressed as business impact measures	• New products • Enhanced products • Productivity • Revenue • Quality • Time • Efficiency • Incidents • Retention • Customer Satisfaction
5–ROI	• Comparison of monetary benefits from the project to project costs	• Benefit Cost Ratio (BCR) • ROI (%) • Payback period

Figure 3.5 Six Categories of Data.

Reaction and Planned Action

Reaction is often omitted from current models of measurement under the assumption that people involved in innovation are involved because they want to be. They see value in the process and they see it as important to their success as well as the success of the organization. But that may be a false assumption. The key is to collect data at this level, to make sure that the people involved in the innovation projects see those projects as relevant to the needs of the organization, important to their individual success and to the success of the organization, and as something that is useful, and helpful, and appropriate. They should intend to make the project successful and are motivated to do it. Perhaps they would even recommend that others be involved as well. Without this proper reaction, the efforts will be minimal at best. Some of the people involved in innovation may see these activities as a waste of time or money. Others would see these efforts as additional work. Still others may see efforts to focus on creativity and innovation as silly and inappropriate. When this is the case, the results will not materialize. Consequently, our first set of data is a very important first outcome level.

Learning

The next logical step is learning, and this is closely related to reaction. In fact, the reaction would normally be influenced by what the people involved in the project are learning. This is knowing about the process that they're involved in, the rules and the conditions under which they are operating, and the power of what they're working with and how it can make a big difference. The more they know, the more the resistance reduces and motivation increases.

Some authors equate innovation with learning. It's all about learning new ways, new processes, and new products through exploring, experimenting, and adjusting. As Thomas Edison famously said, he spent more time learning from the things that don't work than he spent learning from the things that do work. Learning is critical, and we must measure it. Learning measurements ensure that the knowledge, skills, and competencies are there, with the confidence to make it work, and the contacts to make it successful. Learning measurement is necessary, but is still a long way from the end game.

Application and Implementation

For some stakeholders, the big challenge of getting innovation going is this level. We have people doing something. They're generating new ideas. They're testing new concepts, trying new processes, exploring options, and identifying other possibilities. The group is mobilized, making progress, and there are actions. This is helpful because at this level of outcome, resistance has been reduced to a certain extent, as well as the inertia that holds people back from getting things done. It's also critical because innovation must follow certain procedures, such as the drug development protocol in the pharmaceutical industry. Application and implementation includes all processes and procedures necessary to make the trials successful, such as tasks, actions, checkouts, and policies. This is powerful and it can only be accomplished when participants learn what to do.

Impact

The level or measure is critical to funders. The impact is the consequence of actions, such as the new idea is working, the new product is developed, the new approach is seamless, or the new system is functional. The impact is new products, increased productivity, improved quality, or improved times. These impacts are in the system, and they define the organization. They are the impacts that will make the difference. Not only do we have the tangible impacts that we've just described, but the intangible ones as well. These usually include customer satisfaction, image, stress, teamwork, collaboration, alliances; impacts that are important but maybe not easily converted to money.

Impacts at this level are divided into tangibles and intangibles. The tangibles are those that can be converted to money for the ROI calculation and the intangibles are those that cannot be converted to money credibly with a reasonable amount of effort. This makes it all worthwhile in the minds of some of the supporters and funders. For some, you still need more. You need that ultimate accountability, ROI.

Return on Investment

As mentioned earlier, the return on investment is needed, and this can be measured in three very common ways. One is the benefit-cost ratio, which is the monetary benefits from the innovation project divided by the cost of the innovation. Benefit-cost analysis has been around for a long time and is very meaningful to many executives, particularly those in nonprofits, governments, and NGOs.

Next, there's the ROI, expressed as a percentage, which is the net benefits divided by the cost times 100. The net benefits are the monetary benefits minus the project costs. This is a very common measure in businesses and often is even understood by consumers, as they clearly see their ROI for investing their money in a savings account in a financial institution. The ROI formula comes from the finance and accounting literature.

Finally, the payback period is another possibility and this is basically a calculation of how long it takes to get the money back from this investment. This is also a financial measure. ROI measures keep the CFO and the CEO happy. As Warren Buffett says, the ROI is a way to keep score. And it's the ultimate accountability. For most executives, it shows the efficient use of funds. Just getting the impact is one thing, but seeing how this could be achieved with less cost is another. The higher your ROI, the more efficient the use of the funds.

So, there you have it. Six categories of data that are necessary, arranged in a logical flow so that one block or one category is a precondition for the others. This is a foundation that will be critical for the material in the book, but there's more.

How Does Your Current System Stack Up?

For the most part, the current systems of measuring and evaluating innovation projects fall short of providing the proper system for accountability, process improvement, and results generation. As we examined, the ways in which projects are evaluated, ten criteria are identified for an effective evaluation system. Figure 3.6 lists each issue and presents what is needed for improvement. It also shows how the ROI Methodology, presented in this book, addresses all ten of these areas.

Focus of Use

Sometimes evaluation looks like auditing. Usually during a surprise visit, someone checks to see whether the project is working as planned, and a report is generated (usually too late) to indicate that a problem exists. Evaluation of many capital expenditures, for example, is often implemented this way. The project is approved by the board, and after it is completed, a board-mandated follow-up report is produced by internal auditors and presented to the board. This report indicates what is working and not working, often at a point that is too late to make any changes.

Even in government, social sciences, and education, the evaluations are often structured in a similar way. For example, our friends in the British government tell us that when new projects are approved and implemented, funds are set aside for evaluation. When the project is completed, an evaluation is conducted and a detailed report is sent to appropriate government authorities. Unfortunately, these reports reveal that many of the programs are not working, and it is too late to do anything about them. Even worse,

Topic	Problem or issue	What is needed	ROI methodology
Focus of use	Audit focus; punitive slant; surprise nature	Process improvement focus	This is the number one use for the ROI methodology
Standards	Few, if any, standards exist	Standards needed for consistency and credibility	Twelve standards accepted by users
Types of data	Only one or two data types	Need a balanced set of data	Six types of data representing quantitative, qualitative, financial, and non-financial data
Dynamic adjustments	Not dynamic; does not allow for adjustments early in the project cycle	A dynamic process with adjustments made early and often	Adjusts for improvement at four levels and at different time frames
Connectivity	Not respectful of the chain of value that must exist to achieve a positive impact	Data collected at each stage of the chain	Every stage has data collection and a method to isolate the project's contribution
Approach	Activity based	Results based	Eight steps are used to design for results
Conservative nature	Analysis not very conservative	A conservative approach is needed for buy in	Very conservative: CFO and CEO friendly
Simplicity	Not user friendly; too complex	User friendly, simple steps	Ten logical steps
Theoretical foundation	Not based on sound principles	Should be based on theoretical framework	Endorsed by hundreds of professors and researchers; grounded in research and practice
Acceptance	Not adopted by many organizations	Should be used by many	More than 5,000 organizations using the ROI Methodology

Figure 3.6 Problems and Opportunities with Current Measurement Systems.

the people who implemented the project are either no longer there or no longer care. When accountability issues are involved, the evaluation reports usually serve as punitive information to blame the usual suspects or serve as the basis for performance review of those involved.

It is not surprising that auditing with a punitive twist does not work with innovation projects. These project evaluations must be approached with a sense of process improvement—not performance evaluation. If the project is not working, then changes must take place for it to be successful in the future.

Standards

Unfortunately, many of the approaches to evaluate innovation projects lack standards unless the project is a capital expenditure, in which case the evaluation process is covered by Generally Accepted Accounting Principles (GAAP). However, most innovation projects are not capital expenditures. In these instances, standards must be employed to ensure consistent application and reliable results. Overall, the standards should provide consistency, conservatism, and cost savings as the project is implemented. Use of standards allows the results of one project to be compared to those of another and the project results to be perceived as credible.

Types of Data

The types of data that must be collected vary. Unfortunately, many projects focus on impact measures alone, showing new products, cost savings, less waste, improved productivity, or improved customer satisfaction. These measures will change if this project is implemented. The types of measures also include intangibles.

What is needed is a balanced set of data that contains financial and non-financial measures, as well as qualitative and quantitative data. Multiple types of data not only show results of investing in healthcare projects, but help explain how the results evolved and how to improve them over time. To effectively capture the return on investment, six types of data are needed: reaction, learning, application, impact, ROI, and intangible benefits.

Dynamic Adjustments

As mentioned earlier, a comprehensive measurement system must allow opportunities to collect data throughout project implementation rather than waiting until it has been fully completed (perhaps only to find out it never worked from the beginning). Reaction and learning data must be captured early. Application data must be captured when project participants are applying knowledge, skills, and information routinely.

All these data should be used to make adjustments in the project to ensure success, not just to report post-program outcomes at a point that is too late to make a difference. Impact data are collected after routine application has occurred and represent the consequences of implementation. These data should be connected to the project and must be monitored and reviewed in conjunction with the other levels of data. When the connection is made between impact and the project, a credible ROI is calculated.

Connectivity

For many measurement schemes, such as the balanced scorecard, it is difficult to see the connection between an innovation project and the results. It is often a mystery as to how much of the reported improvement is connected to the project or even whether a connection exists.

Data need to be collected throughout the process so that the chain of impact is validated. In addition, when the business measure improves, a method is necessary to isolate the effects of the project on the data to validate the connection to the measure.

Approach

Too often, the measurement schemes are focused on activities. People are busy. They are involved. Activity is everywhere. However, activities sometimes are not connected to impact. The project must be based on achieving results at the impact and ROI levels. Not only should the project track monetary results, but also, the steps and processes along the way should focus on results. Driving improvement should be inherent to the measurement process.

By having a measurement process in place, the likelihood of positive results increases. A complete focus on results versus activity improves the chances that people will react positively, change their attitude, and apply necessary actions, which lead to a positive impact on immediate and long-term outcomes.

Conservative Nature

Many assumptions are made during the collection and analysis of data. If these assumptions are not conservative, then the numbers are overstated and unbelievable, which decreases the likelihood of accuracy and buy in. The results, including ROI, should be CFO- and CEO- friendly.

Simplicity

Too often, measurement systems are complex and confusing for practical use, which leaves users skeptical and reluctant to embrace them. The process must be user-friendly, with simple, logical, and sequential steps. It must be void of sophisticated statistical analysis and complicated financial information, at least for the projects that involve participants who lack statistical expertise. It must be user-friendly, even to those who do not have statistical or financial backgrounds.

Theoretical Foundation

Sometimes measurement systems are not based on sound principles. They use catchy terms and inconvenient processes that make some researchers and professors skeptical. A measurement system must be based on sound principles and theoretical frameworks. Ideally, it must use accepted processes as it is implemented. The process should be supported by professors and researchers who have used the process with a goal of making it better.

Acceptance

A measurement system must be used by practitioners in all types of organizations. Too often, the measurement scheme is presented as theoretical but lacks evidence of widespread use. The ROI Methodology, first described in publications in the 1970s and 1980s (with an entire book devoted to it in 1997), now enjoys more than 5,000 users. It is used in all types of projects and programs from technology, quality, marketing, and human resources, among others. In recent years it has been adopted for green projects and sustainability efforts and now innovation.

The success of the ROI Methodology will be highlighted in detail throughout this book with examples of applications in innovation. It is a comprehensive process that meets the important needs and challenges of those striving for successful innovation projects.

Using Design Thinking to Deliver and Measure Results

It is useful to think about using an innovation technique to actually deliver the value from the innovation project and actually capture the data. A very popular concept in innovation is the concept of design thinking. This process rests on the assumption that success is clearly defined, and the entire team designs for that definition of success. If you want high quality, everyone works on that. If you want low costs, everyone is focused on that issue. If you want functionality, the focus is there. For innovation projects, success is achieved when the impact has occurred. This can mean low costs in a new product, or better quality, or more convenience.

With that success defined, the team works through a series of steps, using design-thinking principles to reach the success that's desired. Although design thinking had its beginnings a few decades ago with the first book written in 1987, it really gained popularity with a book called *Change by Design* from Tim Brown with IDEO.[3] A more recent book seemed to

Basic principles

1. A problem-solving approach to handle problems on a systems level

2. A mind-set for curiosity and inquiry

3. A framework to balance needs and feasibility

4. A way to take on design challenges by applying empathy

5. A culture that fosters exploration and experimentation

6. A fixed process and a tool kit

7. A storytelling process to inspire Senior Executives

8. A new competitive logic of business strategy

9. A means to solve complex or wicked problems

10. A means to reduce risks

Figure 3.7 Design Thinking.

Mootee, Idris. (2013). *Design Thinking for Strategic Innovation*. Hoboken, NJ: Wiley.

broaden the scope and the flexibility of the process, and this is *Design Thinking for Strategic Innovation*.[4] Figure 3.7 lists some of the common design-thinking principles, though they're not universal from one author to another. This figure lists ten principles that seem to be common, taking the first eight principles and placing them in the classic steps to implement an innovation project that takes eight steps to design an innovation project for results, capture that data, and make the case for more investment.[5] This is fully described in Figure 3.8. For each of these steps, the design-thinking principle used is highlighted.

Start with Why: Aligning Projects with the Business

In this step, the design-thinking principle is to use a problem-solving approach at the systems level. The first step is defining clearly why we're pursuing the innovation project, and this is usually one or more impact measures, described earlier. Obviously, in some innovation where new experiments and ideas are generated, the impact may not be clearly known, but the general categories of impact should certainly be identifiable. Essentially, this requires the person involved in the innovation to ask the question: is it a problem we're trying to solve, or an opportunity we want to pursue? For example, the creators of Uber wanted a lower-cost, more convenient, and efficient way to catch a ride from one place to another. Essentially, the problem was that it was costing too much and taking too long to get it done. Taxis are notoriously inefficient and expensive. At the same time, they saw a great opportunity to build loyal customers, provide

1. **Start with why:** Aligning programs with the business
   - Alignment is the key
   - Is it a problem or opportunity?
   - Need specific business measure(s)

   > Design thinking principle:
   > A problem solving approach to handle problems on a systems level

2. **Make it feasible:** selecting the right solution
   - What are we doing (or not doing) that's influencing the innovation impact measure?
   - How can we achieve this performance?

   > Design thinking principle:
   > A mind-set for curiosity and inquiry

3. **Expect success:** designing for results
   - Set objectives at multiple levels
   - Define success
   - Expand responsibilities

   > Design thinking principle:
   > A framework to balance needs and feasibility

4. **Make it matter:** Designing for input, reaction, and learning
   - Focus on the objectives
   - Think about ROI
   - Make it relevant
   - Make it important
   - Make it action-oriented

   > Design thinking principle:
   > A way to take on design challenges by applying empathy

5. **Make it stick:** designing for application and impact
   - Focus on objectives
   - Ensure transfer of learning to innovation project
   - Design application tools
   - Collect data

   > Design thinking principle:
   > A culture that fosters exploration and experimentation

6. **Make it credible:** measuring results and calculating ROI
   - Isolating the effects of projects
   - Converting data to money
   - Tabulating Costs
   - Calculating ROI

   > Design thinking principle:
   > A fixed process and a tool kit

7. **Tell the Story:** communicating results to key stakeholders
   - Define audience
   - Identify why they need it
   - Select method
   - Move quickly
   - Consider one page summary

   > Design thinking principle:
   > A storytelling process to inspire senior executives

8. **Optimize results:** using black box thinking to increase funding
   - Measure
   - Improve

   > Design thinking principle:
   > A new competitive logic of business strategy

Figure 3.8 Designing for Results.

Taken from Phillips, Patti P. and Jack J. Phillips. (2017). *The Business Case for Learning: Using Design Thinking to Deliver Business Results and Increase the Investment in Talent Development.* West Chester, PA: HRDQ and ATD Press.

a great experience, and also solve the problem of time and costs. In this step, it's important to have as many specific measures identified as possible.

Make it Feasible: Selecting the Right Solution

In this step, the design-thinking principle is a mind-set for curiosity and inquiry. This means that the way in which the innovation project unfolds is identified. If we want to make a better-quality process, what is our way of working through that? What is our technique? Is it a dedicated person? Is it a specific technique? Is there a task force needed? What is the right solution to get there? This defines what people will be experiencing as they use the product or the process. If it's tackling an existing process, this is a clear indication of what we're doing now that is not working or what is it we need to be doing that we're not doing now that would make the impact measure improve? For example, taxis were not using technology to connect with riders for the most part. The solution is to use technology to the fullest extent to connect the automobile to the customer quickly, then quickly take them to the new location.

Expect Success: Designing for Results

Three issues are addressed here. The first is to make sure that objectives are set for the innovation project along the five levels or outcomes mentioned in the previous data categories. These objectives, particularly at the application and impact level, indicate what the individuals involved in the project will be doing and the impact that should occur. This also requires the success definition to be provided to all members of the group, particularly the participants of the process and others who are supporting it. And third, this definition of success is provided to all the designers, developers, and other team members who are supporting the process. All of these stakeholders can clearly see what will be done and their role in making it work. They will also design for the outcome.

Make it Matter: Designing for Input, Reaction, and Learning

In this step, the design-thinking principle is a way to take on design challenges by applying empathy. Here, all members of the group are putting themselves in the position of the people who will use and support the innovation. In the Uber example, this requires the designers and developers working on the technology to think about the driver and how this technology can be used without being distracting and without any delays. Also, thinking about the customer, the customer experience must be designed from their perspective. They may be in a hurry, they may be at a location that's not easy to find, and they need to know not only an accurate description of when someone will be there, but where they are now in the progress they're making to pick them up. This step is focusing on making sure that the innovation will be relevant, important to the parties involved, and it's something that is action-oriented. It's something that they will do to make this work.

Make it Stick: Designing for Application and Impact

The design-thinking principle is a culture that fosters exploration and experimentation. In this process, it's making sure the designers and developers are doing what's necessary to achieve success. They're following through on the plans, they're taking the steps, and there is action in place to achieve what needs to be accomplished to meet the end goal, the impact. This is essentially transferring what needs to be done to the environment where it is actually being done now; transferring it to the workplace, the company, the customer, and where it needs to be. This requires data collection at this level, to make sure that things are going properly, and built-in tools are available to measure, drive, and influence the success at the application and impact.

Make it Credible: Measuring Results and Calculating ROI

In this step, the design-thinking principle is using a fixed process and a toolkit. This step produces data that is important to all stakeholders, but particularly those who fund it. This step shows the actual business results that are achieved with the innovation and the calculated financial ROI of this investment in the innovation project.

This requires you not only to monitor the outcome measure, but also to isolate the effects of innovation from other influences. This is important because when you tackle an impact measure, there may be others working on the same measure. For example, if you're trying to speed up the time for a task with an innovative approach, there may be something inherent in the system or in the environment that's focusing on the same issue. Consequently, isolating the effects of the innovation project from other factors is an absolute must.

This also means converting the impact data to money. What's it worth to be able to improve the time and offer convenience? Sometimes it's easy to convert, such as there may be too many errors and mistakes now, and the new innovative approach is going to reduce them, and there's a monetary value for the mistake. It could be we're trying to attract more new customers with some innovative product, and we already know the value of a new customer. Sometimes the value is not there, such as the convenience of getting an Uber car in three minutes compared to a 30-minute wait for a taxi. But it's worth something, and the challenge for the team is to try to place some monetary value on this. This helps in the pricing of the service, which will influence the ROI of the project. This step will be using standard approaches for isolating the effects of the project and converting data to money.

This also involves tabulating all the costs of the project so that the monetary benefits, when the data is converted to money, are compared to the costs of the classic ROI calculation. And the final part is the actual calculation of ROI and/or benefit cost ratio.

Tell the Story: Communicating Results to Key Stakeholders.

In this step, the design-thinking principle is the use of storytelling. Even with results in hand, the efforts are not finished. The results must be communicated to all the stakeholders as quickly as possible to let them know the success of the project. In case of a lack of success, the data will show what needs to improve to make it better. Storytelling will inspire senior executives and others. Audiences love stories, and now the story can be told with different levels of data. It makes a more powerful story when they can clearly see that the dramatic events, the interesting anecdotes, and the insightful comments are backed up with proof that this project has made a difference.

Optimize the Results: Using Black Box Thinking to Increase Funding

The design principle used is a new competitive logic of business strategy. The next step is to use a concept of black box thinking to analyze the results, and use them to increase funding. The key concept is to make sure that innovation is properly supported and properly funded. This can be accomplished when the improvements are made, especially when there's a lack of improvement. Even when there is success, improvements are made to make it deliver even more value. Ultimately, the ROI is optimized, and this optimization leads to the allocation of more funds, as illustrated in Figure 3.2 earlier in the chapter. This builds the case for more investment (instead of less investment) in innovation because there is a positive return on the investment. This series of events are powerful: design for the needed results, capture data to tell a compelling story, use data to improve the innovation and optimize ROI, and then make the case for more funding. It's a novel way to think about the power of an innovation technique (design thinking) to show the value of innovation.

Requirements for the Value of Innovation: A Measurement Process

Now our work is complete, we identify all the factors and processes that must be in place for an evaluation system. Based on these two chapters, it appears that the following are needed.

1. A process must be in place to systematically show the value of the innovation process as it unfolds logically.
2. The process must be dynamic, to make adjustments along the way, as enablers and inhibitors are identified.
3. A variety of data is necessary, ranging from qualitative to quantitative, taken from different sources in different time frames.
4. Both financial and non-financial data are needed, which means that the financial ROI must be an important part of the process to be CFO-friendly.
5. The hard-to-measure and hard-to-value measures are still important and need to be an important part of this process.
6. The process must be able to predict success before the innovation project is implemented in a ROI forecast, as well as a follow-up ROI evaluation.
7. The process must be based on sound theories and theoretical frameworks. It must be researcher- and professor-friendly.
8. It must have standards that guide the use of the process and these standards must be conservative for executives to buy into, and support, them.
9. The process must be user-friendly, void of complicated mathematics and long, complicated tasks.

When these are considered, the ROI Methodology developed by the ROI Institute meets these requirements. As mentioned earlier, for over a decade the experts and practitioners in the field of innovation have experimented with the use of the ROI Methodology, and have essentially performed a proof of concept in the innovation field, showing how the ROI is developed on a variety of innovation projects. This is not only happening in the United States, but also in other countries - in particular, Copenhagen, Istanbul, and Singapore. It is now, through this book, we bring this to the mainstream of professionals in the innovation area.

Now, let's introduce the ROI Methodology in more detail.

ROI Measurement Methodology™

ROI Methodology measures the success of innovation in all types of organizations: corporations, small businesses, service organizations, universities, cities, states, countries, and non-governmental organizations. The process collects six types of data: reaction, learning, application, impact, ROI, and intangibles. Data are collected, analyzed, and reported using a systematic and logical model. Conservative standards generate results that are both CEO- and CFO-friendly.

The methodology was created and has been continuously improved by ROI Institute, a global center of excellence that focuses exclusively on this methodology. ROI Institute was founded to meet the need to evaluate the results of complex but "softer" non-capital programs. ROI Institute founders are the authors of this book.

During the last 20 years, the ROI Methodology has been applied at more than 5,000 client organizations across the globe, through client ROI projects and capability building sessions. ROI Institute has authored many award winning books that explain how the methodology is best applied in a wide range of organizational applications. Many detailed case studies have been published, to show how the method is tailored to the unique needs of individual organizations.

Most readers are familiar with the Balanced Scorecard, a concept developed in the 1990s to measure indicators of business performance. In the typical Balanced Scorecard, KPIs are developed in each of four quadrants: financials, customers, internal operations, and continuous improvement. [6] Well-conceived and implemented, the Balanced Scorecard approach has proven helpful to many executives for many years. This is a macro-level scorecard for an organization.

The limitation of the Balanced Scorecard is that it is a report of the current status of measures, usually at the business unit level. It is usually one or more of these measurements are not performing very well that drives the need for a new approach, an innovation project.

As the innovation project is implemented, the six types of data, five levels of outcomes plus intangibles are collected. The six types of data can be considered to be leading indicators (Reaction, Learning, and Application) and lagging indicators (Impact, ROI, and Intangible Benefits) as shown in Figure 3.9. For these measures, the focus of the analysis is to make the innovation matter to an important group. In the last three measures the focus is on being credible with the analysis. Objectives for each level are built into the design and planning phase of a project, and these measures are

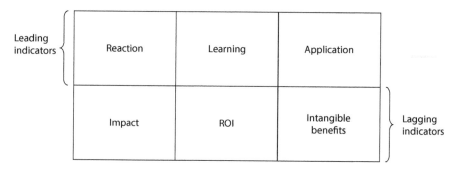

Figure 3.9 The Data from the ROI Methodology.

subsequently evaluated during the implementation and post-implementation. The ROI Methodology is complementary to the Business Scorecard.

Terminology: Projects, Solutions, Participants . . .

In *The Value of Innovation*, the term *project* is used to describe a variety of processes that can be evaluated using the ROI methodology. This is an important issue because readers may vary widely in their perspective. Individuals involved in technology applications may use the terms *system* and *technology* rather than *project*. In public policy, on the other hand, the word *program* is prominent. For a professional meetings and events planner, the word *program* may not be very pertinent, but in human resources, *program* fits quite well. Finding one term that fits all these situations would be difficult. Consequently, the term *project* is used in most. Figure 3.10 lists these and other terms that may be used depending on the context.

The term participant is used to describe the person involved in the innovation project, the person who should make it successful. Examples are provided in the figure. Sometimes there are multiple groups as participants.

Final Thoughts

This chapter makes the case for a new measurement system, describing the different criteria that must be addressed in adopting a new system

Term	Example	Participant
Program	Innovative leadership for senior executives	Senior executives
Project	A reengineering project for the plastics division	Team members
System	A fully interconnected network for all branches	System users
Initiative	An innovative faith-based effort to reduce recidivism	Prisoners
Policy	A new preschool plan for disadvantaged citizens	Students
Procedure	A new scheduling arrangement for truck drivers	Truck drivers
Event	A healthy living event	Attendees
Meeting	U.S. coast guard innovations conference	Delegates
Process	Sampling to improve product quality	Employees
People	Staff additions in the R&D center	Team members
Tool	An innovative approach to selection for the hotel staff	Recruiters

Figure 3.10 Terms and Applications.

for innovation. Clearly, current systems are not working. The funders of innovation are restless and the various supporters and stakeholders need to make sure that value is being delivered so that their participation in the process is at the optimal level. This chapter ends with the introduction to the ROI Methodology, which meets the measurement needs for knowing, proving, and showing the value of innovation. The good news is that it has been used in innovation now for over a decade and with this book we want to bring it to the mainstream of innovation globally.

4

Introducing the ROI
Methodology

A group of hospitals in the Birmingham, Alabama, metro area were seeking an innovative approach to reduce bloodstream infections in the intensive care unit. Participating hospitals comprised a mix of religious-affiliated, government-owned (city, county, and state), university-affiliated, and private-sector organizations. These hospitals were concerned about the excessive number of central line blood infections that were occurring as a result of a central vascular catheter, inserted into a large vein in the chest, introducing infection.

As the group developed and implemented a new set of procedures for reducing the number of infections, they realized that the procedures represented a cultural shift in the way they operated. This comprehensive unit based safety program required participants to use check- lists, gain knowledge, double check, and speak up. For the new procedures to be successful, various levels of data were needed beyond the traditional monitoring of infections, length of stay, and costs associated with these infections. Successive sets of data were needed that would examine the team's reaction

to the new procedures, the extent of learning of new processes and procedures, and correct application of new procedures and tools, all of which
are aimed at the impact: infections, mortality rates, length of stay, and
operating costs. This group envisioned sets of data that represented a chain
of impact that must be present for the project to be effective. These sets
represent four levels of outcome data (reaction, learning, application, and
impact). A fifth level, financial ROI is possible and is some- times necessary to calculate in today's environment. Collecting data along these levels and using a method to isolate the effects of this program from other
factors provides comprehensive data to show the impact of this program.
Figure 4.1 shows the types of data from this study. [1]

The richness of the ROI Methodology is inherent in the types of data
monitored during the implementation of a particular project. These data
are categorized by levels.

The ROI Methodology

The process for showing monetary value, including ROI, is a comprehensive, systematic methodology that includes defining the types of data,
conducting an initial analysis, developing objectives, forecasting value
(including ROI), using the ROI process model, and implementing and sustaining the process. The following sections briefly describe the approach
necessary to achieve the level of innovation accountability demanded in
today's business climate.

Types of Data

The richness of the ROI methodology is inherent in the types of data
monitored during the implementation of a particular innovation program
or project. These data are categorized by levels. Figure 4.2 shows the levels of data, and describes their measurement focus, as were presented in
Chapter 3. Subsequent chapters provide more detail on each level. This
figure is arranged as a pyramid to emphasize the proportion of measures
evaluated at each level. Every project is evaluated at Level 0 while only
about 10% are evaluated at ROI each year, usually. The descriptions are
presented at each level again as a reminder.

Level 0 represents the *Inputs* to an innovation project and details the
numbers of people and hours, the focus, and the cost of the project. These
data represent the activity around a project, as opposed to the contribution

Project: The Comprehensive Unit Based Safety Program

Description: Infections in the bloodstream can be dangerous and hard to treat. According to the Centers for Disease Control and Prevention, almost 250,000 occur in U.S. hospitals each year, often in patients who have a central vascular catheter, a tube inserted into a large vein in the chest, which may be used to provide medication or fluids or check blood oxygen levels and other vital signs. The catheters are very important in treatment but inserting them correctly and keeping the entry site and dressings clean can be complicated.

The Comprehensive Unit Based Safety Program is focused on reducing central blood line infections in intensive care units. The hospital instituted a checklist system that sets up specific steps for doctors, nurses, and technicians to take when inserting and managing a central line. The checklists give nurses explicit permission to challenge their superiors—including doctors—if they don't follow the steps without fear of reprisal. They also require workers to assess each day whether a central line catheter needs to remain in place or can be removed, which reduces the patient's risk of infection

Levels	Objectives
Level 0—Input	• All doctors, nurses, and technicians (participants) in the intensive care units are involved.
Level 1—Reaction	All participants must see this program as: • Necessary • Important • Feasible • Practical.
Level 2—Learning	• All participants must demonstrate knowledge of the checklist and new procedures. • Participants must practice "speak up" conversations with colleagues and visitors.
Level 3—Application	• Checklist will be monitored. • The use of new procedures will be observed. • Extent of "speak up" conversations will be collected.
Level 4—Impact	• Central line bloodstream infections will be reduced by 50% in six months. • Mortality rates reduced by 5%. • Days in hospital reduced by 2%. • ICU costs reduced by 3%.
Level 5—ROI	• ROI objective is 25%.

Figure 4.1 Example of Levels of Evaluation.

Source: Data from Alabama Hospital Association/ROI Institute, Inc.

of the project. Level 0 data represent the scope of the effort, the degree of commitment, and the support for a particular program. For some, this equates to value. However, commitment as defined by expenditures is not evidence that the organization is reaping value.

Reaction (Level 1) marks the beginning of the project's value stream. Reaction data capture the degree to which the participants involved in the project, including the stakeholders, react favorably or unfavorably. The key is to capture the measures that reflect the content of the project, focusing on

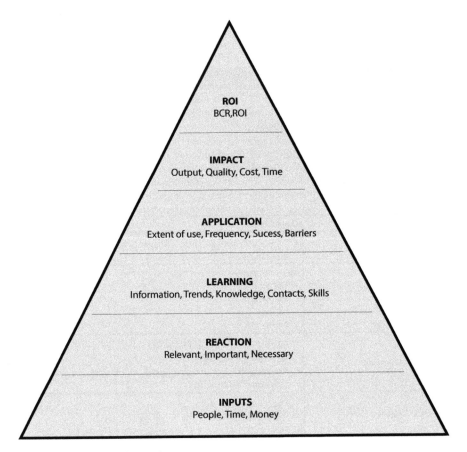

Figure 4.2 The Data Pyramid.

issues such as usefulness, relevance, importance, and appropriateness. Data at this level provide the first sign that project success may be achievable. These data also present innovation leaders with information they need to make adjustments to project implementation, to help ensure positive results.

The next level is *Learning* (Level 2). For every innovation project, there is a learning component. For some – such as projects for new technology, new systems, new competencies, and new processes – this component is substantial. For others, such as a new policy or new procedure, learning may be a small part of the process, but is still necessary to ensure successful execution. In either case, measurement of learning is essential to success. Measures at this level focus on skills, knowledge, capacity, competencies, confidence, and networking contacts.

Application and Implementation (Level 3) measures the extent to which the project is properly applied and implemented. Effective implementation is a must if bottom-line value is the goal. This is one of the most important data categories, and most implementation breakdowns occur at this level. Research has consistently shown that in almost half of all projects, participants and users are not doing what they should to make it successful. At this level, data collection involves measures such as the extent of use of information, task completion, frequency of use of skills, success with use, and actions completed. Data collection also requires the examination of barriers and enablers to successful application. This level provides a picture of how well the system supports the successful transfer of knowledge, skills, and attitude changes.

Impact (Level 4) is important for understanding the business and organizational consequences of the innovation project. Here, data are collected that especially attract the attention of the sponsor and other executives. This level shows the new products, output, productivity, revenue, quality, time, cost, efficiencies, and level of customer satisfaction connected with the project. For some, this level reflects the ultimate reason the project exists: to show the impact on various groups and systems within the organization. Without this level of data, they assert, there is no success. Once this level of measurement is achieved, it is necessary to isolate the effects of the program on the specific measures. Without this extra step, the link between the project and business measures is not evident.

The *ROI* (Level 5) is calculated next. This shows the monetary benefits of the impact measures compared with the cost of the project. This value is typically stated in terms of either a benefits/costs ratio, the ROI as a percentage, or the payback period. This level of measurement requires two important steps: first, the impact data (Level 4) must be converted to monetary values; second, the cost of the project must be captured.

Along with the five levels of results and the initial level of activity (Level 0), there is a sixth type of data (not a sixth level) developed through this methodology. This sixth type of data is the *intangible benefits* – those benefits that are purposefully not converted to money but nonetheless constitute important measures of success.

The Initial Analysis

Our research suggests that the #1 reason for projects failing is misalignment with the business. The first opportunity to obtain business alignment is in the initial analysis. Several steps are taken to make sure that the program or project is absolutely necessary. As shown in Figure 4.3, this is the beginning of the complete, sequential model representing the

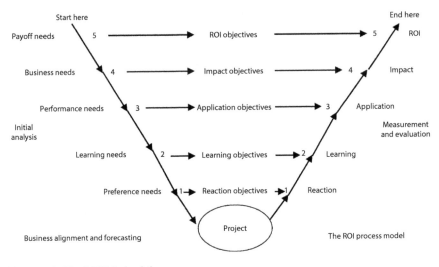

Figure 4.3 The ROI Methodology.

ROI Methodology. The first step in this analysis examines the potential payoff of the innovation. Is this a problem worth solving or an opportunity worth seeking? Or is the project worthy of implementation? For many situations, the answer is obvious: yes, the project is worthy because of its critical nature, its relevance to the issue at hand, or its effectiveness in tackling a major problem or opportunity affecting the organization.

The next step is to ensure that the project is connected to one or more business measures. Defined are the measures that must improve as a result of the overall success of the project. Sometimes the measure is obvious; other times, it is not.

Next, the performance needs are examined, with the question: "What must we do to influence the business measures defined previously?" This step aligns the innovation project with the business, and may involve a series of analytical tools to solve the problem, analyze the cause of the problem, and ensure that the project is connected with business improvement in some way. This may appear to be quite complex, but in fact is a simple approach. A logical series of questions helps: What is keeping the business measure from being where it needs to be? If it is a problem, what is its cause? If it is an opportunity, what is hindering it from moving in the right direction? This step is critical because it provides the link to the project solution.

After performance needs have been determined, the learning needs are next examined by asking: What specific skills or knowledge, need to improve so that performance can change? Every innovation process involves a learning component, and this step defines what the participants or users must know to make the innovation project successful. The needed knowledge may be as simple as understanding a policy, or be as complicated as learning many new competencies.

The final step is pinpointing the perceived value of the project. These are the preference needs. This is important to ensure that necessary knowledge will be acquired and performance will solve the business problem? Participants in the project should see it as important (to their work, to customers, to the organization), relevant (to the user, the organization), and necessary (to their work, for survival, and for growth). This level of analysis could also involve issues surrounding the scope, timing, structure, method, and budget for project implementation and delivery.

Collectively, these steps clearly define the issues that led to initiation of the project. When these preliminary steps are completed, the project can be positioned to achieve its intended results.

Understanding the need for an innovation project is critical to positioning that project for success. Positioning a project requires the development of clear, specific objectives that are communicated to all stakeholders. Objectives should be developed for each level of need, and should define success at each level, answering the question: "How will we know the need has been met?" If the criteria of success are not communicated early and often, process participants will go through the motions, with little change resulting. Developing detailed objectives with clear measures of success will position the project to achieve its ultimate objective.

Before a project is launched, forecasting the outcomes may be important to ensure that adjustments can be made or alternative solutions can be investigated. This forecast can be simple, relying on the individuals closest to the situation, or it can be a more detailed analysis of the situation and expected outcome. Recently, forecasting has become a critical tool for project sponsors who need evidence that the project will be successful, before they are willing to invest in it. Because of its importance, forecasting is the sole focus of Chapter 15.

The ROI Process Model

The next set of activities for many project leaders is to collect a variety of data along a chain of impact that shows the project's value. Figure 4.4 displays the sequential steps that lead to data categorized by the five levels of results. [1] This figure shows the ROI Methodology, a step-by-step process beginning with the objectives and concluding with reporting of data. [2] The model assumes that proper analysis is conducted to define need before the steps are taken.

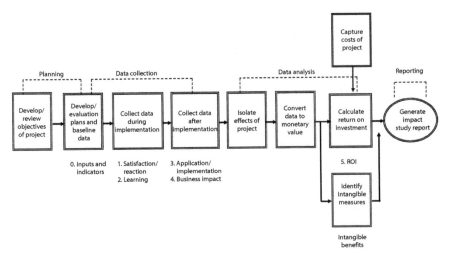

Figure 4.4 The ROI Process Model.

Planning the Evaluation

The first phase of the ROI Methodology is evaluation planning. This phase involves several procedures, including understanding the purpose of the evaluation, confirming the feasibility of the planned approach, planning data collection and analysis, and outlining the details of the project.

Evaluation Purpose

Evaluations are conducted for a variety of reasons:

- To improve the quality of innovation programs and projects, and their outcomes
- To determine whether a project has accomplished its objectives
- To identify strengths and weaknesses in the process
- To enable the cost-benefit analysis
- To assist in the development of projects or programs in the future
- To determine whether the project was the appropriate solution
- To establish priorities for project funding

The purposes of the evaluation should be considered before developing the evaluation plans because the purposes will often determine the scope of the evaluation, the types of instruments used, and the type of data collected. As with any project, understanding the purpose of the evaluation will give it focus, and will help gain support from others.

Feasibility

Another important planning consideration is determining the levels at which the innovation project will be evaluated. Some evaluations will stop at Level 3, where analysis will determine the extent to which participants are using what they have learned. Others will be evaluated through Level 4, where the consequences of application are monitored, and measures linked directly to the project are examined. If the ROI calculation is needed, the evaluation will proceed to Level 5. To reach this level of measurement, two additional steps are required: the Level 4 impact data must be converted to monetary values, and the costs of the program must be captured so that the ROI can be developed. Evaluation at Level 5 is intended for projects that are expensive, are high-profile, and are linked directly to business needs.

The initial analysis, which identifies the needs along the five levels, also defines the objectives at these levels. Programs and projects need crystal-clear direction, and the objectives provide this clarity. Precisely defined objectives provide the participants and other stakeholders with the direction they need to drive project success. The objectives are defined along the same five levels as the needs assessment:

- Reaction objectives (Level 1)
- Learning objectives (Level 2)
- Application and implementation objectives (Level 3)
- Impact objectives (Level 4)
- ROI objectives (Level 5)

These specific objectives take the mystery out of what this project should achieve.

On occasion, the initial analysis may stop with Level 2 objectives, excluding the application and impact objectives that are needed to direct the higher levels of evaluation. If application and impact objectives are not available, they must be developed using input from such groups as job incumbents, analysts, project developers, subject matter experts, facilitators, and on-the-job team leaders.

Three simple planning documents are developed next: the Data Collection Plan, the ROI Analysis Plan, and the Project Plan. These documents should be completed during evaluation planning, and before the evaluation phase is implemented. Appropriate up-front attention will save time later, when data are actually collected.

Data Collection Plan

Figure 4.5 shows a sample Data Collection Plan for an innovative project undertaken to prepare a sales team to sell an upgrade to a major software system. Recognizing that all the sales team could not conveniently come to a regional office, a mobile learning solution was developed for iPad application.

This document provides a place to capture the major elements and issues regarding data collection. Broad objectives are appropriate for planning. Specific, detailed objectives are developed later, before the program is designed. Entries in the Measures column define the specific measure for each objective; entries in the Method/Instruments column describe the technique used to collect the data; in the Sources column, the source of the data is identified; the Timing column indicates when the data are collected; and the Responsibilities column identifies who will collect the data.

ROI Analysis Plan

Figure 4.6 shows a completed ROI Analysis Plan for the same mobile learning project. This planning document captures information on key items that are necessary to develop the actual ROI calculation. In the first column, significant data items are listed. Although these are usually Level 4 impact data, in some cases this column includes Level 3 items as well. These items will be used in the ROI analysis and calculation.

The method employed to isolate the project's effects is listed next to each data item in the second column. The method of converting data to monetary values is included in the third column for those items that will be converted to money. The cost categories that will be captured for the project are outlined in the next column. Normally, the cost categories will be consistent from one project to another. The intangible benefits expected from the program are outlined in the fifth column. This list is generated from discussions about the program with sponsors and subject-matter experts. Communication targets are outlined in the sixth column. Finally, other issues or events that might influence program implementation and its outputs are highlighted in the last column. Typical items include the capability of participants, the degree of access to data sources, and unique data analysis issues.

The ROI Analysis Plan, when combined with the Data Collection Plan, provides detailed information for calculating the ROI, while explaining how the evaluation will develop from beginning to end.

Program: Product Upgrade With Mobile Learning   **Responsibility:**   **Date:**

Level	Broad Program Objective(s)	Measures of Success	Data Collection Method/Instruments	Data Sources	Timing	Responsibilities
1	REACTION & PLANNED ACTIONS Achieve positive reaction on: • Relevance to my work • Recommend to others • Important to my success • Intent to use	Rating of 4 out of 5 on a composite of four measures	LMS survey, built into program	Participant	End of program	Program manager
2	LEARNING Learn to use five concepts to sell new upgrade: • Rationale for upgrade • Features of upgrade • How upgrade will increase client profit • Pricing options • Implementation and support	Achieve 4 out of 5 correct answers on each module Achieve 20 of 25 total correct answers	True/False quiz	Participant	End of program	Program manager
3	APPLICATION/ IMPLEMENTATION Use of five skills: • Explain rationale for upgrade • Identify key features of upgrade • Describe how upgrade increases client profit • Identify pricing options • Explain implementation and support • Make the first call in 5 days	Rating (4 of 5) on a 1-5 scale System Check	Questionnaire, web-based Performance Monitoring	Participant Salesforce.com	1 month after program 1 month after program	Evaluator
4	BUSINESS IMPACT • Increase in sales to $10,000 per month • Sell first upgrade in 3 weeks	Monthly sales per associate Actual sale	Business performance monitoring Business performance monitoring	Salesforce.com Salesforce.com	3 months after program 1 month after program	Evaluator
5	ROI 30%					

Comments:

Figure 4.5 Completed Data Collection Plan.

Program: Product Upgrade with Mobile Learning   **Responsibility:** _____   **Date:** _____

Data Items (Usually Level 4)	Methods for Isolating the Effects of the Program/Process	Methods of Converting Data to Monetary Values	Cost Categories	Intangible Benefits	Communication Targets for Final Report	Other Influences/Issues During Application	Comments
• Monthly sales per associate	• Control group analysis • Participant estimates (Both measures)	• Direct conversion using standard profit contribution	• Needs assessment • Design • Content development • Mobile device • Participants' salaries plus benefits (time) • Cost of coordination and administration (time) • Project management time • Evaluation	• Customer engagement and satisfaction • Job satisfaction of sales associates • Stress reduction • Reputation	• Program participants • Sales managers • Product manager • Senior executives, regional and headquarters • Learning coordinators, designers, and managers • All sales associates	• No communication with control group	
• Time to first sale	• Control group analysis • Participant estimates (Both measures)	N/A					

Figure 4.6 Completed ROI Analysis Plan.

	F	M	A	M	J	J
Decision to conduct ROI study	▓					
Evaluation planning complete	▓					
Instruments designed	▓					
Instruments are pilot tested		▓				
Data collected		▓				
Data tabulation preliminary summary			▓			
Analysis conducted				▓		
Report is written				▓		
Report printed					▓	
Results communicated						▓
Improvements initiated						▓
Implementation complete						▓

Figure 4.7 Project Plan.

Project Plan

The final plan developed for the evaluation planning phase is a Project Plan, as shown in Figure 4.7. The Project Plan consists of a project description, including brief details such as duration, target audience, and number of participants. It also shows the timeline of the project, from the planning through final communication of the results. This Plan becomes an operational tool to keep the project on track.

Collectively, these three planning documents provide the direction necessary for the ROI impact study. Most of the decisions regarding the process are made as these planning tools are developed. Thereby, the remainder of the project becomes a methodical, systematic process of implementing the plans. This is a crucial step in the ROI Methodology, where valuable time allocated to planning will save precious time later.

Collecting Data

Data collection is central to the ROI Methodology. Both hard data (representing output, quality, cost, and time) and soft data (including job satisfaction and customer satisfaction) are collected. Data are collected using a variety of methods, including:

- Surveys
- Questionnaires
- Tests
- Observations
- Interviews

- Focus groups
- Action plans
- Performance contracts
- Business performance monitoring

The important challenge in data collection is to select the method or methods appropriate for the setting and the specific program, within the time and budget constraints of the organization. Data collection methods are covered in more detail in Chapter 6.

Isolating the Effects of the Project

An often overlooked issue in evaluation is the process of isolating the effects of the innovation project. In this step, specific strategies are explored that determine the amount of impact that is directly related to the project. This step is essential because many factors can influence performance data. The specific strategies of this step pinpoint the amount of improvement directly related to the project, resulting in increased accuracy and credibility of ROI calculations. The following techniques have been used by organizations to tackle this important issue:

- Control groups
- Trend line analysis
- Forecasting models
- Participant estimates
- Managers' estimates
- Senior management estimates
- Experts' input
- Customer input

Collectively, these techniques provide a comprehensive set of tools to handle the important and critical issue of isolating the effects of projects. Chapter 11 is devoted to this important step in the ROI Methodology.

Converting Data to Monetary Values

To calculate the return on investment, Level 4 impact data are converted to monetary values and compared with innovation project costs. This requires that a value be placed on each unit of impact data connected with the project. Many techniques are available to convert data to monetary values. The specific technique selected depends on the type of data and the situation. The techniques include:

- Use of output data, as standard values
- Cost of quality, usually as a standard value
- Time savings converted to participant wage and employee benefits
- An analysis of historical costs
- Use of internal and external experts
- Search of external databases
- Use of participant estimates
- Use of manager estimates
- Soft measures mathematically linked to other measures

This step in the ROI model is absolutely necessary to determine the monetary benefits of a project. The process is challenging, particularly with soft data, but can be methodically accomplished using one or more of these strategies. Because of its importance, this step in the ROI Methodology is described in detail in Chapter 12.

Identifying Intangible Benefits

In addition to tangible or monetary benefits, intangible benefits – those not converted to money – are identified for most projects. Intangible benefits include items such as:

- Increased employee engagement
- Increased brand awareness
- Improved networking
- Improved customer service
- Fewer complaints
- Reduced conflict

During data analysis, every attempt is made to convert all data to monetary values. All hard data – such as output, quality, and time – are converted to monetary values. The conversion of soft data is also attempted for each data item. However, if the process used for conversion is too subjective or inaccurate, and the resulting values lose credibility in the process, then the data are listed as an intangible benefit with the appropriate explanation. For some innovation projects, intangible, nonmonetary benefits are extremely valuable, and often carry as much influence as the hard data items. Chapter 13 is devoted to the intangible benefits.

Tabulating Project Costs

An important part of the ROI equation is the denominator, or the calculation of project costs. Tabulating the costs involves monitoring or developing all the related costs of the innovation project targeted for the ROI calculation. Among the cost components to be included are:

- Initial analysis costs
- Cost to design and develop the project
- Cost of all project materials
- Costs for the project team
- Cost of the facilities for the project
- Travel, lodging, and meal costs for the participants and team members
- Participants' salaries (including employee benefits)
- Administrative and overhead costs, allocated in some convenient way
- Evaluation costs

The conservative approach is to include all these costs so that the total is fully loaded. Chapter 14 includes this step in the ROI Methodology.

Calculating the Return on Investment

The return on investment is calculated using the project benefits and costs. The benefits/costs ratio (BCR) is calculated as the project benefits divided by the project costs. In formula form:

$$BCR = \frac{\text{Project Benefits}}{\text{Project Costs}}$$

The return on investment is based on the net benefits divided by project costs. The net benefits are calculated as the project benefits minus the project costs. In formula form, the ROI becomes:

$$ROI(\%) = \frac{\text{Net Project Benefits}}{\text{Project Costs}} \times 100$$

This is the same basic formula used in evaluating other investments, in which the ROI is traditionally reported as earnings divided by investment. Chapter 14 provides more detail.

Reporting

The final step in the ROI Process Model is reporting, a critical step that is often deficient in the degree of attention and planning required to ensure its success. The reporting step involves developing appropriate information in impact studies and other brief reports. At the heart of this step are the different techniques used to communicate to a wide variety of target audiences. In most ROI studies, several audiences are interested in and need the information. Careful planning to match the communication method with the audience is essential to ensure that the message is understood and that appropriate actions follow. Chapter 16 is devoted to this critical step in the ROI process.

Operating Standards and Philosophy

To ensure consistency and replication of impact studies, operating standards must be applied as the process model is used to develop ROI studies. The results of the study must stand alone and must not vary with the individual who is conducting the study. The operating standards detail how each step and issue of the process will be handled. Figure 4.8 shows the Twelve Guiding Principles of the ROI Methodology that form the basis for its operating standards.

---

1. When conducting a higher-level evaluation, collect data at lower levels.
2. When planning a higher-level evaluation, the previous level of evaluation is not required to be comprehensive.
3. When collecting and analyzing data, use only the most credible sources.
4. When analyzing data, select the most conservative alternative for calculations.
5. Use at least one method to isolate the effects of a project.
6. If no improvement data are available for a population or from a specific source, assume that little or no improvement has occurred.
7. Adjust estimates of improvement for potential errors of estimation.
8. Avoid use of extreme data items and unsupported claims when calculating ROI.
9. Use only the first year of annual benefits in ROI analysis of short-term solutions.
10. Fully load all costs of a solution, project, or program when analyzing ROI.
11. Intangible measures are defined as measures that are purposely not converted to monetary values.
12. Communicate the results of ROI methodology to all key stakeholders.

Figure 4.8 Twelve Guiding Principles of ROI.

The guiding principles serve not only to consistently address each step, but also to provide a much-needed conservative approach to the analysis. A conservative approach may lower the actual ROI calculation, but it will also build credibility with the target audience.

Implementing and Sustaining the Process

A variety of environmental issues and events will influence the successful implementation of the ROI process. These issues must be addressed early to ensure its success. Specific topics or actions include:

- A policy statement concerning results-based projects
- Procedures and guidelines for different elements and techniques of the evaluation process
- Formal meetings to develop staff skills with the ROI process
- Strategies to improve management commitment to and support for the ROI process
- Mechanisms to provide technical support for questionnaire design, data analysis, and evaluation strategy
- Specific techniques to place more attention on results

The ROI process can fail or succeed based on these implementation issues.

The ROI process should undergo periodic review by the organization. An annual review is recommended to determine the extent to which the process is adding value. This final element involves checking satisfaction with the process, and determining how well it is understood and applied. Essentially, this review follows the process described in this book to determine the ROI of the ROI Methodology. Chapter 17 focuses on implementing and sustaining the use of ROI.

Benefits of This Approach

The methodology presented in this book has been used consistently and routinely by thousands of organizations worldwide over the past 20 years. It is more prominent in some fields and industries than in others. Much has been learned about the success of this methodology, and what it can bring to the organizations using it.

Aligning with Business

The ROI Methodology ensures alignment with the business, enforced in three steps. First, even before the innovation project is initiated, the Methodology ensures that alignment is achieved upfront, at the time the project is validated as the appropriate solution. Second, by requiring specific, clearly defined objectives at the impact level, the project focuses on the ultimate outcomes, in essence driving the business measure by its design, delivery, and implementation. Third, in the follow-up data, when the business measures may have changed or improved, a method is used to isolate the effects of the project on that data. Consequently, this proves the connection to that business measure (i.e., showing the amount of improvement directly connected to the project and ensuring there is business alignment).

Validating the Value Proposition

Most innovation projects are undertaken to deliver value. As described in this chapter, however, the definition of value may on occasion be unclear, or may not be what a project's various sponsors, organizers, and stakeholders desire. Consequently, shifts in value often occur. When the values are finalized, the project's value proposition is detailed. The ROI Methodology can forecast the value in advance; and if the value has been delivered, it verifies the value proposition agreed to by the appropriate parties.

Improving Processes

The ROI Methodology is a process improvement tool, by design and by practice. It collects data to evaluate how things are, or are not, working. When things are not where they should be – as when projects are not proceeding as effectively as expected – data are available to indicate what must be changed to make the project more effective. When things are working well, data are available to show what else could be done to make them better. Thus, this is a process improvement system designed to provide feedback to make changes. As a project is conducted, the results are collected, and feedback is provided to the various stakeholders for specific actions for improvement. These changes drive the project to better results, which are then measured while the process continues. This continuous feedback cycle is critical to process improvement, and is inherent in the ROI Methodology approach. In essence, the process uses design thinking principles to design for the results needed.

Enhancing the Image and Building Respect

Many functions, and even entire professions, are criticized for being unable to deliver what is expected. For this, their public image suffers. The ROI Methodology is one way to help build the respect a function or profession needs.

The ROI Methodology can make a difference in any function, and not just those under fire. Many executives have used ROI to show the value of a project, perhaps changing the perception of a project from one based on activity to one that credibly adds value. This methodology shows a connection to the bottom line, and shows the value delivered to stakeholders. It removes issues about value and a supposed lack of contribution to the organization. Consequently, this methodology is an important part of the process of changing the image within the function of the organization, and building needed respect innovation.

Improving Support

Securing support for innovation programs and projects is critical, particularly at the middle manager level. Many projects enjoy the support of the top-level managers who allocated the resources to make the projects viable. Unfortunately, some middle-level managers may not support certain projects because they do not see the value the projects deliver in terms these managers appreciate and understand. Having a methodology that shows how a project or program is connected to the manager's business goals and objectives can change this support level. When middle managers understand that a project is helping them meet specific performance indicators or departmental goals, they will usually support the process, or will at least resist it less. In this way, the ROI Methodology can improve manager support.

This is more important when many individuals are involved in innovation activities. For example, as innovation becomes a part of everyone's job, the support level needs to move from "we are involved in innovation activities when we have time" to "innovation is our top priority."

Justifying or Enhancing Budgets

Some organizations have used the ROI Methodology to support proposed budgets. Because the methodology shows the monetary value expected or achieved with specific projects, the data can often be leveraged into budget requests. When a particular function is budgeted, the amount budgeted is often in direct proportion to the value that the function adds. If little or no credible data support the contribution, the budgets are often trimmed – or at least not enhanced. Bringing accountability to this level is one of the best ways to secure future funding.

Building a Partnership with Key Executives

Almost every function attempts to partner with operating executives and key managers in the organization. Unfortunately, some managers may not want to be partners. They may not want to waste time and effort on a relationship that does not help them succeed. They want to partner only with groups and individuals who can add value and help them in meaningful ways. Showing the project results will enhance the likelihood of building these partnerships, with the results providing the initial impetus for making the partnerships work.

Earning a Seat at the Table

Many organizational functions want a "seat at the table", however defined. Typically, a seat at the table means participating in strategy and important tactical discussions at the top of the organization. Department and program leaders hope to be involved in strategic decision making, particularly in areas that will affect their functions, and the projects and processes in their functions. The person leading innovation in an organization should have a seat at the table. Most do; some do not. Showing the actual contribution, and getting others to understand how the function adds value, can help earn the coveted seat at the table. Most executives want to include those who are genuinely helping the business, and will seek input that is valuable and constructive. The use of the ROI Methodology may be the single most important action that can be taken to earn the seat at the table.

Final Thoughts

This chapter introduced the overall ROI Methodology that underlies the Value of Innovation approach. It presented the different elements and steps in the Methodology, the standards, and the different concepts necessary to understand how ROI process works. This chapter brings the Methodology into focus. Before one can accept the approach, the steps and the detail have to be shown.

Let's continue in this regard, by taking a closer look at how to establish the needs and objectives for your innovation project, next.

5

Aligning Innovation Projects to the Organization

If you're concerned about monitoring your exercise with the goal of becoming more fit and losing a few extra pounds, then the odds are that you're aware of Fitbit. Whether it's a device that clips to your pocket or worn on your wrist, Fitbit monitors steps, hours of sleep, and even more. The company behind it has been a phenomenal success. Since its beginning in 2008 Fitbit has sold more than 63 million devices, and the stock peaked at $48 a share shortly after it went public in 2015. Today, it's just over $5. The most recent quarterly sales were 40% lower than the previous period a year ago. Meanwhile in July, Jawbone, maker of the UP wristband fitness tracker who at one time started up fresh with venture capital funding and 3 billion dollar evaluation is liquidating its assets. [1]

Does this mean that this is a fad that is going away, like so many others? Perhaps not. One thing for certain, the Fitbit has more competition than before. Some of the competition is promising all types of measurement tracking, including monitoring blood sugar for diabetes without piercing the skin, for example. The problem with Fitbit might need a little more explanation.

Of Fitbit's over 50 million registered users, less than half, 23.2 million, remain active. The first generation of fitness trackers has largely run its course, it seems. Three major issues appear to have caused the decline of Fitbit. First, they are a victim of their own success. Tracking is now popular, and smart phones and smart watches have all the functionality of the fitness tracker. Second, the devices have been notoriously inaccurate. For example, a recent study published in The Journal of Personalized Medicine found that seven popular fitness trackers all significantly miscalculated the number of calories that participants burned. The third issue concerns the success of the fitness tracker to actually cause weight reduction. Most experts would agree that if a person needs to lose weight, there's a combination of fitness and diet involved. Perhaps Fitbit has not done enough to study how that could be more closely related. Consider this study.

No Magic Bullet – In a 2016 study published in JAMA, 470 overweight participants were put on an exercise plan as well as a low-calorie diet. They were divided into two groups: One self-reported their diet and exercise, while the second was given fitness trackers to measure their activity. After two years, the group that had been given the fitness trackers lost, on average, around five fewer pounds than the group without the devices (5.7 pounds vs. 13).

For John Jakicic, a professor of health and physical activity at the University of Pittsburgh and the study's lead author, the results were surprising. He's currently working on new research exploring why fitness-tracking data doesn't necessarily translate to health results. (His personal hunch is that the device spat out lots of data without providing the support and context to incur a response.)

If you have a device and it works for you, "by all means, keep using it," says Jakicic. But "let's not make this too complicated." Weight loss is about moving more and eating less. [2]

The problem may be focusing users' efforts on one important measure, causing them to ignore the other. This is classic in many systems. Focusing on productivity sometimes has an adverse effect on quality. Focusing on quality can have an adverse effect on productivity. A focus on the cost of sales can have an effect on customer satisfaction.

We were working with a group of Healthy Living professionals in Alberta, Canada, and one of the projects undertaken by a group of people in an ROI

Certification was the effect of Fitbits distributed to a group of people. The study would track the weight loss of the group and try to monetize the weight loss for that health care system, which is largely funded by the government, and to calculate the ROI. The question becomes: Is the money spent on buying the Fitbits and providing them to citizens worth it in the health care system in the long run? The study never got completed because according to the researchers, when they contacted the Fitbit company, there was not much interest on their part in assisting with this kind of study.

The major problem here is a failure to have a good measurement system with proper alignment that can show the value of a new innovation, not only initially, but consistently. When the accuracy of the device itself is called into question and there's a lack of evidence available to users about how it connects directly to weight loss, then it's value comes into question. This may be the reason that less than half of the registered users are still active. While no one knows for sure what happened at Fitbit, we suggest that a balanced measurement system with proper alignment would help. Ample studies should be conducted on the success of the Fitbit in terms of weight loss, keeping diet as an important part of the process. This could have shown more convincing data that Fitbit does make a difference, and it might have made a difference with users.

Creating Business Alignment

Based on approximately 2,000 published and unpublished case studies, the #1 cause of project failure is moving forward without a clearly defined business need. The second most common cause of failure is misalignment between the project objectives and business needs.

The Purpose of Alignment

Most innovation projects should begin with a clear focus on the desired outcome. The end must be specified in terms of business needs and business measures so that the outcome – the actual improvement in the measures – and the corresponding ROI are clear. This establishes the expectations throughout the analysis and project design, development, delivery, and implementation stages.

Beginning with the end in mind requires pinning down all the details to ensure that the project is properly planned and executed according to schedule. But conducting this up-front analysis is not as simple as one might think. It requires a disciplined approach.

Disciplined Analysis

Proper analysis requires discipline and determination to adhere to a structured, systematic process supported by standards. This standardized approach adds credibility and allows for consistent application, so that the analysis can be readily replicated. A disciplined approach maintains process efficiency, as various tools and templates are developed and used. This initial phase of project development calls for focus and thoroughness, with little allowance for major shortcuts.

Not every innovation project should be subjected to the type of comprehensive analysis described in this chapter. Some needs are obvious and require little analysis other than that necessary to develop the project. Additional analysis may be needed to confirm that the project addresses the perceived need, and perhaps to fine tune the project for future application. The amount of analysis required often depends on the expected opportunity to be gained if the project is appropriate, or the negative consequences anticipated if the project is inappropriate.

When analysis is proposed, individuals may react with concern or resistance. Some are concerned about the potential for "paralysis by analysis," where requests and directives lead only to additional analyses. Such reactions are problematic for an organization because analysis is necessary to ensure that the project is appropriate. Unfortunately, analysis is often misunderstood – conjuring up images of complex problems, confusing models, and a deluge of data with complicated statistical techniques to cover all bases. In reality, analysis need not be so complicated. Simple techniques can uncover the cause of a problem or the need for a particular project.

Organizations often resist needed analysis because:

1. *The specific need appears to point to a particular solution.* Sometimes the information gained from asking individuals what they need appears to indicate a legitimate solution, but in fact the solution is inadequate or inappropriate. A few years back, Xerox was losing market share to Canon. Xerox continued to focus on speed and quality, their core advantage. However, Canon focused on cost and size, what the customer wanted.
2. *The solution appears to be obvious.* In the process of examining a problem or identifying a potential opportunity,

some solutions will arise that seem obvious. For example, if employees take too long to complete a particular task, the immediate conclusion may be that a new technology is needed that will reduce task completion time. Although this solution appears obvious, deeper analysis may reveal that other solutions – such as increasing motivation, minimizing resistance, removing obstacles, and eliminating bottlenecks – are more appropriate.

3. *Everyone has an opinion about the cause of a problem.* The person requesting a particular project may think that he or she has the best solution. Choosing the solution championed by the highest-ranking or most senior executive is often tempting. Unfortunately, this person may not be close enough to the situation to offer a solution that will have a lasting effect on the problem.

4. *Analysis takes too much time.* Yes, analysis takes time and consumes resources. However, the consequences of inadequate analysis can be more expensive. If the implemented solution does not appropriately address the needs, time and money may be wasted, and the problem is left unsolved. The consequences of ill-advised solutions implemented without an analysis can be devastating. When designed properly and conducted professionally, an analysis can be completed within the budgetary and time constraints of most organizations. The secret is to focus on the right tools for the situation.

5. *Analysis sounds confusing.* Determining a problem's causes may seem complex and puzzling. However, analyses can be simple and straightforward, and achieve excellent results. The challenge is to select the level of analysis that will yield the best solution with minimal effort and the simplest techniques.

In the face of these misconceptions, the difficulty of promoting additional analysis is apparent. But this step is critical and should not be omitted, or else the process will be flawed from the outset.

The remainder of the chapter delves into the components of analysis that are necessary for a solid alignment between a project and the business. First, however, reviewing the model introduced in the previous chapter may be helpful. It is presented again here, as Figure 5.1.

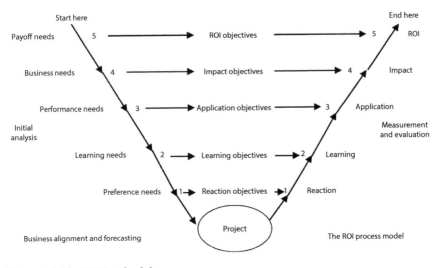

Figure 5.1 The ROI Methodology.

Determining the Potential Payoff

The first step in up-front analysis of an innovation project is to determine the potential payoff of solving a problem or seizing an opportunity. This step begins with answers to a few crucial questions: Is this project worth doing? Is it feasible? What is the likelihood of a positive ROI?

For innovation projects addressing significant problems, or opportunities with high potential rewards, the answers are obvious. However, these questions may take longer to answer for lower-profile projects, or those for which the expected payoff is less apparent. In any case, these are legitimate questions, and the analysis can be as simple or as comprehensive as required.

Essentially, a project will pay off in profit increases or in cost savings. Profit increases are generated by projects that drive revenue (e.g., that improve sales, increase market share, introduce new products, open new markets, enhance customer service, or increase customer loyalty). Other revenue-generating measures include increasing membership, increasing donations, obtaining grants, and generating tuition from new and returning students – all of which, after subtracting the cost of doing business, should leave a profit.

Many projects drive cost savings. Cost savings can come through cost reduction or cost avoidance. Improved quality, reduced cycle time, lowered downtime, reduced complaints, reduced employee turnover, and minimized delays are all examples of cost savings.

Cost avoidance projects are implemented to reduce risks, avoid problems, or prevent unwanted events. Some finance and accounting professionals may view cost avoidance as an inappropriate measure to use to determine monetary benefits and calculate ROI. However, if the assumptions prove correct, an avoided cost (e.g., compliance fines) can be more rewarding than reducing an actual cost. Preventing a problem is more cost-effective than waiting for the problem to occur and then having to focus on solving it.

Determining the potential payoff is the first step in the needs analysis process. This step is closely related to the next one, determining the business need, since the potential payoff is typically based on a consideration of the business. The payoff depends on two factors: the monetary value derived from the business measure's improvement and the approximate cost of the project. Identifying these monetary values in detail usually yields a more credible forecast of what can be expected from the chosen solution. However, this step may be omitted in situations where the problem (business need) must be resolved regardless of the cost, or if it becomes obvious that this is a high-payoff activity.

The target level of detail may also hinge on the need to secure project funding. If the potential funding source does not recognize the value of the project compared with the potential costs, more detail may be needed to provide a convincing case for funding.

Knowledge of the actual payoff is not necessary if widespread agreement exists that the payoff from the project will be high, or if the problem in question must be resolved regardless of cost. For example, if the problem involves a safety concern, a regulatory compliance issue, or a competitive matter, a detailed analysis is not needed.

Obvious Versus not-so-obvious Payoff

The potential payoff is obvious for some projects, and not so obvious for others. Opportunities with obvious payoffs may include:

- Excessive product returns: 30 percent higher than previous year
- Very low market share in a market with few players
- Operating costs 47% higher than industry average
- Customer satisfaction rating of 3.89 on a 10-point scale
- A cost to the city of $75,000 annually for each homeless person
- Noncompliance fines totaling $1.2 million, up 82% from last year

- Turnover of critical talent 35% above benchmark figure
- The time to process a claim has increased 30 percent in two years
- Sexual harassment complaints per 1,000 employees are the highest in the industry
- System downtime is double last year's performance
- Safety record is among the worst in the industry
- Excessive absenteeism in call centers: 12.3 percent, compared to 5.4 percent industry average

Here, each item appears to reflect a serious problem that needs to be addressed by executives, administrators, or politicians.

For other projects, the issues are sometimes unclear and may arise from political motives or bias. These potential opportunities are associated with payoffs that may not be so obvious. The opportunities may include:

- Implement an innovation culture
- Teach employees how to be creative
- Improve the customer experience
- Conduct a design thinking workshop
- Implement extraordinary customer service
- Improve branding for all products
- Create new products
- Become a technology leader
- Become a "green" company
- Improve leadership competencies for all managers
- Grow the business
- Create a great place to work
- Improve customer satisfaction
- Organize a business development conference
- Establish a project management office
- Develop an "open book" company"
- Become a technology leader
- Implement Lean training throughout the system
- Implement a transformation program involving all employees
- Implement a career advancement program
- Create a wellness and fitness center
- Build capability for future growth
- Create an engaged workforce

With each of these opportunities, there is a need for more specific detail regarding the measure. For example, if the opportunity is to become a "green" company, one might ask: How is "green" defined? What is a green company? What are the advantages of becoming a green company? Projects with not-so-obvious payoffs require greater analysis than those with clearly defined outcomes.

The potential payoff establishes the fundamental reason for pursuing new or enhanced projects. But the payoff, whether obvious or not, is not the only reason for moving forward with a project. The cost of a problem is another factor. If the cost is excessive, it should be addressed. If not, then a decision must be made as to whether the problem is worth solving.

The Cost of a Problem

Problems are expensive and their solution can result in high returns, especially when the solution is inexpensive. To determine the cost of the problem, its potential consequences must be examined and converted to monetary values. Problems may encompass time, quality, productivity, and team or customer issues. All of these factors must be converted to monetary values if the cost of the problem is to be determined. Inventory shortages are often directly associated with the cost of the inventory as well as with the cost of carrying the inventory. Time can easily be translated into money by calculating the fully loaded cost of an individual's time spent on unproductive tasks. Calculating the time for completing a project, task, or cycle involves measures that can be converted to money. Errors, mistakes, waste, delays, and bottlenecks can often be converted to money because of their consequences. Productivity problems and inefficiencies, equipment damage, and equipment under use are other items whose conversion to monetary value is straightforward.

In examining costs, it is crucial to consider *all* the costs and their implications. For example, the full cost of an accident includes not only the cost of lost workdays and medical expenses, but their effects on insurance premiums, the time required for investigations, damage to equipment, and the time spent by all involved employees addressing the accident. The cost of a customer complaint includes not only the cost of the time spent resolving the complaint, but also the value of the item or service that has to be adjusted because of the complaint. The costliest consequence of a customer complaint is the price to the company of lost future business and goodwill from the complaining customer, and from potential customers who learn of the complaint.

Placing a monetary value on a problem helps in determining if the problem's resolution is economically feasible. The same applies to opportunities.

The Value of an Opportunity

Just as the cost of a problem can be easily tabulated in most situations, the value of an opportunity can also be calculated. Examples of opportunities include implementing a new process, exploring new technology, increasing research and development efforts, and upgrading the workforce to create a more competitive environment. A problem may not exist in these situations, but there is an opportunity to get ahead of the competition or to prevent a problem's occurrence by taking immediate action. Assigning a proper value to this opportunity requires considering what may happen if the project is not pursued, or acknowledging the windfall that could be realized if the opportunity is seized. The value is determined by following the different possible scenarios to convert specific business impact measures to money. The difficulty in this process is conducting a credible analysis. Forecasting the value of an opportunity entails many assumptions, in contrast to calculating the value of a known outcome.

To Forecast or not to Forecast?

The need to seek and assign value to opportunities leads to an important decision: to forecast or not to forecast ROI. If the stakes are high and support for the innovation project is shaky, a detailed forecast may be the only way to gain the needed support and funding for the project, or to inform the choice between multiple potential projects. In developing the forecast, the rigor of the analysis is an issue. In some cases, an informal forecast is sufficient, given certain assumptions about alternative outcome scenarios. In other cases, a detailed forecast is needed that uses data collected from a variety of experts, previous studies from another project, or perhaps more sophisticated analysis. Chapter 15 provides techniques useful for developing forecasts.

Once the potential payoff, including its financial value, has been determined, the next step is to clarify the business needs.

Determining Business Needs

Determining the business needs requires the identification of specific measures, so that the business situation can be clearly assessed. The concept of business needs refers to gains in productivity, quality, efficiency, time, and cost. This is true for the private sector as well as in government, nonprofit, and academic organizations.

The Opportunity

A business need is represented by a business measure. Any process, item, or perception can be measured, and such measurement is critical to this level of analysis. If the project focuses on solving a problem, preventing a problem, or seizing an opportunity, the measures are usually identifiable. The important point is that the measures are present in the system, and ready to be captured for this level of analysis. The challenge is to define the measures, and to find them swiftly and economically.

Hard Data Measures

To focus on the desired measures, distinguishing between hard data and soft data may be helpful. Hard data are primary measures of improvement presented in the form of rational, undisputed facts that are usually gathered within functional areas throughout an organization. These are the most desirable type of data because they are easy to quantify, and are easily converted to monetary values. The fundamental criteria for gauging the effectiveness of an organization are hard data items such as revenue, productivity, and profitability, as well as measures that quantify such processes as cost control and quality assurance.

Hard data are objective and credible measures of an organization's performance. Hard data can usually be grouped in four categories, as shown in Figure 5.2. These categories – output, quality, costs, and time – are typical performance measures in any organization.

Hard data from a particular innovation project may involve new products or improvements in products or improvements in the output of a work unit, section, department, division, or entire organization. Every organization, regardless of the type, must have basic measures of output, such as number of patients treated, students graduated, tons produced, or packages shipped. Since these values are monitored, changes can easily be measured by comparing "before" and "after" outputs.

Quality is a very important hard data category. If quality is a major priority for the organization, processes are likely in place to measure and monitor quality. The rising prominence of quality improvement processes (such as Total Quality Management, Continuous Quality Improvement, and Six Sigma) has contributed to the tremendous recent successes in pinpointing the proper quality measures, and assigning monetary values to them.

Cost is another important hard data category. Many projects and programs are designed to lower, control, or eliminate the cost of a specific process or activity. Achieving cost targets has an immediate effect on the

Output	Quality	Costs	Time
New products	Failure rates	Shelter costs	Cycle time
Enhanced products	Dropout rates	Treatment costs	Equipment
Revenue	Scrap	Budget variances	downtime
Production	Waste	Unit costs	Overtime
Items assembled	Rejects	Cost by account	On time
Money collected	Error rates	Variable costs	shipments
Items sold	Rework	Fixed costs	Time to project
New accounts	Shortages	Overhead cost	completion
generated	Product defects	Operating costs	Processing time
Forms processed	Deviation from	Project cost savings	Supervisory time
Loans approved	standard	Accident costs	Time to
Inventory turnover	Product failures	Program costs	proficiency
Patients visited	Inventory adjustments	Sales expense	Learning time
Applications processed	Time card corrections		Adherence to
Students graduated	Incidents		schedules
Tasks completed	Compliance		Repair time
Output per hour	discrepancies		Efficiency
Productivity	Agency fines		Work stoppages
Work backlog			Order response
Incentive bonus			Late reporting
Shipments completion			Lost-time days
rate			

Figure 5.2 Examples of Hard Data.

bottom line. Some organizations focus narrowly on cost reduction. For example, consider Wal-Mart, whose tagline is "Always low prices. Always." All levels of the organization are dedicated to lowering costs on processes and products and passing the savings along to customers.

Time is a critical measure in any organization. Some organizations gauge their performance almost exclusively in relation to time. When asked what business FedEx is in, company executives say, "We engineer time."

Soft Data Measures

Soft data are probably the most familiar measures of an organization's effectiveness, yet their collection can present a challenge. Values representing attitude, motivation, and satisfaction are examples of soft data. Soft data are more difficult to gather and analyze, and therefore, they are used when hard data are not available, or to supplement hard data. Soft data are also more difficult to convert to monetary values, a process requiring subjective methods. They are less objective as performance measurements, and are usually behavior related, yet organizations place great emphasis on them. Improvements in these measures represent important business needs, but many organizations omit them from the ROI equation because

INITIATIVE/INNOVATION	CUSTOMER SERVICE
Creativity	Customer complaints
Patents	Customer satisfaction
New ideas	Customer dissatisfaction
Suggestions	Customer impressions
Trademarks	Customer loyalty
Copyrights	Customer retention
Process improvements	Lost customers
Partnerships/alliances	
	EMPLOYEE DEVELOPMENT/
WORK CLIMATE	ADVANCEMENT
Teamwork	Promotions
Culture	Capability
Employee complaints	Intellectual capital
Job satisfaction	Programs completed
Organization Commitment	Requests for transfer
Employee engagement	Performance appraisal ratings
Employee loyalty	Readiness
Intent to leave	Networking
Stress	
	IMAGE
HABITS	Brand awareness
Inattention	Reputation
Tardiness	Leadership
Carelessness	Social responsibility
Violations of safety rules	Environmental friendliness
Communication breakdowns	Social consciousness
	Diversity
	External awards

Figure 5.3 Examples of Soft Data.

they are soft values. However, they can contribute to economic value to the same extent as hard data measures. Figure 5.3 shows common examples of soft data by category. The key is not to focus too much on the hard versus soft data distinction. A better approach is to consider data as tangible or intangible.

Tangible versus Intangible Benefits: A Better Approach

A challenge with regard to soft versus hard data is converting soft measures to monetary values. The key to this problem is to remember that, ultimately, all roads lead to hard data. Although creativity may be categorized as a form of soft data, a creative workplace can develop new products or new patents, which leads to greater revenues – clearly a hard data measure. Although it is possible to convert the measures listed in Figure 5.3 to monetary amounts, it is often more realistic and practical to leave them in nonmonetary form. This decision is based on considerations of credibility and the cost of the conversion. According to the standards of the ROI Methodology, an intangible measure is defined as a measure that is intentionally not converted to money. If a soft data measure can be converted to a monetary amount credibly using minimal resources, it is considered tangible, reported as a monetary value, and incorporated in the ROI calculation. If a data item cannot be converted to money credibly with minimal resources, it is listed as an intangible measure. Therefore, in defining business needs, the key difference between measures is not whether they represent hard or soft data, but whether they are tangible or intangible. In either case, they are important contributions toward the desired payoff and important business impact data.

Impact Data Sources

The sources of impact data, whether tangible or intangible, are diverse and usually involve routine reporting systems in the organization. In many situations, these items have led to the need for the project or program. A vast array of documents, systems, databases, and reports can be used to select the specific measure or measures to be monitored throughout the project. Impact data sources include quality reports, service records, suggestion systems, and employee engagement data.

Some project planners and project team members assume that corporate data sources are scarce because the data are not readily available to them. However, data can usually be located by investing a small amount of time. Rarely do new data collection systems or processes need to be developed in order to identify data representing the business needs of an organization.

In searching for the proper measures to connect to the project and to identify business needs, it is helpful to consider all possible measures that could be influenced. Sometimes, collateral measures move in harmony with the project. For example, efforts to improve safety may also improve productivity and increase job satisfaction. Weighing adverse impacts on certain measures may also help. For example, when cycle times are reduced, quality may suffer; or when sales increase, customer satisfaction may deteriorate. Finally, project team members must anticipate unintended consequences and capture them as other data items that might be connected to or influenced by the project.

In the process of settling on the precise business measures for the project, it is useful to examine various "what if" scenarios. If the organization does nothing, the potential consequences of inaction should be made clear. The following questions may help in understanding the consequences of inaction:

- Will the situation deteriorate?
- Will operational problems surface?
- Will budgets be affected?
- Will we lose influence or support?

Answers to these questions can help the organization settle on a precise set of measures, and can provide a hint of the extent to which the measures may change as a result of the project.

Determining Performance Needs

The next step in the needs analysis is to understand what led to the business need. If the proposed innovation project addresses a problem, this step focuses on the cause of the problem. If the project makes use of an opportunity, this step focuses on what is inhibiting the organization from taking advantage of that opportunity.

Analysis Techniques

Uncovering the causes of the problem or the inhibitors to success requires a variety of analytical techniques. These techniques – such as problem analysis, nominal group technique, force field analysis, and just plain brainstorming – are used to clarify performance needs. The technique that is used will depend on the organizational setting, the apparent depth of the problem, and the budget allocated to such analysis. Multiple techniques can be used since performance may be lacking for a number of reasons. Detailed approaches of techniques can be found in many sources. [1]

A Sensible Approach

Analysis takes time and adds to a project's cost. Examining records, researching databases, and observing individuals can provide important data, but a more cost-effective approach might include employing internal and/or external experts to help analyze the problem. Performance needs can vary considerably, and may include ineffective behavior, a dysfunctional work climate, inadequate systems, a disconnected process flow, improper procedures, a nonsupportive culture, outdated technology, and a nonaccommodating environment, to name a few. When needs vary and with many techniques to choose from, the risk exists for overanalysis and excessive costs. Consequently, a sensible approach is needed.

Determining Learning Needs

The solution to performance needs uncovered in the previous step often requires a learning component – such as participants and team members learning how to perform a task differently, or learning how to use a process, system, or technology. In some cases learning is the principal solution, as in competency or capability development, major technology change, and system installations. For other innovation projects, learning is a minor aspect of the solution, and may involve simply understanding the process, procedure, or policy. For example, in the implementation of a new suggestion system for an organization, the learning component requires understanding how the policy works as well as the participant's role in the policy. In short, a learning solution is not always needed, but all solutions have a learning component.

A variety of approaches are available for measuring specific learning needs. Often, multiple tasks and jobs are involved in a project and should be addressed separately. Sometimes the least effective way to identify the skills and knowledge that are needed is to ask the participants involved in implementing the project. They may not be clear on what is needed, and may not know enough to provide adequate input. One of the most useful ways to determine learning needs is to ask the individuals who understand the process. They can best determine what skills and knowledge are necessary to address the job performance issues that have been identified. This may be the appropriate time to find out the extent to which the knowledge and skills already exist.

Job and task analyses are effective when a new job is created or when an existing job description changes significantly. As jobs are redesigned and the new tasks must be identified, this type of analysis offers a systematic way of detailing the job and task. Essentially, a job analysis is the collection and evaluation of work-related information. A task analysis identifies the specific knowledge, skills, tools, and conditions necessary to perform a particular job.

Observation of current practices and procedures in an organization may be necessary, as the project is implemented. This can often indicate the level of capability, and help to identify the correct procedures. Observations can be used to examine work flow and interpersonal interactions, including those between management and team members. Observers may be previous employees, third-party participant observers, or mystery shoppers.

Sometimes, the demonstration of knowledge surrounding a certain task, process, or procedure provides evidence of what capabilities exist, and what is lacking. Demonstration can be as simple as a skill practice or role play, or as complex as an extensive mechanical or electronic simulation.

The point is to use this as a way of determining if employees know how to perform a particular process. Through demonstration, specific learning needs can evolve.

Testing as a learning needs assessment process is not used as frequently as other methods, but it can be very useful. Employees are tested to reveal what they know about a particular situation. This information helps to guide learning issues.

When implementing innovation projects in organizations where there is an existing manager or team leader, input from the management team may be used to assess the current situation, and to indicate the knowledge and skills required by the new situation. This input can be elicited through surveys, interviews, or focus groups. It can be a rich source of information about what the users of the project, if it is implemented, will need to know to make it successful.

Where learning is a minor component, learning needs are simpler. Determining learning needs can be time-consuming for major projects where new procedures, technologies, and processes must be developed. As in developing job performance needs, it is important not to spend excessive time analyzing learning needs, but rather to collect as much data as possible with minimal resources.

Determining Preference Needs

The final level of needs analysis determines the preferences that drive the innovation project requirements. Essentially, individuals prefer certain processes, schedules, or activities for the structure of the project. These preferences define how the particular project will be implemented. If the project is a solution to a problem, this step defines how the solution will be installed. If the project leverages an opportunity, this step outlines how the opportunity will be addressed, taking into consideration the preferences of those involved in the project.

Preference needs typically define the parameters of the project in terms of scope, timing, budget, staffing, location, technology, deliverables, and the degree of disruption allowed. Preference needs are developed from the input of several stakeholders, rather than from one individual. For example, participants in the project (those who must make it work) may have a particular preference, but the preference could exhaust resources, time, and budgets. The immediate manager's input may help minimize the amount of disruption and maximize resources. The funds that can be allocated are also a constraining resource.

The urgency of project implementation may introduce a constraint in the preferences. Those who support or own the project often impose preferences on the project in terms of timing, budget, and the use of technology. Because preferences correspond to a Level 1 need, the project structure and solution will relate directly to the reaction objectives and to the initial reaction to the project.

In determining the preference needs, there can never be too much detail. Projects often go astray and fail to reach their full potential because of misunderstandings and differences in expectations surrounding the project. Preference needs should be addressed before the project begins. Pertinent issues are often outlined in the project proposal or planning documentation.

Case Study: Southeast Corridor Bank

At this point, following a case study through the different levels of needs may be helpful. This case shows an innovative approach to solve a typical problem.

Payoff Needs

The following discussion explores the analysis at Level 5, determining payoff needs. Southeast Corridor Bank (SCB) operated branches in four states. (SCB has since been acquired by Regions Bank, one of the nation's top ten banks.) Like many other fast-growing organizations, SCB faced merger and integration problems, including excessive employee turnover.

SCB's annual employee turnover was 57%, compared with an industry average of 26% for front line staff. The bank needs an innovative approach to the problem. The typical solution is to "train the managers." However, that may not be the solution. Also, pay was probably an issue, but the bank could not just increase pay levels for all front line staff.

The first step in addressing the problem was answering these questions:

- Is this a problem worth solving?
- Is there a potential payoff to solving the problem?

To the senior vice president of human resources, the answers were clear. After reviewing several published studies about the cost of turnover, including one from a financial institution, he concluded that the cost of employee turnover ranged between 110–125% of annual pay. At the current rate, employee turnover was costing the bank more than $6 million per year. Lowering the rate to the industry average would save the bank at least $3 million annually. Although the structure and cost of the solution had not been determined at this point, it became clear that this problem was worth solving. Unless the solution appeared to be very expensive, solving the problem would have a tremendous impact. This was the only analysis that was needed at this level.

Business Needs

The specific measure in question was voluntary turnover: the number of employees leaving voluntarily divided by the average number of employees, expressed as a percentage. Clearly defining the measure was important. Still, with improvement in any one measure, other measures should also improve, depending on the specific solution. For example, staffing levels, job satisfaction, customer service, sales revenue, and other measures could change. These considerations are detailed in the context of determining the solution.

Performance Needs

To identify the performance needs, the cause of the problem had to be determined. When the cause was known, a solution could be developed.

The nominal group technique was selected as the analysis method because it allowed unbiased input to be collected efficiently and accurately across the organization. Focus groups were planned consisting of 12 employees from each region, for a total of six groups representing all the regions. In addition, two focus groups were planned for the clerical staff in the corporate headquarters. This approach provided approximately a 10% sample, which was considered sufficient to pinpoint the problem.

The focus group participants who represented areas in which turnover was highest described why their colleagues were leaving, not why they would leave. Data were collected from individuals using a carefully structured format – during two-hour meetings at each location, with third-party facilitators – and were integrated and weighted so that the most important reasons were clearly identified. This process had the advantages of low cost and high reliability, as well as a low degree of bias. Only two days of external facilitator time were needed to collect and summarize the data for review.

Following are the ten major reasons given for turnover in the bank branches:

1. Lack of opportunity for advancement
2. Lack of opportunity to learn new skills and gain new product knowledge
3. Pay level not adequate
4. Not enough responsibility and empowerment
5. Lack of recognition and appreciation of work
6. Lack of teamwork
7. Lack of preparation for customer service problems
8. Unfair and nonsupportive supervisor
9. Too much stress at peak times
10. Not enough flexibility in work schedules

Recognizing that not all causes of the turnover could be addressed immediately, the bank's management concentrated on the top five reasons and considered a variety of options.

The Solution

Management determined that a skill-based pay system would address the top five reasons for employee turnover. The program was designed to expand the scope of the jobs, with increases in pay awarded for the acquisition of skills, and a clear path provided for advancement and improvement. Jobs were redesigned from narrowly focused duties to an expanded role with a new title. Every Teller became a Banking Representative I, II, or III.

A branch employee would be designated a Banking Representative I if he or she could perform one or two simple tasks, such as processing deposits and cashing checks. As an employee at this level took on additional responsibilities and learned to perform different functions, he or she would be eligible for a promotion to Banking Representative II. A Representative who could perform all the basic functions of the branch, including processing consumer loan applications, would be promoted to Banking Representative III.

Training opportunities were available to help employees develop the needed skills, and structured on-the-job training was provided by the branch managers, assistant managers, and supervisors. Self-study information was also available. The performance of multiple tasks was introduced to broaden responsibilities, and enable employees to provide excellent customer service. Pay increases were used to recognize skill acquisition, demonstrated accomplishment, and increased responsibility.

Although the skill-based system had obvious advantages from the employee's perspective, the bank also benefited. Not only was turnover expected to decline, but required staffing levels were expected to decrease in the larger branches. In theory, if all employees in a branch could perform all the necessary duties, fewer employees would be needed. Previously, certain critical jobs required minimum staffing levels, and employees in those positions were not always available for other duties.

In addition, the bank anticipated improved customer service. The new approach would prevent customers from having to wait in long lines for specialized services. For example, in the typical bank branch, long lines for special functions – such as opening a checking account, closing out a certificate of deposit, or accepting a consumer loan application – were not unusual under the old setup, whereas routine activities such as paying bills and receiving deposits often required little or no waiting. With each employee now performing all the tasks, shorter waiting lines could be expected.

To support this new arrangement, the marketing department featured the concept in its publicity about products and services. Included with checking account statements was a promotional piece stating: "In our branches, there are no tellers." This document described the new process, and announced that every employee could now perform all branch functions and consequently provide faster service.

Learning Needs

At Level 2, learning needs fell into two categories. First, for each learning program, both skill acquisition and knowledge development needs were identified. Learning measurements included self-assessment, testing, and demonstrations, among others, and were connected to each specific program.

Second, it was necessary for employees to learn how the new program worked. As the program was introduced in meetings with employees, a simple measurement of learning was necessary to capture employee understanding of the following issues:

- How the program is being pursued
- What employees must do to succeed in the program
- How promotion decisions are made
- The timing of various stages of the program

These major learning needs were identified, and connected specifically with the solution being implemented.

Preference Needs

As the project was rolled out and the solution was developed, the preference needs were defined. The project had to be rolled out as soon as possible so that its effects could be translated into lower employee turnover. All the training programs had to be in place and available to employees. The amount of time employees needed to spend away from their jobs for training was an issue, as was the managers' control over the timing of promotions. This process had to move swiftly, or it would result in disappointment to employees who were eager to be trained and promoted. At the same time, the staffing and workload concerns had to be balanced, so that the appropriate amount of time was devoted to training and skill building. More specifically, with the program's announcement, the desired employee reaction was defined. Project leaders wanted employees to view the program as challenging, motivational, rewarding, and fair, and as a solid investment in their futures. These needs were readily translated into the solution design.

This is an excellent example of developing an innovative solution to a common and persistent problem. The key is to follow the process to ensure that the proper solution is implemented to drive the impact measure. The project was very successful, yielding an ROI of 201%. [3]

Developing Objectives for Innovation Projects

Innovation programs and projects are driven by objectives. These objectives will position the project for success if they represent the needs of the business, and include clearly defined measures of achievement. A project may be aimed at implementing a solution that addresses a particular dilemma, problem, or opportunity. In other situations, the initial project is designed to develop a range of feasible solutions, with one specific solution selected before implementation. Regardless of the project or program, multiple levels of objectives are necessary. These levels follow the five-level data categorization scheme, and define precisely what will occur as a project is implemented. They correspond to the levels of evaluation and the levels of needs presented in Figure 5.1.

Reaction Objectives

For a project to be successful, the stakeholders immediately involved in the process must react favorably, or at least not negatively, to the project. Ideally, those directly involved should be satisfied with the innovation project and see the value in it. This feedback must be obtained routinely during the project in order to make adjustments, keep the project on track, and redesign certain aspects as necessary. Unfortunately, for many projects, specific objectives at this level are not developed, nor are data collection mechanisms put in place to allow channels for feedback.

Developing reaction objectives should be straightforward and relatively easy. The objectives reflect the degree of immediate as well as long-term satisfaction, and explore issues important to the success of the program. They also form the basis for evaluating the chain of impact, and they emphasize planned action, when this is feasible and needed. Typical issues addressed in the development of reaction objectives are relevance, usefulness, importance, appropriateness, intent to use, rewards, and motivation.

Learning Objectives

Every innovation project or program involves at least one learning objective, and most involve more. With projects entailing major change, the learning component is quite important. In situations narrower in scope, such as the implementation of a new policy, the learning component is minor but still necessary. To ensure that the various stakeholders have learned what they need to know to make the project successful, learning objectives are developed. The following are examples of learning objectives:

- Identify the six features of the new suggestion system.
- Demonstrate the use of each software routine within the standard time.
- Score 75 or better on the new-product quiz.
- Explain the value of brainstorming in a work group.
- Successfully complete the leadership simulation.
- Know how to apply research procedures.

Objectives are critical to the measurement of learning because they communicate the expected outcomes from the learning component, and define the competency or level of performance necessary to make project implementation successful. They provide a focus to allow participants to clearly identify what it is they must learn and do – sometimes with precision.

Application and Implementation Objectives

The application and implementation objectives clearly define what is expected of the innovation project or program and often the target level of performance. Application objectives are similar to learning objectives but relate to actual performance. They provide specific milestones indicating when one part or all of the process has been implemented. Typical application objectives are illustrated below.

When the project or program is implemented. . .

- At least 99.1% of software users will be following the correct sequences after three weeks of use.
- Within one year, 10% of employees will submit documented suggestions for saving costs.
- Customers will use the new app properly.
- 95% of high-potential employees will complete individual development plans within two years.
- 40% of the city's homeless population will apply for special housing within one year of program launch.
- 80% of employees will use one or more of the three cost containment features of the health care plan.
- 50% of conference attendees follow up with at least one contact from the conference.

Application objectives are critical because they describe the expected outcomes in the intermediate area, between the learning of new tasks and procedures and the delivery of the impact of this learning. Application and implementation objectives describe how things should be or the desired state of the workplace once the project solution has been implemented. They provide a basis for evaluating on-the-job changes and performance.

Impact Objectives

Impact objectives indicate key business measures that should improve as the application and implementation objectives are achieved. The following are typical impact objectives:

- Sales of the new product should be $15,000 per month in four months.
- Sales of the new software upgrade should be $10,000 per month per sales rep in four months.
- Product returns should be reduced from 75 per month to no more than ten per month in six months.
- Cycle time should decrease by 20% within the next calendar year.

- The average number of product defects should decrease from 200 to 150 per month in the Midwest region in six months.
- The company-wide job satisfaction index should rise by 2% during the next calendar year.
- There should be a 10% increase in Pharmaceuticals Inc. brand awareness among physicians during the next two years.
- The dropout rate for high school students in the Barett County system should decrease by 5% within three years.
- Turnover of critical should be no more than 10% in one year.

Impact objectives are critical to measuring business performance because they define the ultimate expected outcome from the project. They describe the business unit performance that should result from the project. Above all, impact objectives emphasize achievement of the bottom-line results that key client groups expect and demand.

ROI Objectives

The fifth level of objectives for projects or programs represents the acceptable return on investment (ROI), or the monetary impact. Objectives at this level define the expected payoff from investing in the project. An ROI objective is typically expressed as an acceptable ROI percentage, which is calculated as annual monetary benefits minus cost, divided by the actual cost, and multiplied by 100. A 0% ROI indicates a breakeven project. A 50% ROI indicates recapture of the project cost and an additional 50% "earnings" (50 cents for every dollar invested).

For some projects, such as the purchase of a new company, a new building, or major equipment, the ROI objective is large relative to the ROI of other expenditures. However, the calculation is the same for both. For many organizations, the ROI objective for a project or program is set slightly higher than the ROI expected from other "routine investments" because of the relative newness of applying the ROI concept to the types of projects or programs described in this book. For example, if the expected ROI from the purchase of a new company is 20%, the ROI from a new advertising project might be around 25%. The important point is that the ROI objective should be established up front and in discussions with the project sponsor. Excluding the ROI objective leaves stakeholders questioning the economic success of a project. If a project reaps a 25% ROI, is that successful? Not if the objective was a 50% ROI.

Final Thoughts

In this chapter we outlined the starting point of the ROI Methodology, by showing how a project can be structured from the outset, with detailed needs identified, and ultimately leading to project objectives at five levels. This kind of detail ensures that the project is aligned with business needs, and remains results focused throughout the process. Without this analysis, the project runs the risk of failing to deliver the value that it should, or of not being in alignment with one or more business objectives. The outputs of the analysis are objectives, which provide a focus for project designers, developers, and implementers, as well as participants and users who must make the project successful. Issues surrounding data collection are discussed in the next several chapters.

In the next chapter, we'll start with a treatment of data collection methods.

6

Collecting Data Along Chain of Impact with a Toolbox of Methods

Some of the most ambitious innovation projects occurred at Sears Roebuck & Company. Faced with serious difficulties due to poor financial performance, Sears underwent a transformational project that changed the culture of the company. Led by the CEO with 100 top-level executives at Sears, the organization developed a business model that tracked the success of management behavior through employee attitudes, customer satisfaction, and financial performance.[1] This connection was made evident through multiple linkages and was referred to as the Employee-Customer-Profit Chain. In this model, employee attitudes were directly correlated with customer satisfaction. For example: 10 questions from their 70-question employee survey correlated with a 1.3-point improvement in customer satisfaction measured on a 10-point scale. The survey demonstrated that job satisfaction drives customer satisfaction. The 1.3-point improvement in customer satisfaction was shown to drive a 0.5 percent increase in revenue growth.

Applying the store-level profit margin to this revenue growth showed the profits achieved from investing in employee attitudes.

At the heart of this project were five task forces collecting a massive amount of data:

- A customer task force reviewed customer surveys for several years and conducted 80 videotaped customer focus groups in the United States so every member of the task force could watch.
- An employee task force conducted 26 employee focus groups and studied all the data on employee attitudes and behavior, including a 70-item opinion survey given to employees every other year.
- The values task force collected 80,000 employee surveys and identified six core values that Sears employees thought strongly about.
- The innovation task force conducted external benchmarking, undertook a research project on the nature of change, and suggested an effort to generate 1 million ideas from employees.
- A financial task force built a model for the drivers of a total shareholder return over a 20-year period and drew emphasis about what Sears would have to do to be in the top quartile of Fortune 500 companies. A large quantity of data involved a variety of sources, and when combined with the appropriate analysis, developed the model described earlier.

The project was the cornerstone of the trans- formation that dramatically improved the financial results at Sears, turning around a loss of $3.9 billion.

Although every innovation project involves data collection, the Sears project was one of the most extensive. This case study underscores the point that data must be collected from a variety of sources, using a variety of techniques, sometimes at different time frames. These methods become an important part of the overall planning for data collection described in this chapter.

Having established project needs and objectives that are aligned with the business or organization, we are ready to begin collecting data along the chain of impact that shows the project's value. The first step in this phase of the analysis is to develop the Data Collection Plan, which tabulates the broad program objectives, measures, data collection methods, data sources, timing, and responsibilities. Essentially, data are collected at four different levels (reaction, learning, application, and impact), following the process outlined in Chapter 4.

This chapter presents the methods of data collection that span all levels. The list is comprehensive, including surveys, questionnaires, interviews, focus groups, tests, simulation, observation, actions plans, performance contracts, and monitoring business performance data from the system and records. We will examine each technique in detail, with an eye toward effective application at one or more of the four levels. The chapter concludes with tips on selecting the data collection methods to use on specific projects.

Questionnaires and Surveys

The questionnaire is probably the most common data collection method. Questionnaires come in all sizes, ranging from short surveys to detailed instruments. They can be used to obtain subjective data about participant perceptions, as well as to document data for use in a projected ROI analysis. With this versatility and popularity, it is important for questionnaires and surveys to be designed properly to satisfy both purposes.

Types of Questions and Statements

Five basic types of questions or statements are available. Depending on the purpose of the evaluation, the questionnaire may contain any or all of the following types of questions:

1. *Open-ended question* – Has an unlimited answer. The question is followed by ample blank space for the response.
2. *Checklist* – A list of items. A participant is asked to check those that apply to the situation.
3. *Range of responses* – Has alternate responses, a yes/no, or other possibilities. This type of question can also include a range of responses from Disagree to Agree.
4. *Multiple-choice question* – Has several choices, and the participant is asked to select the most appropriate.
5. *Ranking scales* – Requires the participant to rank a list of items.

Figure 6.1 shows examples of each of these types of questions.

1. Open-ended Question:

    What problems will you encounter when attempting to use the new system implemented in this project?

2. Checklist:

    For the following list, check all of the business measures that may be influenced by the innovation project.

    ☐ Productivity   ☐ Response Time
    ☐ Quality   ☐ Customer Satisfaction
    ☐ Efficiency   ☐ Job Satisfaction
    ☐ Cost Control

3. Range of Responses:

    As a result of this project, I have a better appreciation for the power of innovation.

    ☐ DEFINITELY YES   ☐ MAYBE   ☐ DEFINITELY NO

4. Multiple Choice Question:

    Since the innovation project has been initiated, the customer response time has:

    a. Increased
    b. Decreased
    c. Remained the same
    d. Don't know

5. Ranking Scales:

    The following list contains five important factors that will influence the success of this innovation project. Place a one (1) by the item that is most influential, a two (2) by the item that is second most influential, and so on. The item ranked five (5) will be the least influential item on the list.

    Rewards Systems   Training
    Job Responsibility   Management Support
    Communications   Resources

Figure 6.1 Types of Questions.

Design Issues

Questionnaire design is a simple and logical process. An improperly designed or worded questionnaire will not collect the desired data, and is confusing, frustrating, and potentially embarrassing. The following steps will help ensure that a valid, reliable, and effective instrument is developed.

- *Determine the information needed* – The first step of any instrument design is to itemize the topics, issues, and success factors for the project. Questions are developed later. It may be helpful to develop this information in outline form so that related questions can be grouped together.
- *Select the type(s) of questions* – Determine whether open-ended questions, checklists, ranges, multiple-choice questions, or a ranking scale is most appropriate for the purpose

of the questions. Take into consideration the planned data analysis and variety of data to be collected.

- *Develop the questions, keeping them simple* – The next step is to develop the questions based on the types of questions planned and the information needed. The questions should be simple and straightforward enough to avoid confusion, or leading the participant to a desired response. Unfamiliar terms or expressions should be avoided.

- *Test the questions* – After the questions are developed, they should be tested for understanding. Ideally, the questions should be tested on a small sample of participants in the project. If this is not feasible, the questions should be tested on employees at approximately the same job level as the participants. Collect as much input and criticism as possible, and revise the questions as necessary.

- *Prepare a data summary* – A data summary sheet should be developed so data can be tabulated quickly for summary and interpretation. This step will help ensure that the data can be analyzed quickly, and presented in a meaningful way.

A Detailed Example

One of the most difficult tasks is determining specific issues that need to be addressed on a follow-up questionnaire. Although the content items on a follow-up questionnaire can be the same as questionnaires used in measuring reaction and learning, certain content items are more desirable for capturing application and impact information (Level 3 and 4 data).

Figure 6.2 presents a questionnaire used in a follow-up evaluation of an innovative project to create a sales culture at the bank. The evaluation was designed to capture the ROI, with the primary method of data collection being the follow-up questionnaire. This example, for Progressive Bank, is used to illustrate many of the issues involving potential content items for a follow-up questionnaire.

Progress Bank, following a carefully planned acquisition of smaller banks, initiated a project to strengthen the collective sales culture. The project involved four solutions. Through a competency-based learning intervention, all branch personnel were taught how to aggressively pursue new customers, and cross-sell to existing customers in a variety of product lines. The software and customer database were upgraded to provide faster access and enhanced routines to assist selling. The incentive compensation system was also redesigned to enhance payments for new

Are you currently in a sales capacity at a branch?   Yes   ☐   No   ☐

1.   Listed below are the objectives of the sales culture project. After reflecting on this project, please indicate the degree of success in meeting the objectives. Use the following scale:

1   = No success
2   = Limited success
3   = Moderate success
4   = Generally successful
5   = Very successful

As a result of this project, branch employees will:	1	2	3	4	5
a. Use the tools and techniques to determine customer needs and concerns.	☐	☐	☐	☐	☐
b. Match needs with specific projects and services.	☐	☐	☐	☐	☐
c. Use the tools and techniques to convince customers to buy/use Progress Bank products and services.	☐	☐	☐	☐	☐
d. Build a productive, long-term relationship with customers.	☐	☐	☐	☐	☐
e. Increase sales of each product line offered in the branch.	☐	☐	☐	☐	☐

2.   Did you implement an on-the-job action plan for this project?

Yes   ☐   No   ☐

If yes, please describe the nature and outcome of the plan. If not, explain why. _____
_____
_____
_____

3.   Please rate the relevance to your job of each of the following components of the project using the following scale:

1   = No relevance
2   = Limited relevance
3   = Moderate relevance
4   = General relevance
5   = Very relevant

Figure 6.2 Example of Follow-up Questionnaire (*Continued*).

customers, and increase sales of all branch products. Finally, a management coaching and goal-setting system was implemented to ensure that ambitious sales goals were met. All branch employees were involved in the project.

Six months after the project was implemented, an evaluation was planned. Each branch in the network had a scorecard that tracked performance through several measures, such as new accounts, total deposits, and growth by specific products. All product lines were monitored. All branch employees provided input on the questionnaire shown in Figure 6.2. Most of the questionnaire data covered application and impact.

	1	2	3	4	5
Job Aids	☐	☐	☐	☐	☐
Group Learning Activities	☐	☐	☐	☐	☐
Incentive Opportunities	☐	☐	☐	☐	☐
Networking Opportunities w/Other Branches	☐	☐	☐	☐	☐
Reading Material/Videos	☐	☐	☐	☐	☐
Coaching Sessions	☐	☐	☐	☐	☐
Software/System Changes	☐	☐	☐	☐	☐
Database Enhancements	☐	☐	☐	☐	☐

4.   Have you used the job aids provided during the project?

Yes   ☐   No   ☐

Please explain. _____
_____
_____
_____

5.   Please indicate the change in the application of knowledge and skills as a result of your participation in the sales culture project. Use the following scale:

1   = No change
2   = Limited change
3   = Moderate change
4   = Much change
5   = Very much change

		1	2	3	4	5	No Opportunity To Use Skill
a.	Probing for customer needs.	☐	☐	☐	☐	☐	☐
b.	Helping the customer solve problems.	☐	☐	☐	☐	☐	☐
c.	Understanding the features and benefits of all products and services.	☐	☐	☐	☐	☐	☐
d.	Comparing products and services to those of competitors.	☐	☐	☐	☐	☐	☐
e.	Selecting appropriate products and services.	☐	☐	☐	☐	☐	☐
f.	Using persuasive selling techniques.	☐	☐	☐	☐	☐	☐
g.	Using follow-up techniques to stay in touch with the customer.	☐	☐	☐	☐	☐	☐
h.	Using new software routines for data access and transactions.	☐	☐	☐	☐	☐	☐

Figure 6.2 Example of Follow-up Questionnaire (*Continued*).

This type of follow-up feedback helps innovation leaders know which parts of an intervention are most effective and useful, and thereby how best to replicate or scale the innovation.

Improving the Response Rate for Questionnaires and Surveys

Given the wide range of potential issues to explore in a follow-up questionnaire or survey, asking all of the potential questions can reduce the response rate considerably. The questionnaire becomes too long. The challenge, therefore, is to approach questionnaire and survey design and

6.   What has changed about your work (actions, tasks, activities) as a result of this project?

_____
_____
_____
_____

7.   Indicate the extent to which you think this program has influenced each of these measures in your branch. Use the following scale:

    1 = No influence
    2 = Limited influence
    3 = Moderate influence
    4 = Much influence
    5 = Very much influence

	1	2	3	4	5
a. New Accounts	☐	☐	☐	☐	☐
b. Sales	☐	☐	☐	☐	☐
c. Customer Response Time	☐	☐	☐	☐	☐
d. Cross-Sales Ratio	☐	☐	☐	☐	☐
e. Cost Control	☐	☐	☐	☐	☐
f. Employee Satisfaction	☐	☐	☐	☐	☐
g. Customer Satisfaction	☐	☐	☐	☐	☐
h. Customer Complaints	☐	☐	☐	☐	☐
i. Customer Loyalty	☐	☐	☐	☐	☐

8.   Please define the most improved measure above. Use a unit of value such as one sale, one new account, one customer complaint.

_____
_____
_____
_____

9.   Provide the actual change in the unit measure since the project began. This would take the pre-program baseline data and subtract it from the current level to indicate a change.

_____
_____
_____
_____

10.   Indicate the actual unit value for the specific measure in question. If it is a measure that is desired to improve, indicate the value-add, such as one additional sale. If it is a value that needs to be minimized, such as one customer complaint, indicate the money saved when the customer complaint is avoided. Although this can be very difficult, please follow the instructions of how this value may be obtained.

_____
_____
_____
_____

Figure 6.2 Example of Follow-up Questionnaire (*Continued*).

administration for maximum response rate. This is a critical issue when the questionnaire is a key data collection activity, and much of the evaluation hinges on the questionnaire results.

The following actions can be taken to increase response rate. Although the term questionnaire is used, the same rules apply to surveys.

- *Provide advance communication* – If appropriate and feasible, project participants and other stakeholders should

11.   Provide the basis for the above unit value. If it is a standard value, please indicate that it is a standard value; if it is an expert input, indicate that it is an expert input; if it is based on an estimate, indicate how the estimate was derived.

_____
_____
_____
_____

12.   Provide the total impact of the change. This involves taking the unit value times the change in the value for one year. This takes into account the frequency. If it is a monthly data item, then it would be times 12. If it is a weekly value, it would be times 52.

_____
_____
_____
_____

13.   List other factors that could have influenced this improvement. Be very thoughtful and specific in listing the other influences.

_____
_____
_____
_____

14.   Indicate the percent of improvement directly related to this project using a scale of 0% to 100%. Zero percent is no improvement connected to the project. One hundred percent is all the improvement is connected to the project.

_____
_____
_____
_____

15.   What level of confidence do you place in the above estimations? (0% = No Confidence, 100% = Certainty) _____%

Please explain. _____
_____
_____

Note: Participants may cycle through questions 8-15 with other measures.

16.   Do you think the sales culture project represented a good investment for Progress Bank?

       Yes ☐   No   ☐

Please explain. _____
_____
_____
_____

Figure 6.2 Example of Follow-up Questionnaire (*Continued*).

receive advance communications about the questionnaire or survey. This minimizes some of the resistance to the process, provides an opportunity to explain in more detail the circumstances surrounding the evaluation, and positions the evaluation as an integral part of the consulting project rather than an add-on activity that someone initiated three months after the project is completed.

- *Communicate the purpose* – Stakeholders should understand the reason for the questionnaire, including who or what

17.   Please rate the success of the immediate project team and the quality of the team's leadership. Use the following scale:

1 = No success
2 = Limited success
3 = Moderately successful
4 = Generally successful
5 = Very successful

Team Characteristic	1	2	3	4	5
Capability	☐	☐	☐	☐	☐
Motivation	☐	☐	☐	☐	☐
Cooperation	☐	☐	☐	☐	☐
Communication	☐	☐	☐	☐	☐

Leadership Quality	1	2	3	4	5
Leadership Style	☐	☐	☐	☐	☐
Organization	☐	☐	☐	☐	☐
Communication	☐	☐	☐	☐	☐
Team Support	☐	☐	☐	☐	☐
Team Training	☐	☐	☐	☐	☐

18.   What barriers, if any, have you encountered that prevented this project from being successful. Please explain, if possible.

_____
_____
_____
_____

19.   What has helped this project be successful? Please explain.

_____
_____
_____
_____

20.   Which of the following statements best describes the level of management support?

☐ There was no management support.
☐ There was limited management support.
☐ There was a moderate amount management support.
☐ There was much management support.
☐ There was very much management support.

21.   Could other program solutions have been effective in meeting the business need(s)?

Yes ☐   No ☐

Please explain. _____
_____
_____
_____

22.   What specific suggestions do you have for improving this project?

_____
_____
_____
_____

23.   Other comments about this project:

_____
_____
_____
_____

Figure 6.2 Example of Follow-up Questionnaire.

initiated this specific evaluation. They should know if the evaluation is part of a systematic process or a special request for this innovation project only.

- *Explain who will see the data* – It is important for respondents to know who will see the data and the results of the questionnaire. If the questionnaire is anonymous, it should clearly be communicated to participants what steps will be taken to ensure anonymity. If senior executives will see the combined results of the study, the respondent should know that.

- *Describe the data integration process* – The respondents should understand how the questionnaire results will be combined with other data, if available. Often the questionnaire is only one of the data collection methods utilized. Participants should know how the data are weighted and integrated into the entire impact study, as well as interim results.

- *Keep the questionnaire/survey as simple as possible* – A simple questionnaire does not always provide the full scope of data necessary for a comprehensive analysis. However, the simplified approach should always be kept in mind when questions are developed, and the total scope of the questionnaire is finalized. Every effort should be made to keep it as simple and brief as possible.

- *Simplify the response process* – To the extent possible, it should be easy to respond to the questionnaire. If appropriate, a self-addressed stamped envelope should be included. Perhaps e-mail could be used for responses, if it is easier. In still other situations, a response box is provided near the project work area.

- *Utilize local management support* – Management involvement at the local level is critical to response-rate success. Managers can distribute the questionnaires themselves, make reference to the questionnaire in staff meetings, follow up to see if questionnaires have been completed, and generally show support for completing the questionnaire. This direct managerial support will prompt many participants to respond with usable data.

- *Let the participants know they are part of the sample* – For large innovation projects, a sampling process may be utilized. When that is the case, participants should know they are part of a carefully selected sample, and that their input will be used to make decisions regarding a much larger target audience. This action often appeals to a sense of responsibility for participants to provide usable, accurate data for the questionnaire.

- *Consider incentives* – A variety of incentives can be offered, and they usually are found in three categories. First, an incentive is provided in exchange for the completed questionnaire. For example, if participants return the questionnaire personally or through the mail, they will receive a small gift, such as a T-shirt or mug. If identity is an issue, a neutral third party can provide the incentive. In the second category, the incentive is provided to make participants feel guilty about not responding. Examples are money clipped to the questionnaire or a pen enclosed in the envelope. Participants are asked to "Take the money, buy a cup of coffee, and fill out the questionnaire." A third group of incentives is designed to obtain a quick response. This approach is based on the assumption that a quick response will ensure a greater response rate. If an individual delays completing the questionnaire, the odds of completing it diminish considerably. The initial group of participants may receive a more expensive gift, or they may be part of a drawing for an incentive. For example, in one project, the first 25 returned questionnaires were placed in a drawing for a $400 gift certificate. The next 25 were added to the first 25 in the next drawing. The longer a participant waits, the lower the odds of winning.
- *Have an executive sign the introductory letter* – Participants are always interested in who sent the letter with the questionnaire. For maximum effectiveness, a senior executive who is responsible for a major area where the participants work should sign the letter. Employees may be more willing to respond to a senior executive than to a member of the outside team.
- *Use follow-up reminders* – A follow-up reminder should be sent a week after the questionnaire is received, and another sent two weeks later. Depending on the questionnaire and the situation, these times can be adjusted. In some situations, a third follow-up is recommended. Sometimes the follow-up is sent in a different media. For example, a questionnaire may be sent through regular mail, whereas the first

follow-up reminder is from the immediate supervisor, and a second follow-up is sent via e-mail.

- *Send a copy of the results to the participants* – Even if it is an abbreviated report, participants should see the results of the questionnaire. More important, participants should understand that they will receive a copy of the impact study when they are asked to provide the data. This promise will often increase the response rate, as some individuals want to see the results of the entire group along with their particular input.

- *Estimate the length of time to complete the questionnaire* – Respondents often have a concern about the time it may take to complete the questionnaire. A very lengthy questionnaire may quickly discourage the participants, and cause it to be discarded. Sometimes lengthy questionnaires can be completed quickly because they contain forced-choice questions or statements that make it easy to respond. However, the number of pages may put off the respondent. Therefore, it is helpful to indicate the estimated length of time needed to complete the questionnaire, perhaps in the letter itself or at least noted in the communications. This provides extra information so that respondents can decide if they are willing to invest the required amount of time in the process. A word of caution: the amount of time must be realistic. Purposely underestimating it can do more harm than good.

- *Explain the timing of the planned steps* – Sometimes the respondents want to learn more about the process, such as when they can see the results. It is recommended that a timeline of the different phases be presented, showing when the data will be analyzed, when the data will be presented to different groups, and when the results will be returned to the participants in a summary report. This provides some assurance that the process is well organized and professional, and that the length of time to receive a data summary will not be too long. Another word of caution: The timetable must be followed to maintain the confidence and trust of the individuals.

- *Make it appear professional* – While it should not be an issue in most organizations, unfortunately, there are too many cases in which a questionnaire is not developed properly, does not appear professional, or is not easy to follow and understand. The participants must gain respect for the process and for the organization. To do this, a sense of professionalism must be integrated throughout data collection, particularly in the appearance and accuracy of the materials. Sloppy questionnaires will usually elicit sloppy responses, or no response at all.

- *Explain the questionnaire during the project meetings* – Sometimes it is helpful to explain to the participants and other key stakeholders that they will be required or asked to provide certain types of data. When this is feasible, questionnaires should be reviewed question by question so that the participants understand the purpose, the issues, and how to respond. This will take only 10–15 minutes but can increase the response rate, enhance the quality and quantity of data, and clarify any confusion that may exist on key issues.
- *Collect data anonymously, if necessary* – Participants are more likely to provide frank and candid feedback if their names are not on the questionnaire, particularly when the project is going astray or is off target. When this is the case, every effort should be made to protect the anonymous input, and explanations should be provided as to how the data are analyzed, while minimizing the demographic makeup of respondents so that the individuals cannot be identified in the analysis.

Collectively, these items help boost response rates of follow-up questionnaires. Using all of these strategies can result in a 70–90% response rate, even with lengthy questionnaires that might take 30 minutes to complete.

Using Interviews

Another helpful collection method is the interview, although it is not used as frequently as the questionnaire. Internal staff or an outside third party can conduct interviews. Interviews can secure data not available in performance records, or data difficult to obtain through written responses or observations. Also, interviews can uncover success stories that can be useful in communicating evaluation results. Participants may be reluctant to describe their results in a questionnaire, but will volunteer the information to a skillful interviewer using probing techniques. The interview is versatile and appropriate for reaction, learning, and application data. A major disadvantage of the interview is that it is time consuming. It also requires time and training of interviewers to ensure that the process is consistent.

Types of Interviews

Interviews usually fall into two basic types: structured and unstructured. A structured interview is much like a questionnaire. Specific questions are asked with little room to deviate from the desired responses. The primary advantages of the structured interview over the questionnaire are that the interview process can ensure the questionnaire is completed, and that the interviewer understands the responses supplied by the participant.

The unstructured interview permits probing for additional information. This type of interview uses a few general questions, which can lead to more detailed information as important data are uncovered. The interviewer must be skilled in the probing process. Typical probing questions include:

- Can you explain that in more detail?
- Can you give me an example of what you are saying?
- Can you explain the difficulty that you say you encountered?

Interview Guidelines

The design steps for interviews are similar to those of the questionnaire. A brief summary of key issues with interviews is outlined here.

- *Develop questions to be asked* – After the decision has been made about the type of interview, specific questions need to be developed. Questions should be brief, precise, and designed for easy response.
- *Test out the interview* – The interview should be tested on a small number of participants. If possible, the interviews should be conducted as part of the early stages of the project. The responses should be analyzed and the interview revised, if necessary.
- *Prepare the interviewers* – The interviewer should have appropriate skills, including active listening, the ability to form probing questions, and the ability to collect and summarize information into a meaningful form.
- *Provide clear instructions* – The interviewee should understand the purpose of the interview, and know what will be done with the information. Expectations, conditions, and rules of the interview should be thoroughly discussed. For example, the participant should know if statements will be

kept confidential. If the participant is nervous during an interview and develops signs of anxiety, he or she should be encouraged to relax and feel at ease.

- *Administer interviews with a plan in mind* – As with other evaluation instruments, interviews need to be conducted according to a predetermined plan. The timing of the interview, the person who conducts the interview, and the location of the interview are all issues that become relevant when developing an interview plan. For a large number of stakeholders, a sampling plan may be necessary to save time and reduce the evaluation cost.

Using Focus Groups

As an extension of the interview, focus groups are particularly helpful when in-depth feedback is needed. The focus group involves a small-group discussion conducted by an experienced facilitator. It is designed to solicit qualitative judgments on a planned topic or issue. Group members are all required to provide their input, as individual input builds on group input.

When compared to questionnaires, surveys, or interviews, the focus group strategy has several advantages. The basic premise of using focus groups is that when quality judgments are subjective, several individual judgments are better than only one. The group process, where participants often motivate one another, is an effective method for generating new ideas and hypotheses. It is less expensive than the interview, and can be quickly planned and conducted. Its flexibility makes it possible to explore an innovation project's unexpected outcomes or applications.

Applications for Evaluation

The focus group is particularly helpful when qualitative information is needed about the success of an innovation project. For example, the focus group can be used in the following situations:

- Assessing the potential impact of the project
- Evaluating the reaction to the consulting project and the various components of it
- Assessing learning of specific procedures, tasks, schedules, or other components of the project

- Assessing the implementation of the project, as perceived by the participants immediately following the project's completion
- Sorting out the reasons for success

Essentially, focus groups are helpful when evaluation information is needed but cannot be collected adequately with a simple questionnaire or survey.

Guidelines

While there are no set rules on how to use focus groups for evaluation, the following guidelines should be helpful:

- *Plan topics, questions, and strategy carefully* – As with any evaluation instrument, planning is the key. The specific topics, questions, and issues to be discussed must be carefully planned and sequenced. This enhances the comparison of results from one group to another, and ensures that the group process is effective and stays on track.
- *Keep the group size small* – While there is no perfect group size, a range of 6.12 is appropriate for most focus group applications. A group has to be large enough to ensure different points of view, but small enough to give every participant a chance to talk freely and exchange comments.
- *Ensure a representative sample of the target population* – It is important for groups to be stratified appropriately so that participants represent the target population. The group should be homogeneous in experience, rank, and influence in the organization.
- *Insist on facilitators with appropriate expertise* – The success of a focus group rests with the facilitator, who must be skilled in the focus group process. Facilitators must know how to control aggressive members of the group, and diffuse the input from those who want to dominate the group. Also, facilitators must be able to create an environment in which participants feel comfortable to offer comments freely and openly. Consequently, some organizations use external facilitators.

In summary, the focus group is an inexpensive and quick way to determine the strengths and weaknesses of projects. However, for a complete evaluation, focus group information should be combined with data from other instruments.

Measuring with Tests

Testing is important for measuring learning in project evaluations. Baseline and post-project comparisons using tests are very common. An improvement in test scores shows the change in skill, knowledge, or capability of the participant attributed to the consulting project. The questionnaires and surveys, described earlier, can be used in testing for learning.

Performance testing allows the participant to exhibit a skill (and occasionally knowledge or attitude) that has been learned in a project. The skill can be manual, verbal, or analytical, or a combination of the three. For example, computer systems engineers are participating in a system-reengineering project. As part of the project, participants are given the assignment to design and test a basic system. The test observer watches participants as they check out the system, then carefully builds the same design, and compares his or her results with those of the participants. These comparisons and the performance of the design provide an evaluation of the project and represent an adequate reflection of the skills learned in the project.

Measuring with Simulation

Another technique for measuring learning is job simulation. This method involves the construction and application of a procedure or task that simulates or models the work involved in the innovation project. The simulation is designed to represent, as closely as possible, the actual job situation. Participants try out their performance in the simulated activity, and have it evaluated based on how well the task is accomplished. Simulations may be used during the project, or as part of a follow-up evaluation.

Task Simulation

One approach involves a participant's performance in a simulated task as part of an evaluation. For example, in a new system implementation, users are provided a series of situations, and they must perform the proper sequence of tasks in a minimum amount of time. To become certified to use this system, users are observed in a simulation where they perform all the necessary steps on a checklist. After they have demonstrated that they possess the skills necessary for the safe performance of this assignment, they are certified by the designated evaluator. This task simulation serves as the evaluation.

Role-Playing/Skill Practice

When skill building is part of the consulting project, role-playing may be helpful. This is sometimes referred to as skill practice. Participants practice a newly learned skill, and are observed by other individuals. Participants are given their assigned role with specific instructions, which sometimes include an ultimate course of action. The participants then practice the skill with other individuals to accomplish the desired objectives. This is intended to simulate the real-world setting to the greatest extent possible. Difficulty sometimes arises when other participants involved in the skill practice make the practice unrealistic by not reacting in the same way that individuals would in an actual situation. To help overcome this obstacle, trained role players (nonparticipants trained for the role) may be used in all roles except that of the participant. This can possibly provide a more objective evaluation.

Using Observation

Observing participants, and recording changes in behavior and specific actions taken, may be appropriate to measure application. This technique is useful when it is important to know precisely how the consulting partici-pants are using new skills, knowledge, tasks, procedures, or systems. For example, participant observation is often used in sales and sales support projects. The observer may be the participant's supervisor, a member of a peer group, or an external resource, such as a mystery customer.

Guidelines for Effective Observation

Observation is often misused or misapplied to evaluation situations, forc-ing some to abandon the process. The effectiveness of observation can be improved with the following guidelines:

- *Observers must be fully prepared* – Observers must fully under-stand what information is needed and what skills are covered in the intervention. They must be prepared for the assignment, and provided a chance to practice observation skills.

- *The observations should be systematic* – The observation process must be planned so that it is executed effectively without any surprises. The individuals observed should know in advance about the observation and why they are being observed, unless the observation is planned to be invisible. In this case, the individuals are monitored unknowingly. Observations are planned when work situations are normal. Eight steps are necessary to accomplish a successful observation:

  1. Determine what behavior will be observed.
  2. Prepare the forms for the observer's use.
  3. Select the observers.
  4. Prepare a schedule of observations.
  5. Prepare observers to observe properly.
  6. Inform participants of the planned observation, providing explanations.
  7. Conduct the observations.
  8. Summarize the observation data.

- *The observers should know how to interpret and report what they see* – Observations involve judgment decisions. The observer must analyze which behaviors are being displayed, and what actions the participants are taking. Observers should know how to summarize behavior and report results in a meaningful manner.
- *The observer's influence should be minimized* – Except for "mystery" or "planted" observers and electronic observations, it is impossible to completely isolate the overall effect of an observer. Participants will display the behavior they think is appropriate, performing at their best. Therefore, the presence of the observer must be minimized. To the extent possible, the observer should blend into the work environment and be unnoticeable.
- *Select observers carefully* – Observers are usually independent of the participants. They are typically members of an outside internal staff or external resource. The independent observer is usually skilled at recording behavior and making interpretations of behavior, and is unbiased in these interpretations.

Using an independent observer reduces the need to prepare observers. However, the independent observer may have the appearance of an outsider, and participants may resent the observer. Sometimes it is more feasible to recruit observers from inside the organization.

Observation Methods

Five methods of observation are suggested and are appropriate, depending on the circumstances surrounding the type of information needed. Each method is briefly described below.

- *Behavior checklist and codes* – A behavior checklist is useful for recording the presence, absence, frequency, or duration of a participant's behavior or action as it occurs. A checklist does not provide information on the quality, intensity, or possible circumstances surrounding the behavior observed. The checklist is useful, though, since an observer can identify exactly which behaviors should or should not occur. The number of behaviors listed in the checklist should be minimized, and behaviors should be listed in a logical sequence if and as they normally occur in a sequence. A variation of this approach involves coding behaviors or actions on a form. While this method is useful when there are many behaviors, it is more time consuming because a code is entered that identifies a specific behavior or actions instead of checking an item. A variation of this approach is the 360-degree feedback process in which surveys are completed on other individuals based on observations within a specific time frame.
- *Delayed report method* – With a delayed report method, the observer does not use any forms or written materials during the observation. The information is either recorded after the observation is completed or at particular time intervals during an observation. The observer tries to reconstruct what has been witnessed during the observation period. The advantage of this approach is that the observer is not as noticeable, and there are no forms being completed or notes being taken during the observation. The observer becomes more a part of the situation and less of a distraction. This approach is typical of the mystery shopper for retail stores. An obvious disadvantage is that the information written

may not be as accurate and reliable as the information collected at the time it occurred.

- *Video recording* – A video camera records behavior or actions in every detail. However, this intrusion may be awkward and cumbersome, and the participants may be unnecessarily nervous or self-conscious while they are being videotaped. If the camera is concealed, the privacy of the participant may be invaded. Because of this, video recording of on-the-job behavior is not frequently used.

- *Audio monitoring* – Monitoring conversations of participants is an effective observation technique. For example, in a large communication company's telemarketing department, sales representatives were prepared to sell equipment by telephone. To determine if employees were using the skills and procedures properly, telephone conversations were monitored on a randomly selected basis. While this approach may stir some controversy, it is an effective way to determine if skills and procedures are being applied consistently and effectively. For it to work smoothly, it must be fully explained and the rules clearly communicated.

- *System monitoring* – For employees who work regularly with checklists, tasks, and technology, system monitoring is becoming an effective way to "observe" participants as they perform job tasks. The system monitors times, sequence of steps, use of routines, and other activities to determine if the participant is performing the work according to specific steps and guidelines of the intervention. As technology continues to be a significant part of the workplace, system monitoring holds increasing promise.

Using Action Plans

In some cases, follow-up assignments can develop application and impact data. In a typical follow-up assignment, the innovation project participant is asked to meet a goal or complete a particular task or project by a set date. A summary of the results of the completed assignments provides further evidence of the success of the project.

With this approach, participants are required to develop action plans as part of the innovation project. Action plans contain detailed steps to accomplish specific objectives related to the project. The process is one of the most effective ways to enhance support for a project, and build the ownership needed for the successful application and impact of the project.

The plan is typically prepared on a printed form, such as the one shown in Figure 6.3. The action plan shows what is to be done, by whom, and the date by which the tasks should be accomplished. The action plan approach is a straightforward, easy-to-use method for determining how participants will implement the project and achieve success.

Using Action Plans Successfully

The development of the action plan requires two major tasks: determining what measure to improve, and writing the action items to improve it. As shown in Figure 6.3, an action plan can be developed for a safety improvement project. The plan presented in this figure requires participants to develop an objective, which is related to the project. In this example, the objective is to reduce the slips and falls on a hospital floor from 11 to 2 in six months. In some cases, there may be more than one objective, which requires additional action plans. Related to the objective are the improvement measure, the current levels, and target of performance. This information requires the participant to anticipate the implementation of the project, and set goals for specific performances that can be realized.

The action plan is completed during the early stages of the innovation project. The project leader approves the plan, indicating that it meets the particular requirements of being Specific, Measurable, Achievable, Realistic, and Time-bound (SMART). The plan can usually be developed in a 1–2 hour time frame, and often begins with action steps related to the implementation of the project. These action steps are actually Level 3 activities that detail the application of the project. All of these steps build support for, and are linked to, business impact measures. Their action elements are listed below:

- *Define the unit of measure* – The next important issue is to define the actual unit of measure. In some cases, more than one measure may be used, and will subsequently be contained in additional action plans. The unit of measure is necessary to break the process down into the simplest steps so that the ultimate value of the project can be determined. The unit can be output data, such as an additional unit manufactured or additional hotel room rented. In terms of quality, the unit can be one reject, error, or defect. Time-based units are usually measured in minutes, hours, days, or weeks, such

Safe Workplace Action Plan

Name: _Ellie Hightower_   Facilitator Signature: _____   Follow-Up Date _____ 2 June

Objective: _Improve workplace safety_   Evaluation Period: _December_   to _May_

Improvement Measure: _Monthly slips and falls_   Current Performance _11/six months_   Target Performance _2/six months_

Action Steps		Analysis
1. Meet with team to discuss reasons for slips and falls	_2 Dec_	A. What is the unit of measure? _1 slip and fall_
2. Review slip and fall records for each incident with safety – look for trends and patterns.	_18 Dec_	B. What is the value (cost) of one unit? _$1750_
3. Make adjustments based on reasons for slips and falls	_22 Dec_	C. How did you arrive at this value? _Safety and Health—Frank M._
4. Counsel with housekeeping and explore opportunities for improvement.		
5. Have safety conduct a brief meeting with team members	_5 Jan_	D. How much did the measure change during the evaluation period? (monthly value) _8_
6. Provide recognition to team members who have made extra efforts for reducing slips and falls.	_11 Jan_	E. What other factors could have caused this improvement? _A new campaign from safety and health._
7. Follow-up with each incident and discuss improvement or lack of improvement and plan other action.	_As needed_	F. What percent of this change was actually caused by this program? _70%_
8. Monitor improvement and provide adjustment when appropriate.	_As needed_ _As needed_	G. What level of confidence do you place on the above information? (100% = Certainty and 0% - No Confidence) _80%_

Intangible Benefits: _Image, risk reduction_

Figure 6.3 Action Plan Example.

as one minute of downtime. Units are specific to their particular type of situations, such as one turnover of key talent, one customer complaint, or one escalated call in the call center. The important point is to break them down into the simplest terms possible.

- *Require participants to provide monetary values for each improvement* – During the innovation project, participants are asked to determine, calculate, or estimate the monetary value for each improvement specified in the plan. The unit value is determined using standard values, expert input, external databases, or estimates. The process used to arrive at the value is described in the action plan. When the actual improvement occurs, participants will use these values to capture the annual monetary benefits of the plan. For this step to be effective, it is helpful to provide examples of common ways in which values can be assigned to the actual data.

- *Participants implement the action plan* – Participants implement the action plan during the innovation project, which often lasts for weeks or months following the intervention. Upon completion, a major portion (if not the entire consulting project) is slated for implementation. Project participants implement the steps in the action plan, and the results are achieved.

- *Participants estimate improvements* – At the end of the specified follow-up period – which is usually three months, six months, nine months, or one year – the participants indicate the specific improvements made, sometimes expressed as a monthly amount. This determines the actual amount of change that has been observed, measured, or recorded. It is important for the participants to understand the need for accuracy as data are recorded. In most cases only the changes are recorded, as those amounts are used to calculate the value of the project. In other cases, before and after data may be recorded, allowing the evaluator to calculate the actual differences.

- *Ask participants to isolate the effects of the project* – Although the action plan is initiated because of the project, the improvements reported on the action plan may be influenced by other factors. Thus, the action-planning process initiated in the innovation project should not take full credit for the improvement. For example, an action plan to reduce employee turnover in a division could take only partial credit for an improvement because of the other variables that affect the turnover rate. While there are several ways to isolate the effects of a project, participant estimation is usually most appropriate in the action-planning process. Consequently, participants are asked to estimate the percentage of the improvement actually related to this particular intervention. This question can be asked on the action plan form or in a follow-up questionnaire.

- *Ask participants to provide a confidence level for estimates* – Because the process to convert data to monetary values may not be exact, and the amount of the improvement actually related to the project may not be precise, participants are asked to indicate their level of confidence in those two values, collectively. On a scale of 0–100%, where 0% means no confidence and 100% means the estimates represent certainty, this value provides participants a mechanism for expressing their uneasiness with their ability to be exact with the process.

- *Collect action plans at specified time intervals* – An excellent response rate is essential, so several steps may be necessary to ensure that the action plans are completed and returned. Usually participants will see the importance of the process, and will develop their plans in detail early in the project. Some organizations use follow-up reminders by e-mail. Others call participants to check progress. Still others offer assistance in developing the final plan as part of the project. These steps may require additional resources, which must be weighed against the importance of having more data.

- *Summarize the data and calculate the ROI* – If developed properly, each action plan should have annualized monetary values associated with improvements. Also, each individual should have indicated the percentage of the improvement directly related to the project. Finally, participants should have provided a confidence percentage to reflect their level of uncertainty with the process and the subjective nature of some of the data that may be provided.

Advantages/Disadvantages of Action Plans

Although there are many advantages to using action plans, there are at least two concerns:

1. The process relies on direct input from the participant. As such, the information can sometimes be inaccurate and unreliable. Participants must have assistance along the way.
2. Action plans can be time consuming for the participant. If the participant's manager is not involved in the process, there may be a tendency for the participant not to complete the assignment.

As this section has illustrated, the action plan approach has many inherent advantages. Action plans are simple and easy to administer, are easily understood by participants, are suitable in a wide variety of projects, and are appropriate for all types of data.

Because of the tremendous flexibility and versatility of the process, and the conservative adjustments that can be made in analysis, action plans have become important data collection tools for project evaluation.

Using Performance Contracts

The performance contract is essentially a slight variation of the action planning process. Based on the principle of mutual goal setting, a performance contract is a written agreement between a participant, the participant's manager, and any external support. The participant agrees to improve performance on measures related to the innovation project. The agreement is in the form of a goal to be accomplished during or after the project. The agreement spells out what is to be accomplished, at what time, and with what results.

The process of selecting the area for improvement is similar to that used in the action-planning process. The topic selected should be stated in terms of one or more objectives. The objectives should state what is to be accomplished when the contract is complete. The objectives should be as follows:

- Written
- Understandable by all involved
- Challenging (requiring an unusual effort to achieve)
- Achievable (something that can be accomplished)
- Largely under the control of the participant
- Measurable and dated

The details required to accomplish the contract objectives are developed following the guidelines for action plans presented in the previous section.

Monitoring Business Performance Data

Data are available in every organization to measure business performance. Monitoring performance data enables management to measure performance in terms of output, quality, costs, time, job engagement, and customer satisfaction. When determining the source of data in the project evaluation, the first consideration should be existing databases and reports. In most organizations, performance data suitable for measuring improvement from an innovation project are available. If not, additional recordkeeping systems will have to be developed for measurement and analysis. Surfacing at this point is the question of economics. Is it economical to develop the recordkeeping systems necessary to evaluate a project? If the costs are greater than the expected return for the entire project, then it is pointless to develop those systems.

Existing Measures

Existing performance measures should be researched to identify those related to the proposed objectives of the project. In many situations, it is the performance of these measures that has created the need for the project in the first place. Frequently, an organization will have several performance measures related to the same item. For example, the efficiency of a production unit can be measured in multiple ways, some of which are listed below:

- Number of units produced per hour
- Number of on-schedule production units
- Percentage utilization of the equipment
- Percentage equipment downtime
- Labor cost per unit of production
- Overtime required per unit of production
- Total unit cost

Each of these, in its own way, measures the efficiency of the production unit. All related measures should be reviewed to determine those most relevant to the intervention.

Occasionally, existing performance measures are integrated with other data, and it may be difficult to keep them isolated from unrelated data. In this situation, all existing related measures should be extracted and retabulated to identify those most appropriate for comparison in the evaluation. At times, conversion factors may be necessary. For example, the average number of new sales orders per month may be presented regularly in the performance measures for the sales department. In addition, the sales costs per sales representative are also presented. However, in the evaluation of a consulting project, the average cost per new sale is needed. The average number of new sales orders and the sales cost per sales representative are required to develop the data necessary for comparison.

Developing New Measures

In some cases, data are not available for the information needed to measure the effectiveness of an innovation project. The organization must develop new recordkeeping systems, if economically feasible. In one organization, for example, a turnover problem with new professional staff prompted a project to fix the problem. To help ensure success of the project, several measures were planned, including early turnover defined as the percentage of employees who left the company in the first three months of employment. Initially this measure was not available. When the intervention was implemented, the organization began collecting early turnover figures for comparison.

In this situation, several questions should be addressed:

- Which department will develop the measurement system?
- Who will record and monitor the data?
- Where will it be recorded?
- Will new forms or documentation be needed?

These questions will usually involve multiple departments. Often the administration department, operations, or the information technology unit may be instrumental in helping determine whether new measures are needed and, if so, how they will be developed.

Selecting the Appropriate Method for Each Level

This chapter presented several methods to capture data. Collectively, these methods represent a wide range of opportunities for collecting data in a variety of situations. Eight specific issues should be considered when deciding which method is appropriate for a situation or evaluation level.

Type of Data

One of the most important issues to consider when selecting the method is the type of data to be collected. Some methods are more appropriate for

Method	Level 1	Level 2	Level 3	Level 4
Surveys	✓	✓	✓	
Questionnaires	✓	✓	✓	✓
Observation		✓	✓	
Interviews	✓	✓	✓	
Focus Groups		✓	✓	
Tests		✓		
Simulations		✓		
Action Planning			✓	✓
Performance Contracting			✓	✓
Performance Monitoring			✓	✓

Figure 6.4 Collecting Application and Impact Data.

Level 4, for example, while others are best for Level 3, 2, or 1. Figure 6.4 shows the most appropriate methods of data collection for each of the four levels. For example, follow-up surveys, observations, interviews, and focus groups are best suited for Level 3 data, sometimes exclusively. Performance monitoring, action planning, and questionnaires can readily capture Level 4 data.

Participants' Time for Data Input

Another important factor in selecting the data collection method is the amount of time participants must spend with data collection and evaluation systems. Time requirements should always be minimized, and the method should be positioned so that it is a value-added activity (i.e., the participants understand that this activity is something valuable, so they will not resist). This requirement often means that sampling is used to keep the total participant time to a minimum. Some methods, such as performance monitoring, require no participant time, while others, such as interviews and focus groups, require a significant investment in time.

Manager Time for Data Input

The time that a participant's direct manager must allocate to data collection is another important issue in the method selection. This time requirement should always be minimized. Some methods, such as performance contracting, may require much involvement from the supervisor, before and after the intervention. Other methods, such as questionnaires administered directly to participants, may not require any supervisor time.

Cost of Method

Cost is always a consideration when selecting the method. Some data collection methods are more expensive than others. For example, interviews and observations are very expensive. Surveys, questionnaires, and performance monitoring are usually inexpensive.

Disruption of Normal Work Activities

Another key issue in selecting the appropriate method – and perhaps the one that generates the most concern among managers – is the amount of disruption the data collection will create. Routine work processes should be disrupted as little as possible. Some data collection techniques, such as performance monitoring, require very little time and distraction from normal activities. Questionnaires generally do not disrupt the work environment, and can often be completed in only a few minutes, or even after normal work hours. On the other extreme, some items such as observations and interviews may be too disruptive to the work unit.

Accuracy of Method

The accuracy of the technique is another factor to consider when selecting the method. Some data collection methods are more accurate than others. For example, performance monitoring is usually very accurate, whereas questionnaires can be distorted and unreliable. If actual on-the-job behavior must be captured, observation is clearly one of the most accurate methods.

Utility of an Additional Method

Because there are many different methods to collect data, it is tempting to use too many data collection methods. Multiple data collection methods add to the time and costs of the evaluation, and may result in little additional value. Utility refers to the added value of the use of an additional data collection method. As more than one method is used, this question should always be addressed: Does the value obtained from the additional data warrant the extra time and expense of the method? If the answer is no, the additional method should not be implemented.

Cultural Bias for Data Collection Method

The culture or philosophy of the organization can dictate which data collection methods are used. For example, some organizations are accustomed to using questionnaires, and find the process fits in well with their culture. Some organizations will not use observation because their culture does not support the potential invasion of privacy often associated with it.

Final Thoughts

In this chapter, we outlined techniques for data collection, a critical issue in determining the success of the innovation project. These essential measures determine not only the success achieved, but areas where improvement is needed and areas where the success can be replicated in the future. Several data collection methods are available, ranging from questionnaires to action planning and business performance monitoring. The method you choose must match the scope of the project resources available and the accuracy needed. Complicated projects require a comprehensive approach that measures all of the issues involved in application and impact. Simple projects can take a less formal approach, and collect data from only a questionnaire.

Armed with this information about methods, we will examine how data is collected and evaluated at each level, starting with Level 1, in the next chapter.

7

Measuring Reaction and Perceived Value

Gram Vikas, which literally means "village development," is a successful non-governmental organization (NGO) that works with rural communities in India and Africa. Gram Vikas partners with these communities to address their critical needs of education, health, safe drinking water, sanitation, livelihoods, and alternative energy in a manner that is sustainable, socially inclusive, gender equitable, and empowering. [1]

Founded by Joe Madiath, this NGO has a reputation for being innovative with their solutions. In a recent interview, the founder reflected on the need for a proper reaction to innovation.

"I think most of the innovations, because I took the initiative, I had an advantage. I happen to be the boss. The boss can innovate and fail. So there was the feeling, 'OK, let Joe do it. Then if it fails, it would be he who fails.' But it's very, very difficult initially to cut through the resistance in the organization. For example, the first idea for a gravity flow. I asked my colleagues and the engineers to implement it. But they were not convinced and they would not do it. They said: You are wasting the organization's money, which is a big challenge. So I said: OK, if it does not work, I will pay for the entire thing, I will slowly pay it back to the organization. At least on the moral ground, you cannot now refuse to work with me." [2]

When the initial analysis is completed and the innovation project is positioned for success, implementation occurs. During implementation, feedback is collected from participants involved in the project. Their reactions and value perceptions with regard to the project provide indications of its potential for success. Additional reaction data may be taken at different intervals.

This chapter focuses on the measurement of reaction and perceived value. Collecting these data at the beginning of the project corresponds to the first operational phase of the ROI methodology. Participant feedback supplies powerful information to use in making adjustments and measuring success. This chapter outlines the most common approaches to collecting data and explores ways to use the information for maximum value.

Why Measure Reaction and Perceived Value?

Robert Safian is the editor of 'First Company Magazine," a publication that covers innovation routinely from many angles. In a recent editorial, Safian commented on the power of reactions:

"Business isn't always about numbers. Actually, it rarely is. It's about people, and emotion. What about the dollars? The cash flow? The share price? Don't kid yourself. Those are the by-products, the results. Anyone who is truly sophisticated about business recognizes this essential truth." [3]

For innovation, the "numbers" are usually inputs (people, time, costs). The outputs are new products, new processes, increased productivity, enhanced quality, improved times, and reduced costs. Rarely do we take the time to measure what occurs between the inputs and outputs. Without a proper reaction, the project is doomed, for example.

It is difficult to imagine an innovation project being conducted without the collection of feedback from those involved in the project, or at least from the sponsor. Collecting reaction and perceived value data serves several purposes. Participant feedback is critical to understanding how well a project serves the customer, and the potential of the project to meet the identified business needs.

Customer Satisfaction

Reaction and perceived value are customer satisfaction measures for the innovation project. The "customers" are the various stakeholders in the project. Without sustained favorable reactions, the project may not succeed. The individuals who have a direct role in the project are immediately affected by it, and often have to change processes or procedures or make other job adjustments in response to the project's initiation. Participant feedback on preferences is critical to making adjustments and changes in the project as it unfolds.

The feedback of project supporters is also important because this group will be in a position to influence the project's continuation and development.

The sponsors, who approve budgets, allocate resources, and ultimately live with the project's success or failure, must be completely satisfied with the project – and their overall satisfaction must be verified early and often.

Immediate Adjustments

An innovation project can go astray quickly, and sometimes a project ends up being the wrong solution for the specified problem. A project can also be mismatched to the solution from the beginning, so getting feedback early in the process is necessary to allow for immediate adjustments. This can help prevent misunderstandings, miscommunications, and, more important, misappropriations. Gathering and using reaction data promptly can enable an improperly designed project to be altered before more serious problems arise.

Predictive Capability

A more recent application of reaction data is predicting the success of an innovation project using analytical techniques. The project participants are asked to estimate the effectiveness of the project's application and, in some cases, the resulting value of that application. The reaction data thus become a forecast. (Forecasting is described in detail in Chapter 15.) Figure 7.1 shows the correlation between reactive feedback and application data. Studies have been conducted to verify this correlation.

In this analysis, the reaction measures are taken as the project is introduced, and the success of the implementation is later judged using the same scale (e.g., a 1–5 rating). When significant positive correlations are present, reaction measures can have predictive capability. Some reaction measures shown to have predictive capability are:

- The project is relevant to my job.
- The project is necessary.

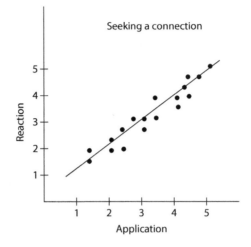

Figure 7.1 Correlations between Reaction and Application.

- The project is important to my success.
- The project contains information that I intend to implement.
- I intend to implement the project.
- I would recommend that others pursue similar projects.

Measures such as these consistently lead to strong positive correlations, and consequently represent more powerful feedback than typical measures of satisfaction with the project. Some organizations collect these or similar reaction measures for every project or program initiated.

Important but not Exclusive

Feedback data are critical to an innovation project's success, and should be collected for every project. Unfortunately, in some organizations, feedback alone has been used to measure project success. For example, at a financial services firm, the traditional method of measuring the effectiveness of a design thinking workshop was to rely entirely on feedback data from employees, by asking them if the workshop was relevant, important, and usable. Positive feedback is obviously critical to the program acceptance but is no guarantee the new program will be successfully executed. As subsequent sessions were conducted, executives became interested in the extent to which employees actually know the content (learning), the extent to which employees used the concepts and techniques (application), and the effectiveness of the program in terms of innovation outputs (impact). Only when these additional measures were taken could the full scope of success be determined.

Sources of Data

Possible sources of reaction and perceived value data concerning the success of an innovation project can be grouped into distinct categories.

Participants

The most widely used data source for project evaluation is the participants, those directly involved in the project. These "users" must take the skills and knowledge they acquired in the project or process, and apply them on the job. They also may be asked to explain the potential impact of that application. Participants are a rich source of data for almost every aspect of a project. They are by far the most credible source of reaction and perceived value data.

Participant Managers

Another key source of data are the individuals who directly supervise or lead the participants. They have a vested interest in the project, and are often in a position to observe the participants as they attempt to apply the knowledge and skills acquired in the project. Consequently, they can report on the successes associated with the project as well as the difficulties and problems. Although managerial input is usually most valuable as a source of reaction, it is also useful for other levels of evaluation.

Other Team Members

When entire teams are involved in the implementation of the project, all employees can provide useful information about the perceived changes prompted by the project. Input from this group is pertinent only to issues directly related to their work. Although data from this group can be helpful and instructive, it is sometimes not elicited because of the potential for introducing inaccuracies to the feedback process. Data collection should be restricted to those team members capable of providing meaningful insight into the value of the project.

Internal or External Customers

The individuals who serve as internal customers of the project are another source of reaction, perceived value, and other types of data. In some situations, internal or external customers provide input on perceived changes linked to the project. This source of data is more appropriate for projects directly affecting the customers. They report on how the project has influenced (or will influence) their work or the service they receive. Although this group may be somewhat limited in their knowledge of the scope of a project, their perceptions can be a source of valuable data that may indicate a direction for change in the project.

Project Leaders and Team Members

The project leader and project team may also provide input on the success of the project. This input may be based on on-the-job observations during the course of the project, and after its completion. Data from this source have limited utility because project leaders often have a vested interest in the outcome of the evaluation, and thus may lack objectivity.

Sponsors and Senior Managers

One of the most useful data sources is the sponsor or client group, usually a senior management team. The perception of the sponsor, be it an individual or a group, is critical to project success. Sponsors can provide input on all types of issues, and are usually available and willing to offer feedback. This is a preferred source for reaction data, since these data usually indicate what is necessary to make adjustments and to measure success.

Records and Previous Studies

In some cases, reaction data can be compared with other data available from innovation projects. Frequently, routine data collection systems are available from which feedback data can be obtained systematically. Also, external benchmarking studies may present data from similar projects. When such sources are available and appropriate, they can be very helpful, although their credibility must be established. It must be ensured that the reaction measures from these sources are directly related to the project at hand.

Noncontent issues	Content issues
• Demographics • Location • Transportation • Registration • Logistics • Service • Media • Food • Breaks and refreshments • Reception • Facilitators • Speakers	• Importance of project to job success • Importance to organization • Relevance of project • Timing of project • Appropriate use of time • Amount of new information • Perceived value • Contacts made • Planned use of material • Forecast of impact

Figure 7.2 Non-Content and Content Issues for Innovation Conference.

Areas of Feedback

In capturing reaction and perceived value data, it is important to focus on the content of the innovation project, program, or initiative. Too often, feedback data reflect aesthetic issues that may not be relevant to the substance of the project. Figure 7.2 distinguishes content and noncontent issues explored in a reaction questionnaire from an innovation conference organized by Qualcomm. The traditional way to evaluate activities is to focus on noncontent issues or inputs. In this figure, the column on the left represents areas important to the activity surrounding the conference, but contains nothing indicating results achieved from the event. The column on the right focuses on content. This is not to suggest that the nature of the service, the atmosphere of the event, and the quality of the speakers are not important; it is assumed that these issues will be taken care of and addressed appropriately. A more important set of data, focused on results, incorporates detailed information about the perceived value of the conference, the importance of the content, and the planned use of material or a forecast of the impact – indicators that successful results were achieved.

Many topics are critical targets for feedback. Feedback is needed in connection with almost every major issue, step, or process, to make sure things are advancing properly. Stakeholders will provide reaction input as to the appropriateness of the project planning schedule and objectives, and the progress made with the planning tools. If the project is perceived as irrelevant or unnecessary to the participants, more than likely it will not succeed in the workplace. Support for the project – including resources – represents an important area of feedback.

Participants must be assured that the innovation project has the necessary commitment. Issues important to project management and the organization sponsoring the project include project leadership, staffing levels, coordination, and communication. Also, it is important to collect feedback on how well the project team is working to address such issues as motivation, cooperation, and capability.

Finally, the perceived value of the project is often a critical parameter. Major funding decisions are made based on perceived value when stronger evidence of value is unavailable.

Data Collection Timing

The timing of data collection centers on particular events connected with the innovation project. As discussed previously, feedback during the early stages of implementation is critical. Ideally, this feedback validates the decision to go forward with the project, and confirms that alignment with business needs exists. The noting of problems in the initial feedback means that adjustments can be made early in its implementation. In practice, however, many organizations omit this early feedback, waiting until significant parts of the project have been implemented, at which point feedback may be more meaningful.

For longer projects, concerns related to the timing of feedback may require data collection at multiple points in time. Measures can be taken at the beginning of the project, and then at routine intervals once the project is under way.

Data Collection Methods

A variety of methods can be used to collect reaction data. Instruments range from simple surveys to comprehensive interviews. The appropriate instrument depends on the type of data needed (quantitative vs. qualitative), the convenience of the method to potential respondents, the culture of the organization, and the cost of a particular instrument. We will touch on the methods relevant to reaction data, without going into the detail that was provided in Chapter 6.

Questionnaires and Surveys

The questionnaire or survey is the most common method of collecting and measuring reaction data. Questionnaires and surveys come in all sizes, ranging from short forms to detailed, multiple-page instruments. They can be used to obtain subjective data about participants' reactions, as well as to document responses for future use in a projected ROI analysis. Proper design of questionnaires and surveys is important to ensure versatility.

Interviews

Interviews, although not used as frequently as questionnaires to capture reaction data, may be conducted by the project team or a third party to secure data that are difficult to obtain through written responses. Interviews can uncover success stories that may help to communicate early achievements of the project. Respondents may be reluctant to describe their experiences using a questionnaire, but may volunteer the information to a skillful interviewer using probing techniques. The interview is versatile and is appropriate for soliciting reaction data as well as application and implementation data. A major disadvantage of the interview is that it consumes time, which increases the cost of data collection. It also requires interviewer preparation to ensure that the process is consistent. Careful consideration is necessary before an organization commits to using interviews to collect reaction and perceived value data, especially when a follow-up evaluation is planned.

Focus Groups

Focus groups are particularly useful when in-depth feedback is needed. The focus group format involves a small-group discussion conducted by an experienced facilitator. It is designed to solicit qualitative judgments on a selected topic or issue. All group members are required to provide input, with individual input building on group input.

Compared with questionnaires, surveys, and interviews, the focus group approach has several advantages. The basic premise behind the use of focus groups is that when quality judgments are subjective, several individual judgments are better than one. The group process, where participants often motivate one another, is an effective method for generating and clarifying ideas and hypotheses. It is inexpensive and can be quickly planned and conducted. Its flexibility allows exploration of a project's unexpected outcomes or applications.

Using Reaction Data

Unfortunately, reaction and perceived value data are often collected and then disregarded. Too many project evaluators use the information to feed their egos, and then allow it to quietly disappear into their files, forgetting the original purpose behind its collection. In an effective evaluation, the information collected must be used to make adjustments or verify success; otherwise, the exercise is a waste of time.

Because this input is the principal measure supplied by key stakeholders, it provides an indication of their reaction to, and satisfaction with, the project. More important, these data provide evidence relating to the potential success of the innovation project. Data collected at this level, Level 1, should be used to:

- Identify the strengths and weaknesses of the project and make adjustments.
- Evaluate project team members.
- Evaluate the quality and content of planned improvements.
- Develop norms and standards.
- Link with follow-up data.
- Market future projects based on the positive reaction.

Final Thoughts

This chapter discussed data collection at the first level of evaluation: reaction and perceived value. Measuring reaction and perceived value is a component of every study, and is a critical factor in an innovation project's success. The data are collected using a variety of techniques, although surveys and questionnaires are most often used because of their cost-effectiveness and convenience. The data are important in allowing immediate adjustments to be made to the project.

While Reaction data are important, data value to executives increases as the evaluation moves up the chain of impact. Let's discuss data collection at the second level, learning, in the next chapter.

8

Measuring Learning

When the Nobel Prize winning physicist Richard Feynman was still working on his graduate degree at Princeton, he was asked to oversee a group of engineers who were tasked, without much context, to perform an endless series of tedious calculations. The math wasn't especially difficult for an engineer, but the work was very slow and full of errors. Growing more frustrated with the team's performance, Feynman made a critical discovery that would dramatically alter the course of events. He realized that the problem wasn't the math but that the engineers were totally disengaged. So he convinced his superiors to let the engineers in on what he already knew - why they were performing the calculations, and why they were sweating their tails off in the New Mexico desert (specifically in Los Alamos, New Mexico).

It was at that time that Feynman's boss, Robert Oppenheimer, pierced the veil of secrecy that had surrounded the work and let the engineers in on the enormity of what they were doing. There weren't simply doing routine math for some inconsequential lab exercise. They were performing calculations that would enable them to complete the race to build the atomic bomb before the Germans did.

Their work would win the war.

The workplace, the work, and the workers' performance completely transformed once the task was imbued with meaning. From that point forward, Feynman reported that the scientists worked ten times faster than before, with fewer mistakes, and with fierce commitment.

Meaning matters. Obviously, not every workplace has as meaningful a backdrop as global conflict. However, when meaning-rich experiences are facilitated and the resultant energy is channeled toward work that truly matters, engagement and productivity will know no limits – and that's something needed more than ever!

"Make it matter" is a critical concept for innovation project input (who's involved), reaction (how participants perceive it), and leaning (what participants will learn). This chapter will show how to make it matter and communicate that to the individuals who will achieve success. [1]

Measuring learning is an important part of the evaluation process, especially when an innovation project is intended to change behaviors or processes. Participant knowledge of what to do and how to do it is critical to a project's success. This chapter focuses on simple, commonly used techniques for measuring learning, and begins with an overarching look at the reasons for measuring learning.

Why Measure Learning and Confidence?

The United Nations (UN) has developed goals to guide different agencies. Many of these goals, called Millennium Development Goals (MDG), focus on healthcare, healthcare delivery, and the health of the citizens. Three of these goals focus directly on HIV and AIDS. [2] The first goal focuses on increasing the awareness of HIV and AIDS. To achieve this first goal, the UN must collect data about the knowledge of HIV and AIDS, what causes it, and how to prevent it. This MDG requires agencies to collect learning data in the form of a simple assessment of the knowledge that has been gained among the citizens of a particular country from the various communiques on the topic. Essentially, it measures the learning of specific knowledge.

Several key principles illustrate the importance of measuring learning during the implementation of an innovation project. Each of these in itself is sufficient to justify the measurement of learning. Collectively, they provide an indication of the full range of benefits that result from measuring the changes in skills, knowledge, and other qualities that occur during a project.

The Importance of Intellectual Capital

Intellectual capital has become an important concept, as organizations progress from agricultural to industrial to knowledge-based systems. Intellectual capital is what the organization knows, and it can be classified in a variety of ways for measurement purposes. Figure 8.1 illustrates one categorization of intellectual capital, showing intellectual capital as a combination of human capital, renewable capital, structural capital, and relationship capital. [3] As projects are implemented, they focus on increasing one or more of these major elements of intellectual capital. For some organizations, intellectual capital translates directly into success, in the form of rewards by the stock market. Up to 80% of the market value of some high technology firms is attributed to intellectual capital. This demonstrates the value of measuring learning in projects aimed at improving intellectual capital.

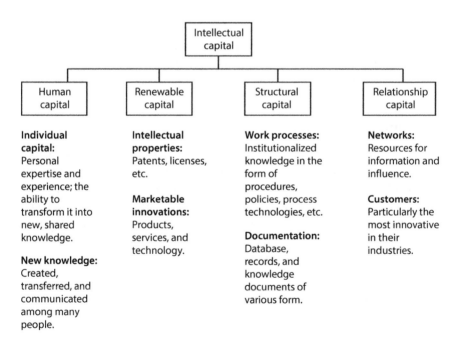

Figure 8.1 Categories of intellectual capital.

The Learning Organization

In recent decades, organizations have experienced a rapid transformation of competitive global markets as a result of economic changes. Organizations must learn new ways to serve customers and use innovations and technology to enhance their efficiency, to restructure, to reorganize, and to execute their functions globally. The concept of the learning organization evolved in response to this need for a change in strategy. This concept requires organizations to use learning proactively in an integrated way, and to support growth for individuals, teams, and entire organizations. Peter Senge popularized the learning organization concept, suggesting that an organization capture, share, and use knowledge so that its members can work together to change how the organization responds to challenges. [4] Managers must question the old social constructs and practice new ways of thinking.

Learning must take place within and support the framework of teams and larger groups where individuals can work together to generate new knowledge. The process must be continuous, because a learning organization is a never-ending journey. [5]

With the new focus on creating learning organizations, where countless activities and processes are in place to promote continuous learning, measurement has become an even more important issue. How do we know if an organization has become a learning organization? How is such an organization measured? Can learning actually be measured on a large scale?

The Compliance Issue

Organizations face an increasing number of regulations with which they must routinely comply. These regulations involve all aspects of business, and are considered essential by governing bodies to protect customers, investors, and the environment. Employees must have a certain amount of knowledge about the regulations to maintain compliance. Consequently, an organization must measure the extent of employee learning and understanding with regard to regulations, to ensure that compliance is not a problem.

The Use and Development of Competencies

The use of competencies and competency models has dramatically increased in recent years. In the struggle for a competitive advantage, many organizations have focused on people as the key to success. Competency models are used to ensure that employees do the right things, clarifying and articulating what is required for effective performance. Competency models help organizations align behavior and skills with the strategic direction of the company. A competency model describes a particular combination of knowledge, skills, and characteristics necessary to perform a role in an organization. Competencies are used as tools for recruiting, selecting, training, reviewing performance, and even removing individuals from the organization. [6] The personas, mentioned in Chapter 2, are similar to competencies.

The Role of Learning in Innovation Projects

Although some projects involve new equipment, processes, and technology, the human factor remains critical to project success. Whether an organization is developing new products, restructuring, or adding new systems, employees must learn how to work in the new products, systems, or environment, and this requires the development of new knowledge and skills. Simple tasks and procedures do not automatically come with new processes. Instead, complex environments, procedures, and tools must be used in an intelligent way to reap the desired benefits for the organization. Employees must learn in different ways – not just in a formal classroom environment, but through technology-based learning and on-the-job practice. Team leaders and managers serve as coaches or mentors in some projects. In a few cases, learning coaches or on-the-job trainers are used in conjunction with a project to ensure that learning is transferred to the job and is implemented as planned. [7]

Innovation project team members and participants don't always fully understand what they must do. Although the chain of impact can be broken at any level, a common place for a break is at Level 2, learning. Employees simply may not know what to do or how to do it properly. When the application and implementation does not go smoothly, project leaders can determine if a learning deficiency is the problem, and if so, they may be able to eliminate it. In other words, learning measurement is necessary to contribute to leaders' understanding of why employees are, or are not, performing the way they should.

The Challenges and Benefits of Measuring Learning

Measuring learning involves major challenges that may inhibit a comprehensive approach to the process. However, besides being an essential part of the ROI Methodology, this measurement provides many other benefits that help ensure an innovation project's success.

Challenges

The greatest challenge in measuring learning is to maintain objectivity without crossing ethical or legal lines, while keeping costs low. A common method of measuring learning is testing, but this approach generates additional challenges.

The first challenge is the "enjoyment" factor. Few people enjoy being tested. Many are offended by it, and feel that their professional prowess is being questioned. Some people are intimidated by tests, which bring back memories of their third-grade math teacher, red pen in hand.

Another challenge with tests is the legal and ethical repercussions of basing decisions involving employee status on test scores. Therefore, organizations use other techniques to measure learning, such as surveys, questionnaires, role plays, and simulations.

The Benefits of Measuring Learning

The benefits of measuring learning are reflected in the reasons for learning measurement described earlier. First, measurement at this level checks the progress of the innovation project against the objectives. Objectives are critical to a project, and they should be established at each level. Fundamentally, the measurement of learning reveals the extent of knowledge and skill acquisition in relation to the project. This is a critical element, particularly for knowledge-based projects, new technology applications, and projects designed to build competencies.

In addition to assessing improvement in skills or knowledge, this level provides feedback to the individuals delivering the skills or knowledge so that adjustments can be made. If project participants are not learning, there may be a problem with the way the learning is being delivered. A learning measure can identify strengths and weaknesses in the method of project presentation or instruction, and may point out flaws in the design or delivery. Thus, measuring learning can pinpoint mismatches among various aspects of a project, and thereby lead to changes or improvement. [8]

Another important benefit is that, in many cases, learning measures enhance participant performance. Verification and feedback concerning the knowledge and skills acquired can encourage participants to improve in certain areas. When employees excel, feedback motivates them to enhance their performance even further. In short, positive feedback on learning builds confidence and the desire to continue improving. Without such measurement, participants will never know their potential to perform.

Lastly, measuring learning helps to maintain accountability. Because projects are aimed at making organizations better – whether a learning organization is being built, competencies are being improved, or systems and processes are being enhanced – learning is an important part of any project, and its measurement is vital in confirming that improvement has in fact occurred.

Measurement Issues

Several items affect the nature and scope of measurement at the learning level. These include project objectives, the measures themselves, and timing.

Project Objectives

The starting point for any level of measurement is development of the innovation project objectives. The measurement of learning builds on the learning objectives. Learning and development professionals are skilled in generating detailed learning objectives following the process described in Chapter 5. However, for projects where the focus is not necessarily on a learning activity – such as implementing a new suggestion system program, initiating a new procedure, or conducting a trial run – the first step again is to ensure that objectives are in place.

Typically, the objectives of the innovation project are broad, and indicate only major skills or general knowledge areas that should be achieved as the project is implemented. These are sometimes called key project learning objectives. They can be divided into subcomponents that provide more detail. This is necessary when a tremendous number of tasks, procedures, or new skills must be learned to make the project successful. For other projects, this level of detail might not be needed; identifying the major objectives and indicating what must be accomplished to meet each objective is often sufficient.

Typical Measures

Measuring learning focuses on knowledge, skills, and attitudes, as well as the individual's confidence in applying or implementing the project or process as desired. Typical measures collected at this level are:

- Skills
- Knowledge
- Awareness
- Contacts

- Capacity
- Readiness
- Confidence

Obviously, the more detailed the knowledge area, the greater the number of objectives. The concept of knowledge is quite general, and often includes the assimilation of facts, figures, and ideas. Instead of knowledge, terms such as awareness, understanding, and information may be used to denote specific categories. In some cases, the issue is developing a reservoir of knowledge and related skills toward improving capability, capacity, or readiness. Networking is often part of a project, and developing contacts who may be valuable later is important. This may occur within or external to an organization. For example, within the organization, a project may include different functional parts of the organization, and an expected outcome from a learning perspective is knowing who to contact at particular times in the future. For projects that involve different organizations, such as a marketing event, new contacts that result from the event can be important and ultimately pay off in terms of efficiency and/or revenue growth.

Timing

The timing of learning measurement can vary. In some situations, a preliminary measure is taken to determine the extent to which the participants know the specific objectives in the program. This may prevent participants from learning information they already know. In these situations, the use of a posttest to compare with the pretest is common. The posttest can be collected early in the project, or as soon as the learning portion is completed. The pretesting and posttesting should be conducted under the same or similar conditions using questions or other test items that are identical or very similar.

Assuming that no pretest is administered, the measurement of learning can occur at various times. If formal learning sessions connected with the project are offered, the measure is taken at the end of those sessions to ensure that participants are ready to apply their newly acquired knowledge. If a project has no formal learning sessions, measuring may occur at different intervals. For long-term projects, as skills and knowledge grow, routine assessment may be necessary to measure both the acquisition of additional skills and knowledge and retention of the previously acquired skills. The timing of measurement is balanced with the need to know the new information. This is offset by the cost of obtaining, analyzing, and responding to the data. In an ideal situation, the timing of measurement is part of the Data Collection Plan, as presented in Chapter 4.

Data Collection Methods

One of the most important considerations with regard to measuring learning is the specific way in which data are collected. Learning data can be collected using many different methods. The following list of instruments are just some of the data collection methods used:

- Questionnaires
- Performance tests
- Technology and task simulations
- Case studies
- Role-playing/skill practice
- Informal assessments

Chapter 6 described these methods in some detail, and we'll provide additional information within the context of Level 2, now.

Questionnaires and Surveys

Questionnaires and surveys were discussed in Chapter 7, with the focus on measuring reaction. Questionnaires are also used to collect data at Level 2. These questionnaires include two-way or true/false questions, where participants are provided with statements and must either agree or disagree. Rating scales are common in surveys gathering learning data. Multiple-choice is probably the most common question type, where participants are asked to choose one or more items from a series of alternative answers. This has the advantage of ease of scoring and is relatively objective. Matching exercises are also useful, where participants match particular items on a choice basis. Short-answer questions can be easy to develop but difficult to score. Essay questions are less likely to be used because they are difficult to score, and rely, to some degree, on the subjective opinion of the scorer rather than the participant. Developing questions in an attempt to measure learning can be fairly simple. The key is to ensure that the questions asked are relevant to the knowledge, skills, or information presented.

Performance Tests

Performance testing allows participants and users to exhibit the skills (and occasionally knowledge or attitudes) that have been learned in an innovation project. A skill can be manual, verbal, or analytical, or a combination of the three. Performance testing is used frequently in task-related projects;

here the participants are allowed to demonstrate what they have learned, and to show how they would use the skill on the job. In other situations, performance testing may involve skill practice or role-playing (e.g., participants are asked to demonstrate discussion or problem-solving skills that they have acquired).

In one situation, computer systems engineers were participating in an innovation project for system reengineering. As part of the project, participants were given the assignment of designing and testing a basic system. A project team manager observed participants as they checked out the system. Then the manager carefully completed the same design and compared his results with those of the participants. These comparisons and the performance of the designs provided an evaluation of the project, and represented an adequate reflection of the skills learned in the project.

Technology and Task Simulations

Another technique for measuring learning is simulation. This method involves the construction and application of a procedure or task that simulates or models the work involved in the innovation project or program. The simulation is designed to represent, as closely as possible, the actual job situation. Participants try out the simulated activity, and their performance is evaluated based on how well they accomplish the task. Simulations offer several advantages. They permit a job or part of a job to be reproduced in a manner almost identical to the real setting. Through careful planning and design, the simulation can have all the central characteristics of the real situation. Even complex jobs, such as that of the manager, can be simulated adequately.

Although the initial development can be expensive, simulations can be cost-effective in the long run, particularly for large projects or situations where a project may be repeated. Another advantage of using simulations is safety. Safety considerations for many jobs require participants to be trained in simulated conditions. For example, emergency medical technicians risk injury and even death if they do not learn the needed techniques prior to encountering a real-life emergency.

Although a variety of simulation techniques are used to evaluate learning, the two most common are technology and task simulation. A technology simulation uses a combination of electronic and mechanical devices to reproduce real-life situations. These simulations are used in conjunction with programs to develop operational and diagnostic skills. Expensive examples are simulated "patients" or a simulation of a nuclear power plant operator. Other, less expensive devices have been developed to simulate equipment operation.

A task simulation involves a participant's performance in a simulated task. For example, a customer service associate must demonstrate the task of creating a new account. This task simulation serves as the evaluation.

Case Studies

A perhaps less effective but still popular technique of measuring learning is the case study. A case study presents a detailed description of a problem, and usually contains a list of several questions posed to the participant. The participant is asked to analyze the case and determine the best course of action. The problem should reflect conditions in the real world and in the content of the project.

This is ideal for innovation projects involving problem solving, brainstorming, or process improvement. An existing case study shows how it works and participants learn from them.

Role-Playing and Skill Practice

Role plays, sometimes referred to as skill practice, require participants to practice a newly learned skill as they are observed by others. Participants are assigned roles and given specific instructions, which sometimes include an ultimate course of action. The participant then practices the skill with other individuals to accomplish the desired objectives. This exercise is intended to simulate real-world conditions to the greatest extent possible. Difficulty sometimes arises when other participants make the practice unrealistic by not reacting the way individuals would in an actual situation. To help overcome this obstacle, trained role players (the actual characters portrayed in the role play) may be used in all roles except that of the participant. For example, some pharmaceutical companies use real physicians when teaching their salespeople to call on physicians to sell new drugs. This requires additional costs but provides a more objective evaluation of a participant's knowledge.

Informal Assessments

Many projects include activities, exercises, or problems that must be explored, developed, or solved. Some of these are constructed in the form of interactive exercises, while others require individual problem-solving skills. When these tools are integrated into the learning activity, they can be effective in gathering learning data.

A commonly used informal method is participant self-assessment. Participants are provided an opportunity to assess their acquisition of skills and knowledge. In some situations, a project leader or a facilitator provides an assessment of the learning that has taken place. Although this approach is subjective, it may be appropriate when project leaders or facilitators work closely with participants.

In many projects, it is sufficient to allow an informal check of learning to provide some assurance that participants have acquired the skills and knowledge needed to implement the project, or that the requisite changes in attitude have occurred. The appropriateness of this approach may depend on other levels of evaluation that are being pursued. For example, if a Level 3 (application and implementation) evaluation is planned, conducting a comprehensive Level 2 evaluation might not be as critical.

An informal assessment of learning is usually sufficient. Moreover, if resources are scarce, a comprehensive evaluation at all levels becomes quite expensive. Informal assessments provide an alternative approach to measuring learning when inexpensive, low-key measurements are all that is needed.

Administrative Issues

Several administrative issues must be addressed in measuring learning. Briefly discussed next, each should be part of the overall plan for administering learning measurement.

Reliability and Validity

Two important issues with regard to test design are validity and reliability. Validity is the extent to which an instrument measures what it is designed to measure. Reliability is the extent to which an instrument is stable or consistent over time. In essence, any instrument used to collect data should be both valid (measure what it should measure) and reliable (be consistent over time). An instrument is reliable if the same data were collected at different times, with nothing intervening to cause the respondent to change his or her knowledge, and the response is the same. Significant deviations indicate that an instrument is unreliable.

Ideally, an instrument should be both reliable and valid. It is not possible for an instrument to be valid if it is not reliable. These two criteria become important when a human resource action (job status change) is taken as a result of a person failing a learning measurement or a specific test. For example, if an individual is promoted, denied promotion, provided an increase in pay, or assigned a job because of his or her performance on the test, the instrument must be defensible. In the vast majority of project work, however, the consequences of not passing the test will not be so severe. The concepts of validity and reliability, and how to verify them, is beyond the scope of this book. Other sources are available to provide detail. [9]

Consistency

Tests, exercises, and assessments for measuring learning must be administered consistently from one group to another, to effectively measure and compare learning between groups. Consistency refers to the time required to respond, the actual learning conditions in which the participants complete the process, the resources available to them, and the amount of assistance from other members of the group. These concerns can easily be addressed in the instructions.

When formal testing is used, participants should be monitored as they complete the test. This ensures that individuals work independently, and also that someone is there to provide assistance or answer questions as needed. This may not be an issue in all situations, but it needs to be addressed in the evaluation plan.

Pilot Testing

Pilot testing an instrument with a small group to ensure that the instrument is both valid and reliable is advisable. A pilot test provides an opportunity to resolve any confusion that might exist about the instructions, questions, and statements. When a pilot test is taken, it should be timed to see how long individuals take to complete it. Also, the individuals taking the pilot test should provide input regarding alternative ways to ask the questions, the flow of information, and any other suggestions for improvement. At a minimum, a test should be piloted for content. All too often, a test or survey is administered that does not cover the content presented that supports implementation.

Scoring and Reporting

Scoring instructions need to be developed for the measurement process so that the person evaluating the responses will be objective and consistent in scoring. Ideally, the potential for bias from the individual scoring the instrument should be completely eliminated by providing proper scoring instructions and other information necessary to guarantee an objective evaluation.

In some situations, the participants are provided with the results immediately, particularly with self-scoring tests or with group-based scoring mechanisms. In other situations, the results may not be known until later. In these situations, a method for providing data on scores should be built into the evaluation plan, unless it has been predetermined that participants are not to know the scores. The worst-case scenario is to promise participants test scores, and then deliver them late or not at all.

Using Learning Data

Data must be used to add value and improve processes. Among the appropriate uses of learning data are the following:

- Provide individual feedback to build confidence.
- Validate that learning has been acquired.
- Provide additional support to ensure successful implementation.
- Evaluate project leaders/facilitators.
- Build a database for project comparisons.
- Improve the project, program, or process.

Final Thoughts

In this chapter we discussed some of the key issues involved in measuring learning, an important ingredient in innovation project success. Even if it is accomplished informally, learning must be assessed to determine the extent to which the participants in a project learn new skills, techniques, processes, tools, and procedures. By measuring learning, facilitators and project leaders can ascertain the degree to which participants are capable of successfully executing the project plan. Measuring learning provides an opportunity to make adjustments quickly so that improvements can be made or additional interventions can be introduced to facilitate project success.

While learning measures indicate potential success with implementation, we will cover an even better measure – application and implementation, at Level 3, next.

9

Measuring Application and Implementation

With several successful brands and a position as a leader in the industry, Fashion Stores, Inc. (FSI) wanted more growth and profitability. Sales growth was not what the executives would like to see, and some operational issues had caused less-than desirable profits.

The executives asked the Chief Talent Officer to be creative and develop the proper approach, not necessarily recycling on typical leadership and management development. The team researched the competencies for high ROI performance and conducted interviews and focus groups with store managers.

After detailed analysis of the issues, it was decided that the store managers needed to drive improvement in store performance by building teams and creating an environment where team members were fully engaged, satisfied with their employer, and perceived FSI as a great place to work. Essentially, the solution was a high-performance team program, preparing the store managers to create a compelling place to shop, a compelling place to work, and a compelling place to invest. Three important business measures—store growth, sales growth, and profitability—provided the business rationale for the program.

With this in mind, the talent development team designed the program to deliver results. They recognized that certain fundamental issues could be addressed at the convenience of the participants through eLearning modules. They also wanted the power of live presentations, networking collaboration, skill-building, and action planning in a high-impact, two-day workshop. From a design perspective, application on the job is the critical issue. To accomplish that, coaches were provided, technology support was made available, and manager involvement was necessary. Action planning was used to capture and track results. Reporting results to the appropriate organization was the way to make sure that they were fully accountable for the results. The design for this program is shown in Figure 9.1.

The initial evaluation for the implementation of this program involved approximately 100 managers across four areas: Europe, South America, North America, and Asia. is group was evaluated all the way to the ROI level to show management the power of this program, to help make it even better, and to influence the allocation of funds for it in the future.

By design, this program was successful, delivering an impressive ROI of 133%. [1]

	Awareness and Alignment	Learning, Engagement, and Practice	Application, Impact, and Reporting
	Technology Based	Classroom 2 Days	On the Job

30 min eLearning	• Awareness
	• Decision to improve
		• Expectations and commitment
		• 360 degree feedback
		• 10 skills of high performance teams
		• Skill videos
		• Realistic practice
		• Engagement and reflection
		• Skill-impact linkage
		• Planning
		  – Business impact
		  – Behaviors/action
			• Connect with manager and coach

30 min eLearning	• Program design • Process flow		• Implement actions • Make adjustments
30 min eLearning	• Customization • Learning styles • Cultural adjustment		• Review videos • Use tools • Use portal
30 min eLearning survey	• 360 degree feedback • Use • Rules		• Impact capture • Analysis • Documentation
30 min eLearning	• Alignment • Business impact measures • Making the connection		• Reporting • Sharing

Figure 9.1 Program Design: Leadership for Performance.

This case clearly illustrates the need for programs to be designed with the results in mind. is means designing content, delivery, expectations, and mechanisms not only to make sure that the right people are there with the right content at the right time but to ensure that their implementation is fully supported and the learning is transferred to the job, with application and business impact. is program was designed for impact and ROI from every perspective.

Many projects fail because of breakdowns in implementation. Project team members and participants just don't do what they should, when they should, or at the frequency they should. Measuring application and implementation is critical to understanding the success of project implementation. Without successful implementation, positive business impact will not occur – and no positive return will be achieved.

This chapter explores the most common ways to evaluate the application and implementation of innovation projects and programs. The possibilities vary from the use of questionnaires to observation, and include action planning. In addition to describing the techniques to evaluate implementation, this chapter addresses the challenges and benefits of each technique.

Why Measure Application and Implementation?

Measuring application and implementation is absolutely necessary. For some projects, it is the most critical data set because it provides an understanding of the degree to which successful project implementation occurs, and of the barriers and enablers that influence success.

Information Value

As briefly discussed in Chapter 4, the value of information increases as progress is made through the chain of impact, from reaction (Level 1) to ROI (Level 5). Thus, information concerning application and implementation (Level 3) is usually more valuable to the client than are reaction and learning data. This is not to discount the importance of the first two levels, but to emphasize the importance of moving up the chain of impact. Measuring the extent to which a project is implemented provides critical data about its success, and about factors that can contribute to greater success as the project is fully implemented.

The Level 1 and Level 2 measures occur during a project's early stages, when more attention and focus are placed on the participants' direct involvement in the project. Measuring application and implementation occurs after the project has been implemented and captures the success of moving the project forward through participants' on-the-job use of knowledge about the project. Essentially, this measure reflects the degree to which the project is implemented by those who are charged with its success. This is the first step in transitioning to a new state, behavior, or process. Understanding the success of the transition requires measuring application and implementation.

Project Focus

Because many innovation projects and programs focus directly on implementation and application of new behaviors and processes, a project sponsor often speaks in these terms and has concerns about these measures of success. The sponsor of a major innovation project designed to transform an organization will be greatly concerned with implementation and application, and will want to know the extent to which key stakeholders adjust to and implement the desired new behaviors, processes, and procedures.

Problems and Opportunities

If the chain of impact breaks at this level, little or no corresponding impact data will be available. Without impact, there is no ROI. This breakdown most often occurs because participants in the project encounter barriers, inhibitors, and obstacles (covered later) that deter implementation. A dilemma arises when reactions to the project are favorable and participants learn what is intended, but they fail to overcome the barriers and don't manage to accomplish what is necessary.

When a project goes astray, the first question usually asked is, "What happened?" More importantly, when a project appears to add no value, the first question should be, "What can we do to change its direction?" In either scenario, it is important to identify the barriers to success, the problems in implementation, and the obstacles to application. At Level 3, measuring application and implementation, these problems are addressed, identified, and examined. In many cases, the stakeholders directly involved in the process can provide important recommendations for making changes or using a different approach in the future.

When a project is successful, the obvious question is, "How can we repeat this or improve it in the future?" The answer to this question is also found at Level 3. Identifying the factors that contribute directly to the success of the project is critical. Those same items can be used to replicate the process, and produce enhanced results in the future. When key stakeholders identify those issues, they make the project successful and provide an important case history of what is necessary for success.

Reward Effectiveness

Measuring application and implementation allows the sponsor and project team to reward those who do the best job of applying the processes and implementing the project. Measures taken at this level provide clear evidence of success and achievement, and provide a basis for performance reviews. Rewards often have a reinforcing value, helping to keep employees on track and communicating a strong message for future improvement.

Challenges

To improve costs and efficiency of a regional healthcare firm, a business process improvement team implemented a new enterprise resource management system. The implementation focuses on the healthcare organization's current procurement, inventory control processes, financial management system, payroll system, discount structures, and specific benchmarks. In addition, cost accounting and capital allocation systems were pinpointed to align with payroll and productivity systems such as scheduling and forecasting. To make this system work properly as it is installed, the users of the system must:

- Manage hospital assets and resources effectively.
- Integrate suppliers.
- Standardize supplies, devices, and equipment across departments and physicians.
- Develop an allocation process.
- Identify areas where the firm is paying too much for specific items.
- Employ more self-service procurement technology.
- Decentralize the inventory management process.
- Employ handheld technology.
- Complete the implementation on schedule.

Although this system will have tremendous payoffs in cost savings, time savings, reductions in unnecessary orders, and overpayments, these benefits will not occur unless the new system is implemented properly and all users are following correct application and use. [2]

Collecting application and implementation data brings into focus key challenges that must be addressed for success at this level. These challenges often inhibit an otherwise successful evaluation.

Linking with Learning

Application data should be linked closely with the learning data discussed in the previous chapter. Essentially, innovation project leaders need to know what has been accomplished, what has been done differently, and what activities have been implemented, based on what the individuals learned to do. This level measures the extent to which participants accurately took what they learned and applied it to their jobs.

Building Data Collection into the Project

Application data are collected after the innovation project's implementation. Because of the time lag between project implementation and data collection, it is difficult to secure a high quality and quantity of data. Consequently, one of the most effective ways to ensure that data are collected is to build data collection into the project from the beginning. Data collection tools positioned as application tools must be built in as part of the implementation. By analogy, consider that many software applications contain overlay software that shows a user performance profile. Essentially, the software tracks the user invisibly, capturing the steps, pace, and difficulties encountered while using the software. When the process is complete, a credible data set has been captured, simply because project leaders built it into the process at the beginning.

Ensuring a Sufficient Amount of Data

Whether collecting data by questionnaire or through action plans, interviews, or focus groups, poor response rates are a problem in most organizations. Having individuals participate in the data collection process is a challenge. To ensure that adequate amounts of high-quality data are available, a serious effort is needed to improve response rates.

Because many projects are planned on the basis of the ROI Methodology, it is expected that sponsors will collect impact data, monetary values, and the project's actual ROI. This need to "show the money" sometimes results in less emphasis being placed on measuring application and implementation. In many cases, it may be omitted or slighted in the analysis. But it is through focused effort on process and behavior change that business impact will occur. Therefore, emphasis must be placed on collecting data that focuses on application and implementation. Doing things differently can result in substantial benefits, but knowing the degree to which things are done differently is essential to guaranteeing those benefits.

Addressing Application Needs at the Outset

During the needs assessment (detailed in Chapter 5), the question is asked, "What is being done on the job, or not being done, that's inhibiting the business measure?" When this question is answered adequately, a connection is made between the solution and the business measure. When this issue is addressed, the activities or behaviors that need to change are identified, serving as the basis of the data collection. The bottom line is that too many evaluations focus on either impact measures, which define the business measure to collect, or on learning, which uncovers what people do not know. More focus is needed at the level in between, Level 3, which involves the tasks, processes, procedures, and behaviors that need to be in place for successful implementation on the job.

Measurement Issues

When measuring the application and implementation of innovation projects and programs, several key issues should be addressed, which are largely similar to those encountered when measuring reaction and learning. (A few issues may differ slightly because of the later time frame for collecting this type of data.)

Methods

A variety of methods are available when collecting data at Level 3. These include traditional surveys and questionnaires, and methods based on observation, interviews, and focus groups. Other powerful methods include action planning, in which individuals plan their parts of the implementation, and follow-up sessions. Data collection methods are described in detail in Chapter 6, and in the context of Level 3 measurement later in this chapter.

Objectives

As with the other levels, the starting point for data collection is the objectives set for project application and implementation. Without clear objectives, collecting data would be difficult. Objectives define what activity is expected. (Chapter 5 discusses the basic principles for developing these objectives.)

Areas of Coverage

To a certain extent, the areas of coverage for this process parallel the areas identified in Chapter 6. The later time frame for data collection changes the measurement to a post-project measure rather than a predictive measure. The key point is that this level focuses on activity or action, not on the ability to act (Level 2) and not on the consequences (Level 4). The sheer number of activities to measure can be mind-boggling. Figure 9.2 shows examples of coverage areas for application, which will vary from project to project.

Data Sources

The sources of data mirror those identified in Chapter 7. Essentially, all key stakeholders are potential sources of data. Perhaps the most important sources of data are the users of the solutions, those directly involved in the application and implementation of the project or program. Good sources may also be the project team or team leaders charged with the implementation. In some cases, the source may be the organizational records or system.

Timing

The timing of data collection can vary significantly. Because this is a follow-up after the project launch, the key issue is determining the best time for a post-implementation evaluation. The challenge is to analyze the nature and scope of the application and implementation, and to determine the earliest time that a trend and pattern will evolve. This occurs when the application of skills becomes routine and the implementation is making significant progress. This is a judgment call. Going in as early as possible is important so that potential adjustments can still be made. At the same time, leaders must wait long enough so that behavior changes are allowed to occur and the implementation can be observed and measured. In projects spanning a considerable length of time, several measures may be taken at three- to six-month intervals. Using effective measures at well-timed intervals will provide successive input on implementation progress, and clearly show the extent of improvement.

Action	Explanation	Example
Increase	Increase a particular activity or action.	Increase the frequency of the use of a particular skill.
Decrease	Decrease a particular activity or action.	Decrease the number of times a particular process has to be checked.
Eliminate	Stop or remove a particular task or activity.	Eliminate the formal follow-up meeting and replace it with a virtual meeting.
Maintain	Keep the same level of activity for a particular process.	Continue to monitor the process with the same schedule as previously used.
Create	Design, build, or implement a new procedure, process, or activity.	Create a procedure for resolving the differences between two divisions.
Use	Use a particular process or activity.	Use the new skill in situations for which it was designed to be used.
Perform	Conduct or do a particular task or procedure.	Conduct post-audit review at the end of each activity.
Participate	Become involved in various activities, projects, or programs.	Submit a suggestion for reducing costs.
Enroll	Sign up for a particular process, program, or project.	Enroll in the career advancement program.
Respond	React to groups, individuals, or systems.	Respond to customer inquiries within 15 minutes.
Network	Facilitating relationships with others who are involved in or have been affected by the program.	Continue networking with contacts on (at minimum) a quarterly basis.

Figure 9.2 Examples of Coverage Areas for Application.

Responsibilities

Measuring application and implementation involves the responsibility and work of others. With data collection occurring later than in Levels 1 and 2, an important issue may surface in terms of who is responsible for this follow-up. Many possibilities exist, ranging from project staff and sponsors to an external, independent consultant. This matter should be addressed in the planning stages so that no misunderstanding arises as to the distribution of responsibilities. More importantly, those who are responsible should fully understand the nature and scope of their accountabilities and what is needed to collect the data.

Data Collection Methods

Some of the techniques previously mentioned that are available to collect application and implementation data are easy to administer and provide quality data. Other techniques are more robust, providing greater detail about success but raising more challenges in administration.

Using Questionnaires to Measure Application and Implementation

Questionnaires have become a mainstream data collection tool for measuring application and implementation because of their flexibility, low cost, and ease of administration. The discussion in Chapter 7 about questionnaires designed to measure reaction and perceived value applies equally to questionnaires developed to measure application and implementation.

Using Interviews, Focus Groups, and Observation

Interviews and focus groups can be used during implementation or on a follow-up basis, to collect data on implementation and application. However, the steps needed to design and administer these instruments apply to Levels 1 and 2, and will not be presented here. Other resources cover this area quite well. [3]

For this level of data collection, observing participants on the job and recording any changes in behavior and specific actions taken is an often-used method. While observation is also used in collecting learning data, a fundamental difference is that participants do not necessarily know they are being observed when observation is used to collect application data. Participant observation is often used in sales and sales support projects. The observer may be a member of the project staff, the participant's manager, a member of a peer group, or an external resource such as a mystery shopper. The most common observer, and probably the most practical one, is a member of the project staff. Technology also lends itself as a tool to assist with observations. Recorders, video cameras, and computers play an important role in capturing application data.

Using Action Plans

In some cases, follow-up assignments can be used to develop implementation and application data. A typical follow-up assignment requires the participant to meet a goal or complete a task or project by a set date. A summary of the results of the completed assignment provides further evidence of the project's success.

The action plan is the most common type of follow-up assignment. With this approach, participants are required to develop action plans as part of the project. Action plans contain the detailed steps necessary to accomplish specific objectives related to the project. The process is one of the most effective ways to enhance project support and build the sense of ownership needed for successful project application and implementation.

The action plan is typically prepared on a printed form that shows what is to be done by whom, and by what date the objectives should be accomplished. The action plan approach is a straightforward, easy-to-use method for determining how participants will change their behaviors on the job and achieve success with project implementation. The approach produces data that answers questions such as:

- What on-the-job improvements have been realized since the project was implemented?
- Are the improvements linked to the project?
- What may have prevented participants from accomplishing specific action items?

Collectively, these data can be used to assess the success of project implementation, and to make decisions regarding modification.

The action plan process can be an integral part of project implementation, and is not necessarily considered an add-on or optional activity. To gain maximum effectiveness from the evaluation data collected from action plans, attempt to implement the steps listed in Figure 9.3.

- Communicate the action plan requirement early
- Identify one or more measures connected to the innovation project
- Describe the action planning process at the beginning of the project
- Teach the action planning process
- Allow time to develop the plan
- Secure the project leader's approval of the action plan
- Require participants to assign a monetary value to each improvement*
- Ask participants to isolate the effects of the project*
- Ask participants to provide a confidence estimate, when appropriate*
- Require action plans to be presented to the group (when possible)
- Explain the follow-up mechanism
- Collect action plans at the predetermined follow-up time
- Summarize the data

*Optional for impact analysis

Figure 9.3 Action Planning Checklist.

Barriers to Application

One of the important reasons for collecting application and implementation data is to uncover barriers and enablers. Although both groups are important, barriers can kill an innovation project. The barriers must be identified and actions must be taken to minimize, remove, or go around them. Barriers are a serious problem that exist in every project. When they can be removed or minimized, the project can be implemented. When barriers are identified, they become important reference points for change and improvement. Typical barriers that will stifle the success of projects include

- My immediate manager does not support the project.
- We have no opportunity to use the project skills, knowledge, or information.
- Technology was not available for the project.
- Resources are not available to implement the project.
- The project is not appropriate for our work unit.
- Another project got in the way.
- The culture in our work group does not support the project.
- We have no time to implement the project.
- My job changed and this no longer applies.
- We didn't see a need to implement the project.

The important point is to identify any barriers, and to use the data in meaningful ways to make the barriers less of a problem.

Application Data Use

Data become meaningless if they are not used properly. As we move up the chain of impact, the data become more valuable in the minds of sponsors, key executives, and others who have a strong interest in the project. Although data can be used in dozens of ways, the following are the principal uses for data after they are collected:

- To report and review results with various stakeholders
- To adjust project design and implementation
- To identify and remove barriers
- To identify and enhance enablers
- To recognize individuals who have contributed to project success

- To reinforce in current and future project participants the value of desired actions
- To improve management support for projects
- To market future projects

Final Thoughts

Measuring application and implementation is critical in determining the success of an innovation project or program. This essential measure not only determines the success achieved, but also identifies areas where improvement is needed, and where success can be replicated in the future. In this chapter, we presented a variety of techniques to collect application data, ranging from observation to use of questionnaires and action plans. The method you choose must match the scope of your project.

Understanding success with application is important in providing evidence that business needs should be met, but it is only through measurement at Level 4, impact and consequences, that a direct link between the project and business impact can be made. Let's examine the business impact level, next.

10

Measuring Impact

Hometown Care is a senior services organization in rural Pennsylvania. This long-term care facility is a skilled nursing and rehabilitative division associated with a retirement community that offers a continuum of care. The health center offers three levels of skilled nursing care: comprehensive, rehabilitative, and memory support. The facility consists of 90 beds and 168 employees. [1]

Healthcare organizations such as Hometown Care are constantly seeking ways to improve quality and efficiency through new and innovative initiatives. Along with this movement, return on investment (ROI) has also become a topic of interest across the healthcare system, particularly with top executives in this facility. Executives wanted to see the ROI calculation on three projects that were being undertaken by eight employees at Hometown Care. These projects used the concept of lean technology, which consists of a variety of tools and processes for problem analysis and measurement. These eight employees tackled three projects in the healthcare area. The first project involved dressing change delays and the concerns when a patient required a dressing change. The second project targeted times for short-term rehab discharge to home. The organization was experiencing delays when short-term rehab patients were discharged to home.

The third project was a chart-to-go project and addressed the documentation system used by the certified nurse assistants (CNAs) to capture activities of daily living (ADL) for each resident in the long-term care unit.

The individuals explored these three healthcare improvement projects using a conservative approach, the ROI Methodology. Each project captured the impact of the major measures, isolated the effects of the programs on the impact, and converted the data to money to get a total benefit. This figure was then compared to the total cost of the project including the cost of the training to learn how to apply these principles. These projects generated ROI results of 590 percent, 154 percent, and 31 percent, respectively. The results of the studies were communicated to a variety of stakeholders, starting with the senior leadership. The leadership team was impressed to the point of making the program the primary quality initiative in their organization. They also assigned a senior leader the responsibility of coordinating and tracking each project to create a database that documents a long-term care organization's transformation to a lean enterprise.

As this case illustrates, impact measures can vary from one team to another, although they are using the same innovation process. This will be the case for many internal processes.

Most sponsors regard business impact data as the most important data type because of its connection to business success. For many projects, inadequate performance in business measures (the business need) is what would have initiated the project. Impact evaluation data close the loop by showing a project's success in meeting the business needs. This chapter examines a variety of business impact measures, and the specific processes needed to collect the measures within a project. First, it addresses the reasons why impact data are measured.

Why Measure Business Impact?

Several rationales support the collection of business impact data related to an innovation project.

Higher-Level Data

Following the assumption that higher-level data create more value for key stakeholders, business impact measures offer more valuable data. Impact data are the consequence of the application and implementation of a project. They represent the bottom-line measures positively influenced when a project is successful. For some stakeholders, these are the most valuable data.

The chain of impact can be broken at Level 4, and it is in many projects. If the project does not drive business impact data, then the corresponding results may be less than satisfactory. In extreme cases, the project can meet with success at the lower levels but fail at Level 4. Participants may react positively to the project (Level 1), they may learn successfully to implement the project (Level 2), and they may follow the correct implementation steps or use the skills needed to implement the project (Level 3). However, when the business impact measure (which the project is expected to influence) does not change, the project does not add value.

What could cause this? There are two possibilities. First, the business alignment for the project may not have been completed properly, which would keep it from being the right solution. Although the project may have been implemented, it has driven activity and not results. The second possibility is that other factors are driving the business measure. Although the project could be connected to the measure, other influences may be affecting the business measure in a direction opposite that desired by project planners.

So it may appear at first glance that the project has no value, but in reality it could. This brings into focus the importance of isolating the effects of a project. The business data may be disappointing, but they would be even more disappointing without the project. The important process of isolating the effects of the project is presented in Chapter 11.

A Business Driver for Projects

For most projects, business impact data represent the initial drivers for the innovation project. The problem of deteriorating or less than expected performance, or the opportunity for improvement of a business measure, usually leads to a project. If the business needs defined by business measures are the drivers for a project, then the key measure for evaluating the project is the business measure. The extent to which measures have changed is the principal determinant of project success.

"The Money" for Sponsors

From the perspective of the sponsor, business impact data reflect key payoff measures. These are the measures often desired by the sponsor, and the ones that the sponsor wants to see changed or improved. They often represent hard, indisputable facts which reflect performance that is critical to the business or operating unit level of the organization. Business impact leads to "the money" – to the actual return on investment in the project. Without credible business impact data linked directly to the project, it would be difficult, if not impossible, to establish a credible monetary value for the project. This makes this level of data collection one of the most critical.

Easy to Measure

One unique feature of business impact data is that they are often easy to measure. Hard and soft data measures at this level often reflect key measures that are plentiful throughout an organization. It is not unusual for an organization to have hundreds or even thousands of measures reflecting specific business impact items. The challenge is to connect the objectives of the project to the appropriate business measures. This is more easily accomplished at the beginning of the project.

Collecting Effective Impact Measures

Chapter 5 defined four hard data categories (output, quality, costs, time). Soft data has several categories as well. Also data can be categorized at several different levels, as shown in Figure 10.1. The figure illustrates that some data are considered strategic, and are linked to the corporate level of an organization. Other data are more operational, and are linked to the business unit level. Still others are considered tactical in nature and scope, and are used at the operating level of an organization.

Data Categories

Examples of data categorized at the strategic level include financial, people-oriented, and internal versus external data. At the business unit level, classifications such as output, quality, cost, time, job satisfaction, and customer satisfaction are critical categories. At the tactical level, the categories are greater in number and include productivity, efficiency, cost control, quality, time, attitudes, and individual and team performance. The importance

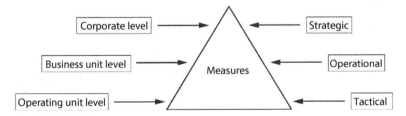

Figure 10.1 Measures at Different Levels.

is not in the classification of data itself but in the awareness of the vast array of data available. Regardless of their categories, these data are consequence measures of project success (Level 4). The challenge is to find the data items connected directly to the project.

Metric Fundamentals

When determining the type of measures to use, reviewing metric fundamentals can be helpful. The first important issue is identifying what makes an effective measure. Figure 10.2 shows some of the criteria of an effective measure. These are issues that should be explored when examining any type of measure.

These criteria serve as a screening checklist as measures are considered, developed, and ultimately added to the list of data to collect. In addition to meeting criteria, the factual basis of the measure should be stressed. In essence, the measure should be subjected to a fact-based analysis, a level of analysis never before applied to decisions about many projects, even when these decisions have involved huge sums of money.

Criteria: effective measures are	Definition: the extent to which a measure...
Important	Connects to strategically important business objectives rather than to what is easy to measure
Complete	Adequately tracks the entire phenomenon rather than only part of the phenomenon
Timely	Tracks at the right time rather than being held to an arbitrary date
Visible	Is visible, public, openly known, and tracked by those affected by it, rather than being collected privately for management's eyes only
Controllable	Tracks outcomes created by those affected by it who have a clear line of sight from the measure to results
Cost-effective	Is efficient to track using existing data or data that are easy to monitor without requiring new procedures
Interpretable	Creates data that are easy to make sense of and that translate into employee action
Simplicity	Simple to understand from each stakeholder's perspective
Specific	Is clearly defined so that people quickly understand and relate to the measure
Collectible	Can be collected with no more effort than is proportional to the measure's usefulness
Team-based	Will have value in the judgment of a team of individuals, not in the judgment of just one individual
Credible	Provides information that is valid and credible in the eyes of management

Figure 10.2 Criteria for Effective Measures.

Distinguishing between the various "types" of facts is beneficial. As shown below, the basis for facts ranges from common sense to what employees "say" to actual data:

- *No facts* – "Common sense tells us that employees will be more productive if they have a stake in the profits of a company."
- *Unreliable facts* – "Employees say they are more likely to stay with a company if they are offered profit sharing."
- *Irrelevant facts* – "We have benchmarked three world-class companies with variable pay plans: a bank, a hotel chain, and a defense contractor. All reported good results."
- *Fact-based* – "Employee turnover in call centers is increasing operational costs" [2].

Identifying Specific Measures Linked to Projects

An important issue that often surfaces when considering ROI applications is the understanding of specific measures that are driven by specific projects. Although no standard answers are available, Figure 10.3 represents a summary of typical payoff measures for specific types of projects. The measures are quite broad for some projects. In general, product and service innovations pay off with a variety of sales and marketing metrics. Process and job related innovations pay off with classic hard and soft data categories, such as productivity, efficiency, quality, costs, time, satisfaction, engagement, and image.

The table also illustrates the immense number of applications of this Methodology, and the even larger set of measures that can be driven or influenced. In most of these situations, assigning monetary values to these measures (as the benefits of a given program are compared to the costs) and developing the ROI become reasonable tasks.

A word of caution: Presenting specific measures linked to a typical project may give the impression that these are the only measures influenced. In practice, a given project can have multiple outcomes, and this can make calculation of the ROI a difficult process. The good news is that most innovation projects are driving business measures. The monetary values are based on what is being changed in the various business units, divisions, regions, and individual workplaces. These are the measures that matter to senior executives. The difficulty often comes in ensuring that the connection to the program exists. This is accomplished through a variety of techniques to isolate the effects of the program on the particular business measures, as will be discussed in Chapter 11.

ROI Applications	
Project	Key impact measures
Sales process innovations	Productivity/output, quality, time savings, efficiency, costs, employee satisfaction, customer satisfaction, compliance
Innovation and creativity workshops	Cost savings, productivity improvement, quality improvement, cycle times, error reductions, job satisfaction, retention
Channel innovations	Sales, market share, brand, loyalty, costs, efficiency, time savings
Innovation task forces	Sales, productivity, output, quality, efficiency cost/time savings, employee satisfaction, engagement
Product use enhancements	Sales, market share, customer loyalty, cost of sales, wallet share, customer satisfaction, branding
Innovation labs	Time savings, quality, costs, sales, brand loyalty, retention, productivity
Ideation systems	Output quality, efficiency, waste, costs, time, customer satisfaction, employee engagement
Innovation through networking	Image, branding, customer satisfaction, investor satisfaction, sales, productivity
Customer engagement	Sales, productivity, quality, cust omer satisfaction
Product performance	Defects, rework, response times, cycle times, costs, sales
New product development	Sales, market share, customer service, quality/service levels, cycle times, cost savings, brand awareness
Brand Initiative	Brand awareness, customer loyalty, net promoter score, market share, sales, quality, time costs, customer service, customer engagement

Figure 10.3 Typical Measures from Different Types of Innovation.

Business Performance Data Monitoring

Data are available in every organization to measure business performance. Monitoring performance data enables management to measure performance in terms of sales output, quality, costs, time, job satisfaction, customer satisfaction, and other measures. In determining the source of data in the evaluation, the first consideration should be existing databases and reports. In most organizations, performance data will be available that are suitable for measuring improvement resulting from a project. If such data are not available, additional recordkeeping systems will have to be developed for measurement and analysis.

At this point, the question of economics surfaces. Is it economical to develop the recordkeeping systems necessary to evaluate a project or program? If the costs will be greater than the expected benefits, developing those systems is pointless.

Identify Appropriate Measures

Existing performance measures should be thoroughly researched to identify those related to the proposed objectives of the project. Often, several performance measures are related to the same item. For example, the efficiency of a production unit can be measured in several ways:

- Number of units produced per hour
- Number of units produced on schedule
- Percentage of equipment used
- Percentage of equipment downtime
- Labor cost per unit of production
- Overtime required per unit of production
- Total unit cost

Each of these in its own way measures the effectiveness or efficiency of the production unit. All related measures should be reviewed to determine those most relevant to the project.

Convert Current Measures to Usable Ones

Occasionally, existing performance measures will become integrated with other data. Keeping existing performance measures isolated from unrelated data may be difficult. In these situations, all existing related measures should be extracted and retabulated to make them more appropriate for comparison in the evaluation. At times, it may be necessary to develop conversion factors. For example, the average number of new sales orders per month may be presented regularly in the performance measures for the sales department. In addition, the sales costs per sales representative may also be presented. However, in evaluating the project, the average cost per new sale is needed. The average number of new sales orders and the average number of lost sales per sales representative are required to develop the data necessary for comparison.

Develop New Measures

In some cases, data needed to measure the effectiveness of a project are not available, and new data are needed. The project staff must work with the client organization to develop record-keeping systems, if economically feasible. In one organization, delays of the sales staff in responding to customer requests were an issue. This issue was discovered from customer feedback. The feedback data prompted a project to reduce the response time. To help ensure the success of the project, several measures were planned, including measuring the actual time to respond to a customer request. Initially, this measure was not available. As the project was implemented, new software was used to measure the time that elapsed in responding to customer requests.

Data Collection Methods

For many innovation projects and programs, business data are readily available to be monitored. However, at times, data won't be easily accessible to the project team or to the evaluator. Sometimes data are maintained at the individual, work unit, or department level, and may not be known to anyone outside that area. Tracking down all those data sets may be too expensive and time-consuming. When this is the case, other data collection methods may be used to capture data sets and make them available for the evaluator. Three other options described in this book are the use of action plans, performance contracts, and questionnaires.

Using Action Plans to Develop Business Impact Data

Action plans can capture application and implementation data, as discussed in Chapter 9. They can also be a useful tool for capturing business impact data. For business impact data, the action plan is more focused and credible than using a questionnaire. The basic design principles and the issues involved in developing and administering action plans are the same for business impact data as for application and implementation data. However, a few issues are unique to business impact and ROI, and are presented here. The following steps are recommended when an action plan is developed and implemented to capture business impact data and to convert the data to monetary values.

An action plan can be developed with a direct focus on business impact data from innovation. The action plan is particularly appropriate for innovation labs, innovation task forces, process innovation, and innovation and creativity workshops. Participants develop an overall objective for the plan, which is usually the primary objective of the project. In some cases, a project may have more than one objective, which requires additional action plans. In addition to the objective, the improvement measure and the current levels of performance are determined. This information requires the participant to anticipate the application and implementation of the project, and to set goals for specific performances that can be realized.

The action plan is completed during project implementation, often with the input, assistance, and facilitation of the project team. The evaluator or project leader actually approves the plan, indicating that it meets the requirements of being Specific, Motivational, Achievable, Realistic, and Time-based (SMART). The plan can be developed in 30–45 minutes, and often begins with action steps related to the implementation of the project. These action steps are Level 3 activities that detail the application and implementation. All these steps build support for and are linked to business impact measures.

For maximum effectiveness, the action plan addresses several issues:

- Define the actual unit(s) of impact measure.
- Place a monetary value on each improvement outlined in the plan.
- List of planned actions, scheduled to the extent that innovation uncertainty permits.
- Specify improvements at the end of each follow-up period.
- Isolate the effects of the project.
- Provide a confidence level of estimated project effects.
- Collect action plans at specified time intervals to maximize response rate.
- Summarize the data, and calculate ROI.

These steps are described in some detail in the review of data collection methods, in Chapter 6.

Because the ROI calculation process may involve estimates, it risks appearing to be inaccurate. Therefore, adjustments during analysis are necessary to make the process credible and more accurate. These adjustments reflect the guiding principles that form the basis of the ROI methodology, as outlined in Chapter 4. The adjustments are made in six steps.

Step 1: If participants provide no data, assume they had no improvement to report. (This is a very conservative approach.) Record zero for this participant.

Step 2: Calculate the actual change in value. This is the new state minus the beginning state. Check the value for realism, usability, and feasibility. Discard extreme values, and omit them from analysis.

Step 3: Calculate the annual improvement. Because the improvement is annualized, assume the project had no improvement after the first year for short-term projects. (Chapter 12 discusses projects that add value after two and three years.)

Step 4: Adjust the annual improvement value by the percentage related directly to the project, recognizing that other factors may have influenced the amount of improvement. The percentage is supplied by the participant.

Step 5: Adjust the allocation calculated in Step 4, using the confidence multiplied by the confidence percentage. The confidence is actually a percentage of error suggested by the participants. For example, a participant indicating 80% confidence with the allocation is reflecting a possibility of 20% error. To be conservative, multiply the confidence factor by the value of the allocated improvement.

Step 6: Knowing the unit cost (or value), calculate the annual monetary benefits.

Total the monetary values determined in these six steps to arrive at the final project benefit. Because these values are annualized, the total of these benefits becomes the annual benefits for the project. Place this value in the numerator of the ROI formula to calculate the ROI. Figure 10.4 provides an example from the fashion store example in Chapter 9.

Using Performance Contracts to Measure Business Impact

Another technique for collecting business impact data is the performance contract. The performance contract is essentially a slight variation of the action plan. Based on the principle of mutual goal setting, a performance contract is a written agreement between a participant and the participant's

Situation: Innovation project to improve product returns. A product return cost is $85	
Step 1	Participant provided data to use in the analysis
Step 2	Product returns were averaging 250 per month. Six months after the improvement was implemented, product returns are now averaging 120 per month.
Step 3	The annual improvement is 1560 product returns.
Step 4	Participants list two other factors that have influenced the improvement in product returns and allocates 40% to innovation project. The improvement connected to the product is: 1560 returns x 40% = 624 products (This is the isolation of results)
Step 5	Participant success an 80% confidence for the allocation in Step 4. This suggests an error of 20% which is removed from the value by multiplying by 80%: 624 x 80% = 499 product returns
Step 6	The annual monetary benefits are: 499 x $85 = $42,415

Figure 10.4 Example Calculation from an Action Plan.

manager. The participant agrees to improve performance in an area of mutual concern related to the project. The agreement is in the form of a goal to accomplish during the project or after the project's completion. The agreement details what is to be accomplished, at what time, and with what results. This is particularly helpful in situations where innovations are expected as part of the job.

Although the steps can vary according to the organization and the specific kind of contract, a common sequence of events follows:

1. The employee (participant) becomes involved in an innovation project implementation.
2. The participant and his or her immediate manager agree on a measure or measures for improvement related to the project.
3. Specific, measurable goals for improvement are set, following the SMART requirements discussed on earlier in this chapter.
4. In the early stages of the project, the contract is discussed and plans are developed to accomplish the goals.
5. During project implementation, the participant works to meet the deadline set for contract compliance.
6. The participant reports the results of the effort to his or her manager.
7. The manager and participant document the results and forward a copy, with appropriate comments, to the project team.

The process of selecting the area for improvement is similar to the process used in an action plan. The topic can cover one or more of the following areas:

- Routine performance related to the project, including specific improvement in measures such as production, efficiency, and error rates
- Problem solving, focused on such problems as an unexpected increase in workplace accidents, a decrease in efficiency, or a loss of morale
- Innovative or creative applications arising from the project, which could include the initiation of improvements in work practices, methods, procedures, techniques, and processes
- Personal development connected to the project, such as learning new information and acquiring new skills to increase individual effectiveness

The topic of the performance contract should be stated in terms of one or more objectives that are:

- Written
- Understandable by all involved
- Challenging (requiring an unusual effort to achieve)
- Achievable (something that can be accomplished)
- Largely under the control of the participant
- Measurable and dated

The performance contract objectives are accomplished by following the corresponding guidelines for action plans presented earlier. The methods for analyzing data and reporting progress are essentially the same as those used to analyze action plan data.

Using Questionnaires to Collect Business Impact Measures

As described in the previous chapters, the questionnaire is one of the most versatile data collection tools, and can be appropriate for collecting Level 1, 2, 3, and 4 data. Essentially, the design principles and content issues are the same as at other levels, except that questionnaires developed for a business impact evaluation will include additional questions to capture those data specific to business impact.

The use of questionnaires for impact data collection brings both good news and bad news. The good news is that questionnaires are easy to implement and low in cost. Data analysis is efficient, and the time required to provide the data is often minimal, making questionnaires among the least disruptive of data collection methods. The bad news is that the data can be distorted and inaccurate, and are sometimes missing. The challenge is to take all the steps necessary to ensure that questionnaires are complete, accurate, and clear, and that they are returned.

Unfortunately, questionnaires can be the weakest methods of data collection. Paradoxically, they are the most commonly used because of their advantages. Of the first 100 case studies published on the ROI Methodology, roughly 50% used questionnaires as a method of data collection. They are popular, convenient, low-cost, and have become a way of life. The challenge is to improve them. The philosophy in the ROI Methodology is to take processes that represent the weakest method, and make them as credible as possible. Here the challenge is to make questionnaires credible and useful by ensuring that they collect all the data needed, that participants provide accurate and complete data, and that return rates are in at least the 70–80% range.

The reason return rates must be high, as explained in Guiding Principle #6 of the ROI Methodology outlined in Figure 4.8: no data, no improvement. If an individual provides no improvement data, it is assumed that the person had no improvement to report. This is a very conservative principle, but necessary to bring the credibility needed. Consequently, using questionnaires will require effort, discipline, and personal attention to ensure proper response rates. Chapter 6 presented suggestions for ensuring high response rates for questionnaires and surveys. The same techniques should be considered here. It is helpful to remember that this is the least preferred method for collecting Level 4 data, and it is used only when other methods do not work (i.e., when business performance data cannot be easily monitored, when action plans are not feasible, or when performance contracting is not suitable).

Measuring the Hard to Measure

The focus of this chapter is on capturing the measures that are easy to collect and easy to measure. These represent the classic definitions of hard data and soft data – or, tangible data and intangible data. Much attention today is focused on the very hard to measure, on some of the classic soft items that are even softer than customer satisfaction and job satisfaction. Although this subject is discussed at length in Chapter 13, a few comments are appropriate here.

Everything Can Be Measured

Contrary to the thinking of some professionals, everything can be measured. Any item, issue, or phenomenon that is important to an organization can be measured. Even images, perceptions, and ideas in a person's mind can be measured. The thorny issue is usually in identifying the best way and the available resources to do the measuring. For example, although the image of an organization in the community, or the way that customers become aware of a brand, can be measured accurately, doing so takes time and money.

A case in point is the project launched by Nissan Motor Company in the 1980s when it located its first auto manufacturing plant in North America. Nissan executives were concerned about how a Japanese automaker would be regarded in a traditional southern community. (This came at a time when common attitudes toward Japanese automakers were less amicable than today.) The project involved extensive surveying in the communities that would host a Nissan plant. The results were impressive, and demonstrate that you can measure anything if you can define it and spend the money to measure it.

Perceptions are Important

Some soft or intangible items are not based on perceptions, but others are. For example, consider innovation. An important component of innovation in a company is image or perception. Some measures reflect innovation of a company in its processes, products, and services (e.g., number of new patents, number of new products). However, concepts like brand awareness are based strictly on perception (i.e., on what a person knows or perceives about an item, product, or service).

In the past, perceptions were considered not so valuable, but today many decisions are based on perceptions. Consider perceptions about service quality from the customer's viewpoint – these perceptions often drive tremendous organizational changes. Employees' perceptions of their employer often drive huge investments in projects to improve job satisfaction, organizational commitment, and engagement.

Perceptions must be part of the measurement plan for the hard to measure.

Every Measure Can Be Converted to Money, but not Every Measure Should Be

In parallel with the adage, "everything can be measured," so, too, can everything be valued. Every measure can be converted to monetary value. The concern has to do with credibility and resources. This is the definition accorded to intangibles in this book: they are measures that cannot credibly be converted to money with minimum resources (listed as Guiding Principle #11 in Figure 4.8). Knowing when to pursue conversion to money and when not to is important. Specific rules are available to guide you in making this decision, which are presented in Chapter 12.

Special Emphasis on Intangibles

Important emphasis must be placed on intangibles, on measuring the hard to measure, and on valuing the hard to value. This book includes an entire chapter on intangibles in which we provide more examples and techniques to measure the hard to measure and address the issue of converting to money.

Final Thoughts

Business impact data are critical to address an organization's business needs. These data lead the evaluation to the "money." Although perceived as difficult to find, business impact data are readily available and very credible. After describing the types of data that reflect business impact, this chapter provided an overview of several data collection approaches that can be used to capture business data. Some methods are gaining greater acceptance for use in capturing impact data. Performance monitoring, follow-up questionnaires, action plans, and performance contracts are used regularly to collect data for an impact analysis.

In this chapter we focused on methods to collect data on project impact and consequences. Linking these consequences directly to the project requires the important step of isolating the effects of the program, which we will cover next.

11

Isolating the Effects of Innovation

In the early 1990s, the crime rate in the United States had been rising relent-lessly. Death by gunfire, intentional and otherwise, had become common-place, as had carjacking, crack dealing, robbery, and rape. Violent crime had become a gruesome, constant companion. And things were about to get even worse, according to all the experts. [1]

The cause was the so-called super-predator: a scrawny, big-city teenager with a cheap gun in his hand and nothing in his heart. Thousands just like him were out there, a generation of killers preparing to send the country into total chaos.

In 1995, criminologist James Alan Fox wrote a report for the US attor-ney general grimly detailing the forthcoming spike in murders by teenag-ers. Fox proposed optimistic and pessimistic scenarios. In the optimistic scenario, he predicted the rate of teen homicides would rise another 15% over the next decade; in the pessimistic scenario, it would more than double.

Other criminologists as well as political scientists and similarly informed forecasters laid out the same horrible picture, as did President Clinton. This dire situation prompted many innovative solutions to solve this persistent problem.

Then, instead of going up and up and up, crime began to fall and fall and fall. The reversal was startling in several respects, with every category of crime falling in every part of the country. It was persistent, with incremental decreases seen year after year. And it was entirely unanticipated – especially by the "experts," who had predicted the very opposite.

The magnitude of the reversal was also astounding. The teenage murder rate fell more than 50% over five years. By 2000, the overall murder rate in the United States had dropped to its lowest level in 35 years, as had the rate of just about every other category of crime, from assault to car theft. Even though the experts had failed to anticipate the crime drop, they now hurried to explain it. Most of their theories sounded perfectly logical. It was the roaring 1990s economy, they said, that helped turn back crime. It was the proliferation of gun control laws, they said. It was the result of the innovative policing strategies put in place in New York City, where the number of murders would fall from 2,245 in 1990 to 596 in 2003.

These theories were not only logical; they were also encouraging, for they attributed the crime drop to specific recent human initiatives. If it was gun control, clever police strategies, and better-paying jobs that was quelling crime, then the power to stop criminals had been within our reach all along. And it would continue to be.

These theories were accepted seemingly without question. They became the conventional wisdom. There was only one problem: they were not true.

Another factor, it seemed, had greatly contributed to the massive crime drop of the 1990s. It had begun to take shape more than 20 years earlier and involved a young woman in Dallas. Norma McCorvey dramatically altered the course of criminal history without intending to. All she had wanted was an abortion. She was a poor, uneducated, unskilled, alcoholic, drug-using 21-year-old woman who had already given up two children for adoption; and now, in 1970, she found herself pregnant again. But in Texas, as in all but a few states at that time, abortion was illegal. McCorvey's cause was taken up by people far more powerful than she. They made her the lead plaintiff in a class action lawsuit seeking to legalize abortion. The defendant was Henry Wade, the Dallas County district attorney. The case ultimately made it to the US Supreme Court, by which time McCorvey's name had been changed to Jane Roe to shield her identity. On January 22, 1973, the court ruled in favor of Ms. Roe, thereby legalizing abortion throughout the country. By this time, of course, it was far too late for

Ms. McCorvey/Roe to have her abortion; she had given birth and put the child up for adoption.

So how did Roe v. Wade help trigger, a generation later, the greatest crime drop in recorded history? Decades of studies have shown that a child born into an adverse family environment is far more likely than other children to become a criminal. And the millions of women most likely to obtain abortions in the wake of Roe v. Wade – poor, unmarried, teenage mothers for whom illegal abortions had been too expensive or too hard to get – were common models of adversity. They were the very women whose children, if born, would have been much more likely to become criminals. But because of Roe v. Wade, these children weren't being born. This powerful ruling would have a drastic, delayed effect; in the years when these children, had they been born, would have entered their criminal primes, the rate of crime began to plummet.

It wasn't gun control or a strong economy or new police strategies that blunted the American crime wave. It was another factor, among these and other factors, that the pool of potential criminals had dramatically shrunk.

Now, as the crime experts spun their new theories on the reversal to the media, how many times did they cite legalized abortion as a cause?

The *Freakonomics* authors provide much detail explaining how they attempted to isolate the effects of the various influences on the crime rate reduction. Their arguments, analysis, and data are credible; however, as you might expect, their conclusion is not without its share of critics. Some found the analysis to be distasteful and perhaps racist. However, these economists were merely trying to report the data in the most credible way, while attempting to isolate the effects of many complicated factors interacting in this situation to improve a particular measure.

Reporting improvement in business impact measures is an important step in a innovation project evaluation that leads to the money. Invariably, however, the question comes up (as it should): How much of this improvement was the result of the innovation project? Unfortunately, the answer is rarely provided with any degree of accuracy and confidence. Although the change in an impact measure may in fact be linked to the innovation project, other factors unrelated to the project may have contributed to the improvement as well. If this issue is not addressed, the results reported will lack credibility.

In this chapter we explore useful techniques for isolating the effects of the project. These techniques have been used in some of the most successful organizations as they attempt to measure the ROI from projects and programs.

Why the Concern over this Issue?

In almost every innovation project, multiple factors influence the business measures targeted by the project. Determining the effect of each factor is imperative. Without this isolation, the project's success cannot be confirmed. Moreover, the effects of the project may be overstated if the change in the business impact measure is attributed entirely to the project. If this issue is ignored, the impact study may be considered invalid and inconclusive. This puts pressure on evaluators and project leaders to demonstrate the actual effects of their projects on business improvement, as opposed to other possible factors.

Reality

Isolating the effects of projects on business measures has led to some important conclusions. First, other influences are almost always present. In almost every situation, multiple factors generate business results. The rest of the world does not stand still while a project is being implemented. Other processes and programs are also operating to improve the same metrics targeted by the implemented project.

Next, if the project effects are not isolated, no business link can be established. Without steps taken to document the project's contribution, there is no proof that the project actually influenced the measures. The evidence will show only that the project might have made a difference. Results have improved, but other factors may have influenced the data.

Also, the outside factors and influences have their own protective owners. These owners will insist that it was their processes that made the difference. Some of them will probably be certain that the results are due entirely to their efforts. They may present a compelling case to management, stressing their achievements.

Finally, isolating the effects of the project on impact data is a challenging task. For complex projects in particular, the process is not easy, especially when strong-willed owners of other processes are involved. Fortunately, a variety of approaches are available to facilitate the procedure.

Myths

The myths surrounding the isolation of project effects create confusion and frustration with the process. Some researchers, professionals, and consultants go so far as to suggest that such isolation is not necessary. Here are the most common myths:

1. *Our project is complementary to other processes; therefore, we should not attempt to isolate the effects of the project.* A project often complements other factors at work, all of which together drive results. If the sponsor of a project needs to understand its relative contribution, the isolation process is the only way to do it. If accomplished properly, it will reveal how the complementary factors interact to drive improvements.

2. *Other project leaders do not address this issue.* Some project leaders do not grapple with the isolation problem because they wish to make a convincing case that all of the improvement is directly related to their own processes. Most customer surveys that are filled out after a purchase or the opening of a new account ask why the purchase was made. This is one way organizations try to isolate the results of multiple variables. They want to know which of their processes or systems persuaded the customer to make the purchase.

3. *If we cannot use a research-based control group, or mathematical modeling, we should not attempt this procedure.* Although an experimental research design using randomly assigned control and experimental groups is the most reliable approach to identifying causes and effects, it is inapplicable to most situations. Consequently, other methods must be used to isolate the effects of a project. The challenge is to find a method that is effective and whose results are reproducible, even if it is not as credible as the group comparison method.

4. *The stakeholders will understand the link to business impact measures; therefore, we do not need to attempt to isolate the effects of the project.* Unfortunately, stakeholders try to understand only what is presented to them. The absence of information makes it difficult for them to understand the business links, particularly when others are claiming full credit for the improvement.

5. *Estimates of improvement provide no value.* It may be necessary to tackle the isolation process using estimates from those who understand the process best. Although this should be done only as a last alternative, it can provide value and credibility, particularly when the estimates have been adjusted for error in order to reduce subjectivity.

6. *Ignore the issue; maybe the others won't think about it.* Audiences are becoming more sophisticated on this topic, and they are aware of the presence of multiple influences. If

no attempt is made to isolate the effects of the project, the audience will assume that the other factors have had a major effect, and perhaps the only effect. A project's credibility can deteriorate quickly.

These myths underscore the importance of addressing the isolation. The emphasis on isolation is not meant to suggest that a project is implemented independently and exclusively of other processes. Obviously, all groups should be working as a team to produce the desired results. However, when funding is parceled out among different functions or organizations with different owners, there is always a struggle to show, and often to understand, the connection between their activities and the results. If you do not undertake this process, others will – leaving your project with reduced budgets, resources, and respect.

Preliminary Issues

The cause-and-effect relationship between an innovation project and performance can be confusing and difficult to prove, but it can be demonstrated with an acceptable degree of accuracy. The challenge is to develop one or more specific techniques to isolate the effects of the project early in the process, usually as part of an evaluation plan conducted before the project begins. Up-front attention ensures that appropriate techniques will be used with minimal cost and time commitments. Two important issues in isolating the effects of a project are covered next, followed by specific methods.

Chain of Impact

Before presentation of isolation methods, it is helpful to reexamine the chain of impact implicit in the different levels of evaluation, starting with application. Measurable results from an innovation project should be derived from the application of the project (Level 3 data). Successful application of the project should stem from project participants learning to do something different, something necessary to implement the project (Level 2 data). Successful learning will usually occur when project participants react favorably to the project's content and objectives (Level 1 data). Without this preliminary evidence, isolating the effects of a project is difficult.

To be sure, if there is an adverse reaction, no learning, or no application, it cannot be concluded that any business impact improvements were caused by the project. From a practical standpoint, this requires data collection at four levels for an ROI calculation (Guiding Principle #1 in Figure 4.8). Although this requirement is a prerequisite to isolating the effects of a project, it does not establish a direct connection, nor does it pinpoint the extent of the improvement caused by the project. It does show, however, that without improvements at previous levels, making a connection between the ultimate outcome and the project is difficult or impossible.

Identify other Factors: A First Step

As a first step in isolating a project's impact on performance, all key factors that may have contributed to the performance improvement should be identified. This step communicates to interested parties that other factors may have influenced the results, underscoring that the project is not the sole source of improvement. Consequently, the credit for improvement is shared among several possible variables and sources – an approach that is likely to garner the respect of the client. Several potential sources are available for identifying major influencing variables:

- Project sponsor
- Participants in the project
- The immediate managers of participants
- Subject matter experts
- Other process owners
- Experts on external issues
- Middle and top management

The importance of identifying all of the factors is underscored by an example. The Royal Bank of Canada had a sophisticated system for identifying the reasons customers make product purchase decisions. At the point of sale, the purchaser records the reasons for the sale; was it the price, the product design, the advertising, or the referral from a satisfied customer? This system, owned by the marketing department, is designed to isolate the factors underlying the success of various marketing programs. However, it omits factors outside marketing. In essence, it assumes that 100% of the improvement in product sales can be attributed to a marketing influence. It ignores the effect of the economy, competition, information technology, reward systems, learning and development, job design, and other factors that could have had an important influence. Without identifying all the factors, the credibility of the analysis will suffer. Thus, competing factions within that organization had to address changing the system so that other factors are considered in the analysis.

Taking the time to focus on outside variables that may have influenced performance adds accuracy and credibility to the process. Project team leaders should go beyond this initial step, and use one or more of the following techniques to isolate the impact of the project.

Isolation Methods

Just as there are many data collection methods available for collecting data at different levels, a variety of methods are also available to isolate the effects of a project.

Control Groups

National Crushed Stone (NCS) is one of the leading firms in the crushed stone industry, with more than 300 locations in many geographic areas. The crushed stone industry is very competitive; profit margins are narrow and cost control is everything. Companies in this industry are constantly seeking ways to control costs to gain a competitive advantage in the marketplace.

There were some concerns that the costs at NCS were not as low as they could be, although they were among the lowest in the industry. Some costs were fixed and not under the control of the quarry team. However, many costs could be controlled. The executives wanted an innovative approach to control costs, perhaps using a behavioral approach. [2]

Based on engagement studies in the literature, the assumption was that if employees were really engaged in quarry operations, taking a very strong interest in maintaining and caring for the equipment, working smarter, and operating efficiently, the costs could be lower, perhaps even significantly so.

The talent development team suggested a simple employee engagement survey and proposed that if employees became more engaged, they would take more interest in their jobs, try to be more efficient, take better care of equipment, take better care of the facility, and even make suggestions for improvement. However, the company culture wasn't very open to employees accepting more responsibility, making recommendations, and being more involved in making decisions. In order to implement this plan, NCS would have to change its culture. To help augment change, the plant superintendents assumed the role of plant managers with the additional expectation of having a more involved and engaged workforce. However, this does not happen just by decree, discussion, meeting, memo, or policy—it comes from changing the mindset of the organization while adjusting job descriptions and encouraging employees to open up and be engaged.

In early discussions, it was suggested that a portion of the cost savings be shared with the employees using the motivational effect of rewards. Using a concept called gainsharing, the decision was made to share half the gains in cost reductions with employees, providing a bonus for exploring options to lower costs.

The new system was planned for implementation in six locations that represented typical NCS plants. The complete process, which would comprise several stages, was developed during a two-month period using an external consultant and the part-time assistance of two internal staff members.

Specific cost measures and other impacts (Level 4) would be monitored at each plant before and after the program, and these data would be compared with a group of similar plants. This control group arrangement involved identifying six other crushed stone plants to compare with the six plants destined for implementation. The section was based on plants with similar operating costs, production volume, age of plant, market served, and employee retention rate.

This approach should ensure that the results achieved were directly related to the new system. The actual cost of the system would be compared with the monetary value of the benefits to develop an actual ROI (Level 5). To be conservative, one year of monetary benefits would be obtained and compared with the fully loaded costs of the program.

The most accurate approach for isolating the impact of a project is an experimental design with control groups. This approach involves the use of an experimental group that goes through the implementation of the project, and a control group that does not. The two groups should be as similar in composition as possible and, if feasible, participants for each group should be randomly assigned. When this is achievable and the groups are subjected to the same environmental influences, any difference in performance between the two groups can be attributed to the project.

As illustrated in Figure 11.1, the control group and experimental group do not necessarily require preproject measurements. Measurements can

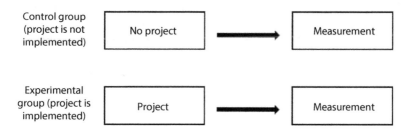

Figure 11.1 Use of Control Groups.

be taken during the project and after the project has been implemented, with the difference in performance between the two groups indicating the amount of improvement that is directly related to the project.

One caution should be observed: the use of control groups may create the impression that the project leaders are reproducing a laboratory setting, which can cause a problem for some executives and administrators. To avoid this perception, some organizations conduct a pilot project using participants as the experimental group. A similarly constituted nonparticipant comparison group is selected but does not receive any communication about the project. The terms pilot project and comparison group are a little less threatening to executives than experimental group and control group.

The control group approach has some inherent problems that can make it difficult to apply in practice. The first major problem is the selection of the groups. From a theoretical perspective, having identical control and experimental groups is next to impossible. Dozens of factors can affect performance, some individual and others contextual. On a practical basis, it is best to select the four to six variables that will have the greatest influence on performance. Essentially, this involves the 80/20 rule or the Pareto principle. The 80/20 rule is aimed at selecting the factors that might account for 80% of the difference. The Pareto principle requires working from the most important factor down to cover perhaps four or five issues that capture the vast majority of the factors having influence.

Another major problem is that the control group process is not suited to many situations. For some types of projects, withholding the program from one particular group while implementing it with another may not be appropriate. This is particularly true where critical solutions are needed immediately; management is typically not willing to withhold a solution from one area to see how it works in another. This limitation keeps control group analyses from being implemented in many instances. However, in practice, many opportunities arise for a natural control group to develop even in situations where a solution is implemented throughout an organization. If it takes several months for the solution to encompass everyone in the organization, enough time may be available for a parallel comparison between the initial group and the last group to be affected. In these cases, ensuring that the groups are matched as closely as possible is critical. Such naturally occurring control groups can often be identified in the case of major enterprise-wide program implementations. The challenge is to address this possibility early enough to influence the implementation schedule to ensure that similar groups are used in the comparison.

Another problem is contamination, which can develop when participants involved in the project group (experimental group) communicate with people in the control group. Sometimes, the reverse situation occurs, where members of the control group model the behavior of the project group. In either case, the experiment becomes contaminated as the influence of the project is carried over to the control group. This hazard can be minimized by ensuring that the control and project groups are at different locations, are on different shifts, or occupy different floors of the same building. When this is not possible, it should be explained to both groups that one group will be involved in the project now, and the other will be involved at a later date. Appealing to participants' sense of responsibility and asking them not to share information with others may help prevent contamination.

A closely related problem involves the passage of time. The longer a control versus experimental group comparison operates, the greater the likelihood that other influences will affect the results; more variables will enter into the situation, contaminating the results. On the other end of the scale, enough time must pass to allow a clear pattern to emerge distinguishing the two groups. Thus, the timing of control group comparisons must strike a delicate balance between waiting long enough for performance differences to show, but not so long that the results become contaminated.

Still another problem occurs when the different groups function under different environmental influences. This is usually the case when groups are at different locations. Sometimes the selection of the groups can prevent this problem from occurring. Another tactic is to use more groups than necessary, and discard those groups that show some environmental differences.

A final problem is that the use of control and experimental groups may appear too research oriented for most business organizations. For example, management may not want to take the time to experiment before proceeding with a program, in addition to the selective withholding problem discussed earlier. Because of these concerns, some project managers will not entertain the idea of using control groups.

Because the use of control groups is an effective approach for isolating impact, it should be considered when a major ROI impact study is planned. In these situations, isolating the project impact with a high level of accuracy is essential, and the primary advantage of the control group process is accuracy.

Trend Line Analysis

Another useful technique for approximating the impact of a project is trend line analysis. In this approach, a trend line is drawn to project the future, using previous performance as a base. When the project is fully

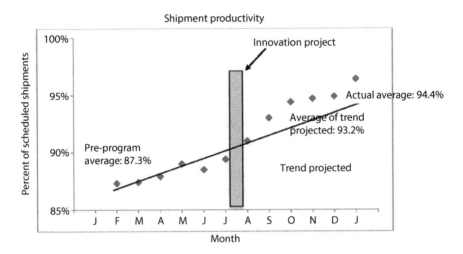

Figure 11.2 Trend Line Analysis.

implemented, actual performance is compared with the trend line projection. Any improvement in performance beyond what the trend line predicted can be reasonably attributed to project implementation. While this is not a precise process, it can provide a reasonable estimate of the project's impact.

Figure 11.2 shows a trend line analysis from the shipping department of a book distribution company. The percentage reflects the level of actual shipments compared with scheduled shipments. Data reflect conditions before and after an innovation project implementation in July. As shown in the figure, an upward trend for the data began prior to project implementation. Although the project apparently had an effect on shipment productivity, the trend line shows that some improvement would have occurred anyway, based on the trend that had previously been established. Project leaders may have been tempted to measure the improvement by comparing the six-month average for shipments prior to the project (87.3%) to the six-month average after the project (94.4%), which would yield a 7.1 percentage point difference. However, a more accurate comparison is the six-month average after the project versus the trend line (92.3%), a difference of 2.1%. Using this more conservative measure increases the accuracy and credibility of the process in terms of isolating the impact of the project.

To use the trend line analysis technique, two conditions must be met:

- It can be assumed that the trend that developed before the project would have continued if the project had not been

implemented to alter it (i.e., had the project not been implemented, this trend would have continued on the same path).
The process owner(s) should be able to provide input to
confirm this assumption. If the assumption does not hold,
trend line analysis cannot be used. If the assumption is a
valid one, the second condition is considered.

- No other new variables or influences entered the process during project implementation. The key word here is new. The
  understanding is that the trend has been established from
  the influences already in place, and no additional influences
  have entered the process beyond the project. If such is not
  the case, another method will have to be used. Otherwise,
  the trend line analysis presents a reasonable estimate of the
  impact of this project.

Preproject data must be available in order for this technique to be used,
and the data should show a reasonable degree of stability. If the variance of
the data is high, the stability of the trend line will be an issue. If the stability
cannot be assessed from a direct plot of the data, more detailed statistical
analyses can be used to determine if the data are stable enough to allow a
projection. The trend line can be projected directly from historical data
using a simple formula that is available in many calculators and software
packages, such as Microsoft Excel.

A primary disadvantage of the trend line approach is that it is not always
accurate. This approach assumes that the events that influenced the performance variable before project implementation are still in place, except
for the effects of the implementation (i.e., the trends established before the
project will continue in the same relative direction). Also, it assumes that
no new influences entered the situation during the course of the project.
This may not be the case.

The primary advantage of this approach is that it is simple and inexpensive. If historical data are available, a trend line can quickly be drawn and
the differences estimated. While not exact, it does provide a quick general
assessment of project impact.

Mathematical Modeling

A more analytical approach to isolation is the use of modeling methods
that predict a change in performance variables. This approach represents a
mathematical interpretation of the trend line analysis when other variables
enter the situation at the time of implementation. With this approach, the

impact measure targeted by the project is forecasted based on the influence of variables that have changed during the implementation or evaluation period for the project. The actual value of the measure is compared with the forecast value, and the difference reflects the contribution of the project.

A major disadvantage to this approach emerges when several variables enter the process. The complexity multiplies, and the use of sophisticated statistical packages designed for multiple variable analyses is necessary. Even with this assistance, however, a good fit of the data to the model may not be possible. Unfortunately, some organizations have not developed mathematical relationships for output variables as a function of one or more inputs, and without them the forecasting method is difficult to use.

Estimates

The most common method of isolating the effects of a project is to use estimates from some group of individuals. Although this is potentially the weakest method, it is practical in many situations, and it can greatly enhance the credibility of the analysis if adequate precautions are taken. The beginning point in using this method is ensuring that the estimates are provided by the most credible source, which is often the participant in an innovation project – not a higher-level manager or executive removed from the process. The individual who provides this information must understand the different factors and, particularly, the influence of the project on those factors.

Essentially, there are four categories of potential input. The participants directly involved in the project are the first source considered. Managers are another possible source. Customers provide credible estimates in particular situations, and external experts may provide insight into causes for improvement. These sources are described in more detail next.

Participants' Estimate of Impact

An easily implemented method of isolating the impact of a project is to obtain information directly from participants during project implementation. The usefulness of this approach rests on the assumption that participants are capable of determining or estimating how much of the performance improvement is related to the project implementation. Because their actions have led to the improvement, participants may provide highly accurate data. Although an estimate, the value they supply is likely to carry considerable weight with management because they know that the participants are at the center of the change or improvement. The estimate is

What is the link between these factors and the improvement?
What other factors have contributed to this improvement in performance?
What percentage of this improvement can be attributed to the implementation of this project?
How much confidence do you have in this estimate, expressed as a percentage? (0% = no
   confidence, 100% = complete confidence)
What other individuals or groups could provide a reliable estimate of this percentage to deter-
   mine the amount of improvement contributed by this project?

Figure 11.3 Questions for Participant Estimation.

Factor causing improvement	Percentage of improvement caused	Confidence (%)	Adjusted percentage of improvement
Project	60	80	48
Process changes	15	70	10.5
Environmental changes	5	60	3
Compensation changes	20	80	16
Other	–	–	–
Total	100		

Figure 11.4 Example of a Participant's Estimationv.

obtained by defining the improvement, and then asking participants the series of questions in Figure 11.3.

Figure 11.4 illustrates this approach with an example of one participant's estimation. Participants who do not provide answers to the questions in are excluded from the analysis. Erroneous, incomplete, and extreme information should also be discarded before the analysis. To obtain a conservative estimate, the confidence percentage can be factored into each of the values. The confidence percentage is a reflection of the error in the estimate. Thus, an 80% confidence level equates to a potential error range of plus or minus 20%. Guiding principle number four (Figure 4.8) suggests that we should be conservative in the analysis and use the minus 20%. To reduce a number by 20%, we should multiply it by 80%. With this approach, the estimate is multiplied by the confidence to be at the lower side of the range. In the example, the participant allocates 60% of the improvement to the project and has a level of confidence in the estimate of 80%. The confidence percentage is multiplied by the estimate to produce a usable project value of 48%. This adjusted percentage is then multiplied by the actual amount of the improvement (postproject minus preproject value) to isolate the portion attributed to the project.

For example, if errors declined 10 per week, 4.8 of the reduced errors would be attributed to the project. The adjusted improvement is now ready for conversion to monetary value and, ultimately, use in the ROI calculation. An example of this was presented in the previous chapter as Figure 10.4.

Although the reported contribution is an estimate, this approach offers considerable accuracy and credibility. Five adjustments are effectively applied to the participant estimate to produce a conservative value:

1. Participants who do not provide usable data are assumed to have observed no improvements.
2. Extreme data values and incomplete, unrealistic, or unsupported claims are omitted from the analysis, although they may be included in the "other benefits" category.
3. For short-term projects, it is assumed that no benefits are realized from the project after the first year of full implementation. For long-term projects, several years may pass after project implementation before benefits are realized.
4. The amount of improvement is adjusted by the portion directly related to the project, expressed as a percentage.
5. The improvement value is multiplied by the confidence level, expressed as a percentage, to reduce the amount of the improvement in order to reflect the potential error.

As an enhancement of this method, the level of management above the participants may be asked to review and concur with each participant's estimate.

In using participants' estimates to measure impact, several assumptions are made:

1. The project encompasses a variety of different activities, practices, and tasks, all focused on improving the performance of one or more business measures.
2. One or more business measures were identified before the project, and have been monitored since the implementation process. Data monitoring has revealed an improvement in the business measure.
3. There is a need to associate the project with a specific amount of performance improvement, and determine the monetary impact of the improvement. This information forms the basis for calculating the actual ROI.

Given these assumptions, the participants can specify the results linked to the project, and provide data necessary to develop the ROI. This can be accomplished using a focus group, an interview, or a questionnaire.

Manager's Estimate of Impact

In lieu of, or in addition to, participant estimates, the participants' manager may be asked to provide input concerning the project's role in improving performance. In some settings, the managers may be more familiar with the other factors influencing performance, and therefore may be better equipped to provide estimates of impact. The questions to ask managers, after identifying the improvement ascribed to the project, are similar to those asked of the participants.

Managers' estimates should be analyzed in the same manner as the participant estimates, and they may also be adjusted by the confidence percentage. When participants' and managers' estimates have both been collected, the decision of which estimate to use becomes an issue. If there is a compelling reason to believe that one estimate is more credible than the other, then that estimate should be used. The most conservative approach is to use the lowest value, and include an appropriate explanation. Another option is to recognize that each estimate source has a unique perspective and that an average of the two may be appropriate, with equal weight placed on each input. It is recommended that input be obtained from both participants and their managers.

In some cases, upper management may provide an estimate of the percentage of improvement attributable to a project. After considering other factors that could contribute to the improvement – such as technology, procedures, and process changes – they apply a subjective factor to represent the portion of the results that should be attributed to the project. Despite its subjective nature, this input by upper management is usually accepted by the individuals who provide or approve funding for the project. Sometimes, their comfort level with the processes used is the most important consideration.

Customer Estimates of Project Impact

An approach that is useful in some narrowly focused project situations is to solicit input on the impact of a project directly from customers. Customers are asked why they chose a particular product or service, or are asked to explain how their reaction to the product or service has been influenced by individuals or systems involved in the project.

This technique often focuses directly on what the project is designed to improve. For example, after the implementation of a customer service project at an electric utility, market research data showed that the level of customer dissatisfaction with response time was 5% lower than the rate before the project implementation. Because response time was reduced by the project and no other factor was found to contribute to the reduction, the 5% improvement in customer satisfaction was attributed to the project.

Routine customer surveys provide an excellent opportunity to collect input directly from customers regarding their reactions to new or improved products, services, processes, or procedures. Pre- and postproject data can pinpoint the improvements spurred by a new project.

Customer input should be elicited using current data collection methods; the creation of new surveys or feedback mechanisms is to be avoided. This measurement process should not add to the data collection systems in use. Customer input may constitute the most powerful and convincing data if it is complete, accurate, and valid.

Internal or External Expert Estimates

External or internal experts can sometimes estimate the portion of results that can be attributed to a project. With this technique, experts must be carefully selected based on their knowledge of the process, project, and situation. For example, an expert in quality might be able to provide estimates of how much change in a quality measure can be attributed to a quality project, and how much can be attributed to other factors.

This approach has its drawbacks, however. It can yield inaccurate data unless the project and the setting in which the estimate is made are quite similar to the program with which the expert is familiar. Also, this approach may lack credibility if the estimates come from external sources and do not involve those close to the process.

This process has the advantage that its reliability is often a reflection of the reputation of the expert or independent consultant. It is a quick and easy form of input from a reputable expert or consultant. Sometimes top management has more confidence in such external experts than in its own staff.

Estimate Credibility: The Wisdom of Crowds

The following story is an example of the large amount of research showing the power of input from average individuals. It is taken from James Surowiecki's best-selling book, *The Wisdom of Crowds*.

One day in the fall of 1906, British scientist Francis Galton left his home in the town of Plymouth, and headed for a country fair. Galton was 85 years old and was beginning to feel his age, but he was still brimming with the curiosity that had won him renown – and notoriety – for his work on statistics and the science of heredity. On that particular day, Galton's curiosity turned to livestock.

Galton's destination was the annual West of England Fat Stock and Poultry Exhibition, a regional fair where the local farmers and towns-people gathered to appraise the quality of each other's cattle, sheep, chickens, horses, and pigs. Wandering through rows of stalls examining workhorses and prize hogs may seem like a strange way for a scientist to spend an afternoon, but there was certain logic to it. Galton was a man obsessed with two things: the measurement of physical and mental qualities, and breeding. And what, after all, is a livestock show but a large showcase for the effects of good and bad breeding?

Breeding mattered to Galton because he believed that only a very few people had the characteristics necessary to keep societies healthy. He had devoted much of his career to measuring those characteristics, in fact, in an effort to prove that the vast majority of people did not possess them. His experiments left him with little confidence in the intelligence of the average person, "the stupidity and wrong-headedness of many men and women being so great as to be scarcely credible." Galton believed, "Only if power and control stayed in the hands of the select, well-bred few, could a society remain healthy and strong."

As he walked through the exhibition that day, Galton came across a weight judging competition. A fat ox had been selected and put on display, and many people were lining up to place wagers on what the weight of the ox would be after it was slaughtered and dressed. For sixpence, an individual could buy a stamped and numbered ticket and fill in his or her name, occupation, address, and estimate. The best guesses would earn prizes.

Eight hundred people tried their luck. They were a diverse lot. Many of them were butchers and farmers, who were presumably expert at judging the weight of livestock, but there were also quite a few people who had no insider knowledge of cattle. "Many non-experts competed," Galton wrote later in the scientific journal, *Nature*. "The average competitor was probably as well fitted for making a just estimate of the dressed weight of the ox, as an average voter is of judging the merits of most political issues on which he votes."

Galton was interested in figuring out what the "average voter" was capable of because he wanted to prove that the average voter was capable of very little. So he turned the competition into an impromptu experiment. When the contest was over and the prizes had been awarded, Galton borrowed the tickets from the organizers, and ran a series of statistical tests on them. Galton arranged the guesses (totaling 787–13 were discarded because they were illegible) in order from highest to lowest, and plotted them to see if they would form a bell curve. Then, among other things, he added up all of the contestants' estimates and calculated the mean. That number represented, you could say, the collective wisdom of the Plymouth crowd. If the crowd were viewed as a single person, that would be the person's guess as to the ox's weight.

Galton had no doubt that the average guess of the group would be way off the mark. After all, mix a few very smart people with some mediocre people and a lot of dumb people, and it seems likely that you would end up with a dumb answer. But Galton was wrong. The crowd had guessed that the slaughtered and dressed ox would weigh 1,197 pounds. In fact, after it was slaughtered and dressed, the ox weighed 1,198 pounds. In other words, the crowd's judgment was essentially perfect. The "experts" were not even close. Perhaps breeding didn't mean so much after all. Galton wrote later: "The result seems more creditable to the trustworthiness of a democratic judgment than it might have been expected." That was something of an understatement.

What Francis Galton stumbled on that day in Plymouth was a simple but powerful truth: under the right circumstances, groups are remarkably intelligent, and are often smarter than the smartest people in them. Groups do not need to be dominated by exceptionally intelligent people in order to be smart. Even if most of the people within a group are not especially informed or rational, collectively they can reach a wise decision [3].

Calculate the Impact of other Factors

It is sometimes possible, although not appropriate in all cases, to calculate the impact of factors (other than the project) that account for part of the improvement, and then credit the project with the remaining part. That is, the project assumes credit for improvement that cannot be attributed to other factors.

An example will help explain this approach. In a consumer lending project for a large bank, a significant increase in consumer loan volume occurred after a project was implemented. Part of the increase in volume was attributed to the project, and the remainder was due to the influence of other factors in place during the same time period. Two additional factors were identified: 1) an increase in marketing and sales promotion; and 2) falling interest rates.

With regard to the first factor, as marketing and sales promotion increased, so did consumer loan volume. The contribution of this factor was estimated using input from several internal experts in the marketing department. As for the second factor, industry sources were used to estimate the relationship between consumer loan volume and interest rates. These two estimates together accounted for a modest percentage of the increase in consumer loan volume. The remaining improvement was attributed to the project.

This method is appropriate when the other factors can be easily identified, and the appropriate mechanisms are in place to calculate their impact on the improvement. In some cases, estimating the impact of outside factors is just as difficult as estimating the impact of the project, limiting this approach's applicability. However, the results can be reliable if the procedure used to isolate the impact of other factors is sound.

Select the Technique

With all of these techniques available to isolate the impact of an innovation project, selecting the most appropriate ones for a specific project can be difficult. Some techniques are simple and inexpensive; others are time-consuming and costly. In choosing among them, the following factors should be considered:

- Feasibility of the technique
- Accuracy associated with the technique
- Credibility of the technique with the target audience
- Specific cost to implement the technique
- Amount of disruption in normal work activities resulting from the technique's implementation
- Participant, staff, and management time required for the technique

The use of multiple techniques or multiple sources of data input should be considered, since two sources are usually better than one. When multiple sources are used, a conservative method should be used to combine the inputs. The reason is that a conservative approach builds acceptance. The target audience should always be provided with an explanation of the process and the subjective factors involved.

Multiple sources allow an organization to experiment with different strategies and build confidence in the use of a particular technique. For example, if management is concerned about the accuracy of participants' estimates, the combination of a control group arrangement and participant estimates could be useful for checking the accuracy of the estimation process.

It is not unusual for the ROI of a project to be extremely large. Even when a portion of the improvement is allocated to other factors, the magnitude can still be impressive in many situations. The audience should understand that even though every effort has been made to isolate the project's impact, it remains an imprecise figure that is subject to error. It represents the best estimate of the impact given the constraints, conditions, and resources available. Chances are it is more accurate than other types of analysis regularly used in other functions within the organization.

Final Thoughts

Isolating the effects of a project is an important step in answering the question of how much of the improvement in a business measure was caused by the project. The techniques presented in this chapter are the most effective approaches available to answer this question, and are used by some of the most progressive organizations. Too often results are reported and linked to a project with no attempt to isolate the exact portion of the outcome associated with the project. This leads to an invalid report trumpeting project success. If professionals wish to improve their images and are committed to meeting their responsibility to obtain results, the need for isolation must be addressed early in the process for all major projects.

When we complete this important step, we must convert the data to monetary values. We will detail this process in the next chapter.

12

Converting Data to Money

One of Canada's largest banks is on a path to truly be a global organization with acquired banks in different countries and expanded divisions within the bank serving a global market.

Recently, the bank conducted a global leaders meeting at its headquarters in Toronto where the heads of the banking units and banks around the world discussed a variety of strategy and leadership topics. The talent development team saw this as an opportunity to enhance networking. Executives had always thought executives could benefit by working together, perhaps sharing some of the same clients and expanding specialized services to other countries. Some units offer services that could be purchased by other parts of the bank. With the urging of executives, the team decided to track the success of the networking and develop the actual monetary value.

The bank used innovative technology where the name tags of individuals could electronically track networking. The devices tracked which executives met other participants, how long they met, and how many times they met. Participants were asked to keep their name badges with them at all times with this message, "We want to try an experiment to see how much networking actually occurs and the value of that networking. This is not a performance issue. It's just an attempt to understand the value of networking." The bank engaged the services of external consultants to measure the monetary value of the networking.

One month after the meeting, armed with the data that showed the networking profile, the consulting firm conducted interviews with each participant to indicate what had actually happened with the networking, explore what has occurred since the meeting, and show how it connects to the business. Another follow up interview was conducted three months after the meeting with the specific goal of tracking any successes from the networking.

Over fifty participants were involved in the meeting and a few had very little networking experience, with no value reported. Some were able to exchange clients or obtain a client from another executive. The headquarters of a client company may be in another country and the participants used the headquarters connection with the bank to sell local financial services. A few were able to use the services of other divisions. Some were able to provide referrals. Each of these actions and consequences were detailed with as much specifics as possible to understand what happened and what was anticipated to happen in the future.

The participants attempted to place a monetary value on the outcome anticipating a profit (or cost savings) that would be generated from the contact. In some cases, a new client was secured and they knew the value of a new client, based on the average tenure of a client and the average profit made with that particular product line. In the interviews with fifty-two executives, twenty-one were able to provide specific data, and seven had very impressive results. Part of the process included the question "How much of this improvement is actually caused by the networking?" There is a chance that the outcome could have happened through normal channels. In some cases there was a possibility that this could have happened as some participants were already thinking about those particular clients. The networking helped. So they gave the percent of the improvement to the meeting.

When all the money was tallied, divided by all fifty-two participants, an average value of the networking was $4,265 per person. Although the total amount was impressive, it wasn't enough to cover the total cost of the meeting, but that wasn't the principal reason for the meeting. This value gave executives some comfort that networking activities can add business value.

This case study illustrates an important trend as executives attempt to convert hard to value measures to money. The monetary value is a way for executives to understand the important of measures typically not converted. This can be an eye-opening exercise.

To show the real money, the improvement in business measures that is attributable to the innovation project (after the effects of the project have been isolated) must be converted to monetary values, which are then compared with project costs. This represents the ultimate level in the five-level evaluation framework presented in Chapter 4. In this chapter we will explain how business and organization leaders develop the monetary values used to calculate ROI.

Why Convert Data to Monetary Values?

The need to convert data to monetary amounts is not always clearly understood by project leaders. A project can be shown to be a success just by providing business impact data, and the amount of change directly attributable to the project. For example, a change in quality, cycle time, market share, or customer satisfaction could represent a significant improvement linked directly to a new project. For some projects, this may suffice. However, many sponsors require the actual monetary value, and more project leaders are taking this extra step of converting data to monetary values.

Value Equals Money

For some stakeholders, the most important value is money. As described in Chapter 6, there are many different types of value. However, monetary value is becoming one of the primary criteria of success, as the economic benefits of projects are pursued. Executives, sponsors, clients, administrators, and other leaders are particularly concerned with the allocation of funds, and want to see evidence of the contribution of a project in terms of monetary value. Any other outcome for these key stakeholders would be unsatisfactory.

Impact is More Understandable

For some projects, the impact is more understandable when stated in terms of monetary value. Consider for example, the impact of a major project to improve the creativity of an organization's employees, and thereby enhance the innovation of the organization. Suppose this project involved literally all employees and had an impact on all parts of the organization. Across all departments, functions, units, and divisions, employees were being more creative, suggesting new ideas, taking on new challenges, driving new products – in short, helping the organization in a wide variety of ways. The only way to understand the value of such a project is to convert the individual efforts and their consequences to monetary values. Totaling the monetary values of all the innovations would provide some sense of the value of the project.

Consider the impact of a leadership for innovation program directed at all of the middle managers in an organization. As part of the program, the managers were asked to select at least two measures of importance to them, and to indicate what would need to change or improve for them to meet their specific goals. The measures must be under the control of their team and can be changed using the innovation techniques with the team. For a given session, measures could number in the dozens, if not hundreds. When the program's impact was studied, a large number of improvements were identified but were hard to quantify. Converting them to monetary values allowed the improvements to be expressed in the same terms, enabling the outcomes to be more clearly reported.

Monetary value is necessary to determine ROI. As described in earlier chapters, an expression of a monetary value is needed to compare against costs in order to develop the benefits/costs ratio, the ROI (as a percentage), and the payback period.

Converting to Monetary Values is Similar to Budgeting

Professionals and administrators are typically occupied with budgets, and are expected to develop budgets for projects with an acceptable degree of accuracy. They are also comfortable with handling costs. When it comes to benefits, however, many are not comfortable, even though some of the same techniques used in developing budgets are used to determine benefits. Some of the benefits of the project will take the form of cost savings or cost reductions, and this can make identification of the costs or value easier for some projects. The monetary benefit resulting from a project is a natural extension of the budget.

Monetary Value is Vital to Organizational Operations

With global competitiveness and the drive to improve the efficiency of operations, awareness of the costs related to particular processes and activities is essential. In the 1990s this emphasis gave rise to activity-based costing (ABC) and activity-based management. ABC is not a replacement for traditional, general ledger accounting. Rather, it is a translator or medium between cost accumulations, or the specific expenditure account balances in the general ledger, and the end users who must apply cost data in decision making. In typical cost statements, the actual cost of a process or problem is not readily discernible. ABC converts inert cost data to relevant, actionable information. ABC has become increasingly useful for identifying improvement opportunities, and measuring the benefits realized from performance initiatives on an after-the-fact basis [1]. Over 80% of the ROI impact studies conducted show projects benefiting the organization through cost savings (cost reductions or cost avoidance). Consequently, understanding the cost of a problem and the payoff of the corresponding solution is essential to proper management of the business.

Monetary Values are Necessary to Understand Problems and Cost Data

In any business, costs are essential to understanding the magnitude of a problem. Consider, for example, the cost of employee turnover. Traditional records and even those available through activity-based costing will not indicate the full value or cost of the problem. A variety of estimates and expert inputs may be necessary to supplement cost statements to arrive at a definite value. The good news is that organizations have developed a number of standard procedures for identifying undesirable costs. For example, Wal-Mart has calculated the cost of one truck sitting idle at a store for one minute, waiting to be unloaded. When this cost is multiplied by the hundreds of deliveries per store and the result then multiplied by 5,000 stores, the cost becomes huge.

Key Steps in Converting Data to Money

Converting data to monetary values involves five steps for each data item:

1. *Focus on a unit of measure.* First, a unit of measure must be defined. For output data, the unit of measure is the item produced (e.g., one item assembled), service provided (e.g., one package shipped), or sale completed. Time measures could include the time to complete a project, cycle time, or customer response time; and the unit here is usually expressed in terms of minutes, hours, or days. Quality is another common measure, with a unit defined as one error, reject, defect, or reworked item. Soft data measures vary, with a unit of improvement expressed in terms of absences, turnover, or a change in the customer satisfaction index. Specific examples of units of measure are:

   - One new product
   - One enhanced product

- One minute of customer time saved
- One point on the net promoter score
- One FTE employee
- One student enrolled
- One loan approved
- One grievance
- One hour of downtime
- One voluntary turnover
- One hour of cycle time
- One customer complaint
- One patient served
- One point increase in customer satisfaction

2. *Determine the value of each unit.* Now comes the challenge: placing a value (V) on the unit identified in the first step. For measures of productivity, quality, cost, and time, the process is relatively easy. Most organizations maintain records or reports that can pinpoint the cost of one unit of production or one defect. Soft data are more difficult to convert to money. For example, the monetary value of one customer complaint or a one-point change in an employee attitude may be difficult to determine. The techniques described in this chapter provide an array of approaches for making this conversion. When more than one value is available, the most credible or lowest value is generally used in the calculation.

3. *Calculate the change in performance data.* The change in output data is calculated after the effects of the project have been isolated from other influences. This change (d) is the performance improvement that is directly attributable to the project, represented as the Level 4 impact measure. The value may represent the performance improvement for an individual, a team, a group of participants, or several groups of participants.

4. *Determine the annual amount of change.* The d value is annualized to develop a value for the total change in the performance data for one year (dP). Using annual figures is a standard approach for organizations seeking to capture the benefits of a particular project, even though the benefits may not remain constant throughout the year. For a short-term solution, first-year benefits are used even when the project

produces benefits beyond one year. This approach is considered conservative. More will be discussed about this later.

5. *Calculate the annual value of the improvement.* The total value of improvement is calculated by multiplying the annual performance change (dP) by the unit value (V) for the complete group in question. For example, if one group of participants is involved in the project being evaluated, the total value will include the total improvement for all participants providing data in the group. This value for annual project benefits is then compared with the costs of the project to calculate the BCR, ROI, or payback period.

An example from an innovation project at a trucking company describes the five-step process of converting data to monetary values. This project was developed and implemented to address customer complaints as the company was experiencing an excessive number of complaints caused by inadequate or improper customer service. The number of complaints was selected as an output measure. Figure 12.1 shows the steps in assigning a monetary value to the data, resulting in a total project impact of $1,350,000.

Setting: Labor-management cooperation project in a manufacturing plant	
Step 1:	*Define the unit of measure.* The unit is defined as one customer complaint based on customer service.
Step 2:	*Determine the value (V) of each unit.* According to internal experts (i.e., the customer care staff), the cost of an average complaint in this category was estimated at $7,500, when time and direct costs are considered $(V = \$7,500)$.
Step 3:	*Calculate the change (Δ) in performance data.* Six months after the project was completed, total complaints per month had declined by 25. Sixty percent of the reductions were related to the project, as determined by the front line customer service staff ("Isolating Project Impact"). Use the six-month value of 25 x 60% = 15 per month.
Step 4:	*Determine an annual amount for the change (ΔP).* This yields an annual improvement value of $15 \times 12 = 180$ $\Delta P = 180$
Step 5:	*Calculate the annual value of the improvement.* Annual value $= \Delta P \times V$ $= 180 \times \$7,500$ $= \$1,350,000$

Figure 12.1 Converting customer complaint data to monetary values.

Standard Monetary Values

Most hard data items (output, quality, cost, and time) have standard values. A standard value is a monetary value assigned to a unit of measurement that is accepted by key stakeholders. Standard values have been developed because these are often the measures that matter to the organization. They reflect problems, and their conversion to monetary values show their impact on the operational and financial well-being of the organization.

For the last two decades, quality programs have typically focused only on the cost of quality. Organizations have been obsessed with placing a value on mistakes, or the payoff from avoiding these mistakes. This assigned value – the standard cost of an item – is one of the critical outgrowths of the quality management movement. In addition, a variety of process improvement programs – such as reengineering, reinventing the corporation, transformation, and continuous process improvement – have included a component in which the cost of a particular measure is determined. Finally, the development of a variety of cost control, cost containment, and cost management systems, such as activity-based costing, have forced organizations, departments, and divisions to place costs on activities and, in some cases, relate those costs directly to the revenues or profits of the organization.

The following discussion describes how measures of output, quality, and time can be converted to standard values.

Converting Output Data to Money

When an innovation project results in a change in output, the value of the increased output can usually be determined from the organization's accounting or operating records. For organizations operating on a profit basis, this value is typically the marginal profit contribution of an additional unit of production or service provided. An example is a team within a major appliance manufacturing firm that was able to boost the production of small refrigerators after a comprehensive work cell redesign innovation project; the unit of improvement is the profit margin associated with one refrigerator.

For organizations that are performance driven rather than profit driven, this value is usually reflected in the savings realized when an additional unit of output is realized for the same input. For example, in the visa section of a government office, one additional visa application may be processed at no additional cost; an increase in output translates into a cost savings equal to the unit cost of processing a visa application.

Most organizations have standard values readily available for performance monitoring and goal setting. Managers often use marginal cost statements and sensitivity analyses to pinpoint values associated with changes in output. If the data are not available, the project team must initiate or coordinate the development of appropriate values.

One of the more important measures of output is productivity, particularly in a competitive organization. Today, most organizations competing in the global economy do an excellent job of monitoring productivity and placing a value on it.

For example, consider the Snapper lawn mower factory in McDonough, Georgia. Ten years ago it produced 40 models of outdoor equipment items; now it makes 145. Ten years ago, all of the manufacturing processes were performed by humans. Today robots do the welding, lasers cut parts, and computers control the steel stamping process. Productivity at the factory is three times what it was ten years ago, and the workforce has been cut by half. At Snapper, each factory worker's output is measured every hour, every day, every month, and every year. And everyone's performance is posted publicly every day for all to see. Production at the Snapper plant is rescheduled every week according to the pace of store sales across the nation. A computer juggles work assignments and balances the various parts of the assembly process. At Snapper, productivity is not only important, it is measured and valued. Snapper knows the value of improving productivity by even a tiny amount. The president knows that the factory must be efficient to compete in a global market with low-cost products. This requires that the performance of every factory worker be measured every hour of every day.

The benefit of converting output data to money using standard values is that these calculations are already available for the most important data items. Perhaps no area has as much experience with standard values as the sales and marketing area. Figure 12.2 shows a sampling of the sales and marketing measures that are routinely calculated and reported as standard values [2].

Calculating the Cost of Quality

Quality and the cost of quality are important issues in most manufacturing and service organizations. Because many projects are designed to increase quality, the project team may have to place a value on the improvement of certain quality measures. For some quality measures, the task is easy. For example, if quality is measured in terms of the defect rate, the value of the improvement is the cost to repair or replace the product.

Metric	Definition	Conversion notes
Sales	The sale of the product or service recorded in a variety of different ways: by product, by time period, by customer	The data must be converted to monetary value by applying the profit margin for a particular sales category.
Profit margin (%)	Price−Cost / Cost for the product, customer, and time period	Factored to convert sales to monetary value add to the organization
Unit margin	Unit price less unit cost	Shows the value of incremental sales
Channel margin	Channel profits as a percentage of channel selling price	Used to show the value of sales through a particular marketing channel
Retention rate	The ratio of customers retained to the number of customers at risk of leaving	The value is the saving of the money necessary to acquire a replacement customer
Churn rate	Ratio of customers leaving to the number who are at risk of leaving	The value is the saving of the money necessary to acquire a new customer
Customer profit	The difference between the revenues earned from and the cost associated with the customer relationship during the specified period	The monetary value added is the profit obtained from customers, which all goes toward the bottom line
Customer value lifetime	The present value of the future cash flows attributed to the customer relationship	Bottom line; as customer value increases, it adds directly to the profits; as a customer is added, the incremental value is the customer lifetime average
Cannibalization rate	The percentage of new product sales taken from existing product lines	This is to be minimized, as it represents an adverse effect on existing product, with the value added being the loss of profits due to the sales loss
Workload	Hours required to service clients and prospects	This includes the salaries, commissions, and benefits from the time the sales staff spend on the workloads

Inventories	The total amount of product or brand available for sale in a particular channel	Since inventories are valued at the cost of carrying the inventory, costs involve space, handling, and the time value of money; insufficient inventory is the cost of expediting the new inventory or the loss of sales because of the inventory outage
Market share	Sales revenue as a percentage of total market sales	Actual sales are converted to money through the profit margins, is a measure of competitiveness
Loyalty	The length of time the customer stays with the organization, the willingness to pay a premium, and the willingness to search	Calculated as the additional profit from the sale or the profit on the premium

Figure 12.2 Examples of Standard Values from Sales and Marketing.

Adapted from *Marketing Metrics: 50+ Metrics Every Executive Should Master* by Paul W. Farris, Neil T. Bendle, Phillip E. Pfeifer, and David J. Ribstein.

The most obvious cost of poor quality is the amount of scrap or waste generated by mistakes. Defective products, spoiled raw materials, and discarded paperwork are all the result of poor quality. Scrap and waste translate directly into a monetary value. In a production environment, for example, the cost of a defective product is the total cost incurred up to the point at which the mistake is identified, minus the salvage value. In the service environment, the cost of a defective service is the cost incurred up to the point at which the deficiency is identified, plus the cost to correct the problem, plus the cost to make the customer happy, plus the loss of customer loyalty.

Employee mistakes and errors can be expensive. The costliest form of rework occurs when a product or service is delivered to a customer, and must be returned for repair or correction. The cost of rework includes both labor and direct costs. In some organizations, rework costs can constitute as much as 35% of operating expenses.

Quality costs can be grouped into six major categories:

1. Internal failure represents costs associated with problems detected prior to product shipment or service delivery. Typically such costs are reworking and retesting.
2. Penalty costs are fines or penalties incurred as a result of unacceptable quality.
3. External failure refers to problems detected after product shipment or service delivery. Typical items here are technical support, complaint investigation, remedial upgrades, and fixes.
4. Appraisal costs are the expenses involved in determining the condition of a particular product or service. Typical costs involve testing and related activities, such as product quality audits.
5. Prevention costs involve efforts undertaken to avoid unacceptable products or service quality. These efforts include service quality administration, inspections, process studies, and improvements.
6. Customer dissatisfaction is perhaps the costliest element of inadequate quality. In some cases, serious mistakes result in lost business. Customer dissatisfaction is difficult to quantify, and arriving at a monetary value may be impossible using direct methods. The judgment and expertise of sales, marketing, or quality managers are usually the best resources to draw upon in measuring the impact of dissatisfaction. More

and more quality experts are measuring customer and client dissatisfaction with the use of market surveys [3].

As with output data, the good news is that a tremendous number of quality measures have been converted to standard values. Some of these measures are

- Defects
- Rework
- Processing errors
- Date errors
- Accidents
- Grievances
- Downtime – equipment and system
- Delay
- Fines
- Days sales uncollected
- Queues

Converting Employee Time Using Compensation

Reducing the workforce or saving employee time is a common outcome for innovation projects. In a team environment, a project may enable the team to complete tasks in less time or with fewer people. A major disruptive innovation project could lead to a reduction of several hundred employees. On an individual basis, a technology project may be designed to help professional, sales, and managerial employees save time in performing daily tasks. The value of the time saved is an important measure, and determining a monetary value for it is relatively easy.

The most obvious time savings stem from reduced labor costs for performing a given amount of work. The monetary savings are found by multiplying the hours saved by the labor cost per hour. For example, a time-saving process in one organization, participants estimated, saved an average of 74 minutes per day, worth $31.25 per day or $7,500 per year, based on the average salary plus benefits for a typical participant.

The average wage, with a percentage added for employee benefits, will suffice for most calculations. However, employee time may be worth more. For example, additional costs for maintaining an employee (office space, furniture, telephones, utilities, computers, administrative support, and other overhead expenses) could be included in calculating the average labor cost. Thus, the wage rate used in the calculation can escalate quickly. In a large-scale employee reduction effort, calculating the costs of additional employees may be more appropriate for showing the value. However, for most projects, the conservative approach of using salary plus employee benefits is recommended.

Beyond reducing the labor cost per hour, time savings can produce benefits such as improved service, avoidance of penalties for late projects, and additional profit opportunities. These values can be estimated using other methods discussed in this chapter.

A word of caution is needed concerning time savings. Savings are realized only when the amount of time saved translates into a cost reduction or a profit contribution. Even if a project produces savings in manager time, monetary value is not realized unless the manager puts the time saved to productive use. Having managers estimate the percentage of time saved that is devoted to productive work may be helpful, if it is followed up with a request for examples of how the extra time was used. If a team-based project sparks a new process that eliminates several hours of work each day, the actual savings will be based on the corresponding reduction in staff or overtime pay. Therefore, an important preliminary step in figuring time savings is determining whether the expected savings will be genuine. FedEx is a primary example of assigning value to time [4].

Finding Standard Values

Standard values are available for all types of data. Virtually every major department will develop standard values that are monitored for that area. Typical functions in a major organization where standard values are tracked include:

- Finance and accounting
- Production
- Operations
- Engineering
- IT
- Administration
- Sales and marketing
- Customer service and support
- Procurement
- Logistics
- Compliance
- Research and development
- HR

Thanks to enterprise-wide systems software, standard values are commonly integrated and made available for access by a variety of people. In some cases, access may need to be addressed to ensure that the data can be obtained by those who require them.

When Standard Values are not Available

When standard values are not available, several alternative strategies for converting data to monetary are available. Some are appropriate for a specific type of data or data category, while others may be used with virtually any type of data. The challenge is to select the strategy that best suits the situation.

Using Historical Costs from Records

Historical records often indicate the value of a measure, and the cost (or value) of a unit of improvement. This strategy relies on identifying the appropriate records and tabulating the proper cost components for the item in question.

For example, suppose a large construction firm initiated a project to improve safety. The project improved several safety-related performance measures, ranging from amounts spent in response to government fines to total workers' compensation costs. From the company's records for one year of data, the average cost for each safety measure was determined. This value included the direct costs of medical payments, insurance payments and premiums, investigation services, and lost-time payments to employees, as well as payments for legal expenses, fines, and other direct services. The amount of time used to investigate, resolve, and correct the issues was also factored in. This time involved not only the health and safety staff, but other personnel as well. In addition, the costs of lost productivity, disruption of services, morale, and dissatisfaction were estimated to obtain a full cost. The corresponding costs for each item were then developed.

This example suggests the challenges inherent in maintaining systems and databases to enable the value for a particular data item to be identified. It also raises several concerns about using historical costs as a technique to convert data to money.

Time

Sorting through databases, cost statements, financial records, and activity reports takes a tremendous amount of time, and time that may not be available for the project. It is important to keep this part of the process in perspective. Converting data to monetary values is only one step in the ROI Methodology. Time needs to be conserved.

Availability

In some cases, data are not available to show all of the costs for a particular item. In addition to the direct costs associated with a measure, an equal number of indirect or invisible costs may be present that cannot be obtained easily.

Access

Compounding the problems of time and availability is access. Monetary values may be needed from a system or record set that is under someone else's control. In a typical implementation, the project leader may not have full access to cost data. Cost data are more sensitive than other types of data, and are often protected for a number of reasons, including competitive advantage. Therefore, access can be difficult and sometimes is even prohibited unless an absolute need to know can be demonstrated.

Accuracy

Finally, the need for accuracy in this analysis should not be overlooked. A measure provided in current records may appear to be based on accurate data, but this may be an illusion. When data are calculated, estimations are involved, access to certain systems is denied, and different assumptions are made (all of which can be compounded by different definitions of systems, data, and measures). Because of these limitations, the calculated values should be viewed as suspect unless means are available to ensure that they are accurate.

Calculating monetary value using historical data should be done with caution, and only when these two conditions exist:

- The sponsor has approved the use of additional time, effort, and money to develop a monetary value from the current records and reports.
- The measure is simple and can be found by searching only a few records.

Otherwise, an alternative method is preferred.

Using Input from Experts

When it is necessary to convert data items for which historical cost data are not available, input from experts on the process might be a consideration. Internal experts can provide the cost (or value) of one unit of improvement in a measure. Individuals with knowledge of the situation and the confidence of management must be willing to provide estimates, as well as the assumptions behind the estimates. Internal experts may be found in the department in which the data originated – sales, marketing, payroll, labor relations, or any number of other functions. Most experts have their own methodologies for developing these values. So when their input is required, it is important to explain the full scope of what is needed, and to provide as many specifics as possible.

If internal experts have a strong bias regarding the measure or are not available, external experts are sought. External experts should be selected based on their experience with the unit of measure. Fortunately, many experts are available who work directly with important measures such as employee attitudes, customer satisfaction, turnover, absenteeism, and grievances. They are often willing to provide estimates of the cost (or value) of these intangibles.

External experts – including consultants, professionals, or suppliers in a particular area – can also be found in obvious places. For example, the costs of accidents can be estimated by the workers' compensation carrier, or the cost of a grievance may be estimated by the labor attorney defending the company in grievance transactions. The process of locating an external expert is similar to the external database search, which is described later.

The credibility of the expert, whether internal or external, is a critical issue if the monetary value placed on a measure is to be reliable. Foremost among the factors behind an expert's credibility is the individual's experience with the process or measure at hand. Ideally, he or she should work with this measure routinely. Also, the person must be unbiased. Experts should be neutral in connection with the measure's value and should have no personal or professional interest in it.

In addition, the credentials of external experts – published works, degrees, and other honors or awards – are important in validating their expertise. Many of these people are tapped often, and their track records can and should be checked. If their estimate has been validated in more detailed studies and was found to be consistent, this can serve as a confirmation of their qualifications in providing such data.

Using Values from External Databases

For some measures, the use of cost (or value) estimates based on the work and research of others may be appropriate. This technique makes use of external databases that contain studies and research projects focusing on the cost of data items. Fortunately, many databases include cost studies of data items related to projects, and most are accessible on the Internet. Data are available on the costs of turnover, absenteeism, grievances, accidents, and even customer satisfaction. The difficulty lies in finding a database with studies or research germane to the particular project. Ideally, the data should originate from a similar setting in the same industry, but that is not always possible. Sometimes, data on industries or organizations in general are sufficient, with adjustments possibly required to suit the project at hand.

Linking with other Measures

When standard values, records, experts, and external studies are not available, a feasible alternative might be to find a relationship between the measure in question and some other measure that can be easily converted to a monetary value. This involves identifying existing relationships that show a strong correlation between one measure and another with a standard value.

A classic relationship is the correlation between job satisfaction and employee turnover. Suppose that in a project designed to improve job satisfaction, a value is needed to reflect changes in the job satisfaction index. A predetermined relationship showing the correlation between increases in job satisfaction and reductions in turnover can directly link the two measures. Using standard data or external studies, the cost of turnover can easily be determined as described earlier. Therefore, a change in job satisfaction can be immediately converted to a monetary value, or at least an approximate value. The conversion is not always exact because of the potential for error and other factors, but the estimate is sufficient for converting the data to monetary values.

In some situations, a chain of relationships may establish a connection between two or more variables. A measure that may be difficult to convert to a monetary value is linked to other measures that, in turn, are linked to measures to which values can be assigned. Ultimately, these measures are traced to a monetary value typically based on profits. Figure 12.3 shows the model used by Sears [5]. The model connects job attitudes (collected directly from the employees) to customer service, which is directly related to revenue growth. The rectangles in the figure represent survey information,

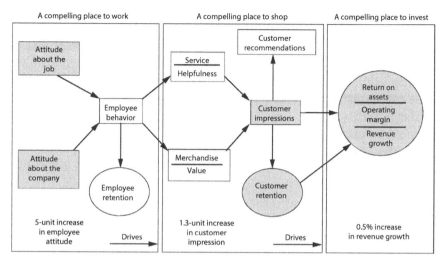

Figure 12.3 Relationship between Attitudes and Profits.

Copyright 1998. President and Fellows of Harvard College 1998. Used with permission.

and the ovals represent hard data. The shaded measurements are collected and distributed in the form of Sears total-performance indicators.

As the model shows, a 5-point improvement in employee attitudes leads to a 1.3-point improvement in customer satisfaction. This, in turn, drives a 0.5 percentage point increase in revenue growth. If employee attitudes at a local store improved by 5 points, and the previous rate of revenue growth were 5%, the new rate of revenue growth would then be 5.5%.

These links between measures, often called the service-profit chain, offer a promising methodology for applying monetary values to hard-to-quantify measures.

Using Estimates from Participants

In some cases, participants in the project should estimate the value of improvement. This technique is appropriate when participants are capable of providing estimates of the cost (or value) of the unit of measure that has improved as a result of the project. With this approach, participants should be provided with clear instructions, along with examples of the type of information needed. The advantage of this approach is that the individuals who are most closely connected to the improvement are often able to provide the most reliable estimates of its value. As with isolating project effects, when estimates are used to convert measures to monetary values, adjustments are made to reduce the error in those estimates.

Using Estimates from the Management Team

In some situations, participants in a project may be incapable of placing a value on the improvement. Their work may be so far removed from the ultimate value of the process that they cannot provide reliable estimates. In these cases, the team leaders, supervisors, or managers of participants may be able to providing estimates. Thus, they may be asked to provide a value for a unit of improvement linked to the project.

In other situations, managers are asked to review and approve participants' estimates and confirm, adjust, or reject those values. For example, suppose a project involving customer service representatives was designed to reduce customer complaints. The project did result in a reduction in complaints, but the value of a single customer complaint had to be identified to determine the value of the improvement. Although customer service representatives had knowledge of certain issues surrounding customer complaints, their scope was limited; so their managers were asked to provide a value. These managers had a broader perspective of the impact of a customer complaint.

Senior management can often provide estimates of the value of data. In this approach, senior managers concerned with the project are asked to place a value on the improvement based on their perception of its worth. This approach is used when calculating the value is difficult or when other sources of estimation are unavailable or unreliable.

Using Project Staff Estimates

The final strategy for converting data to monetary values is using project staff estimates. Using all available information and experience, the staff members most familiar with the situation provide estimates of the value. For example, a particular project for an international oil company was designed to reduce dispatcher absenteeism and address other performance problems. Unable to identify a value using the other strategies, the consulting staff estimated the cost of an absence to be $200. This value was then used in calculating the savings from the reduction in absenteeism that followed the project implementation.

Although the project staff may be qualified to provide accurate estimates, this approach is sometimes perceived as biased. It should therefore be used only when other approaches are unavailable or inappropriate.

Technique Selection and Finalizing Value

With so many techniques available, the challenge is selecting one or more strategies appropriate for the situation and available resources. Developing a table or list of values or techniques for the situation may be helpful. The guidelines that follow may aid in selecting a technique and finalizing the values.

Choose a Technique Appropriate for the Type of Data

Some strategies are designed specifically for hard data, whereas others are more appropriate for soft data. Thus, the type of data often dictates the strategy. Standard values are developed for most hard data items, and company records and cost statements are used in the process. Soft data often involve the use of external databases, links with other measures, and estimates. Experts are used to convert both types of data to monetary values.

Move from Most Accurate to Least Accurate

The techniques in this chapter are presented in order of accuracy. Standard values are always most accurate and therefore the most credible. But, as mentioned earlier, they are not always readily available. When standard values are not available, the following sequence of operational techniques should be tried:

- Historical costs from company records
- Internal and external experts
- External databases
- Links with other measures
- Estimates

Each technique should be considered in turn based on its feasibility and applicability to the situation. The technique associated with the highest accuracy is always preferred if the situation allows.

Consider Source Availability

Sometimes the availability of a particular source of data determines the method selection. For example, experts may be readily accessible. Some standard values are easy to find; others are more difficult. In other situations, the convenience of a technique is a major factor in the selection. The Internet, for example, has made external database searches more convenient

As with other processes, keeping the time investment for this phase to a minimum is important so that the total effort directed to the ROI study does not become excessive. Some techniques can be implemented in much less time than others. Devoting too much time to the conversion process may dampen otherwise enthusiastic attitudes about the use of the methodology, plus drive up the costs of the evaluation.

Use the Source with the Broadest Perspective on the Issue

According to Principle #3 in Figure 4.8, the most credible data source must be used. The individual providing estimates must be knowledgeable of the processes and the issues surrounding the valuation of the data. For example, consider the estimation of the cost of a grievance in a manufacturing plant. Although a supervisor may have insight into what caused a particular grievance, he or she may have a limited perspective. A high-level manager may be able to grasp the overall impact of the grievance and how it will affect other areas. Thus, a high-level manager would be a more credible source in this situation.

Use Multiple Techniques When Feasible

The availability of more than one technique for obtaining values for the data is often beneficial. When appropriate, multiple sources should be used to provide a basis for comparison or for additional perspectives. The data must be integrated using a convenient decision rule, such as the lowest value. The conservative approach of using the lowest value was presented as Guiding Principle #4 in Chapter 4, but this applies only when the sources have equal or similar credibility.

Converting data to monetary values has its challenges. Once the particular method has been selected and applied, several adjustments or tests are necessary to ensure the use of the most credible and appropriate value with the least amount of resources.

Apply the Credibility Test

The discussion of techniques in this chapter assumes that each data item collected and linked to a project can be converted to a monetary value. Highly subjective data, however, such as changes in employee attitudes or a reduction in the number of employee conflicts, are difficult to convert. Although estimates can be developed using one or more strategies, such estimates may lack credibility with the target audience, which can render their use in analysis questionable.

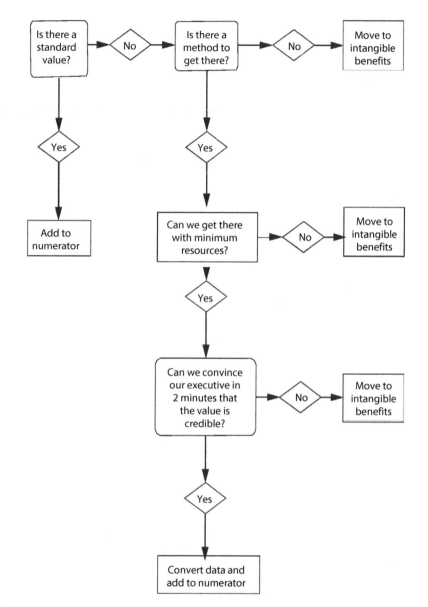

Figure 12.4 To Convert or Not to Convert.

The issue of credibility in combination with resources is illustrated in Figure 12.4. This is a logical way to decide whether to convert data to monetary values or leave them intangible. Essentially, in the absence of standard values, many other ways are available to capture the data or convert them to monetary values. However, there is a question to be answered: can it be done with minimum resources? Some of the techniques mentioned in this chapter – such as searching records or maybe even searching the Internet – cannot be performed with minimal use of resources. However, an estimate obtained from a group or from a few individuals is available with minimal use of resources. Then we move to the next question: will the executive who is interested in the project buy into the monetary value assigned to the measure with minimum explanation? If so, then it is credible enough to be included in the analysis; if not, then move it to the intangibles. The intangible benefits of a project are also important and are covered in much more detail in the next chapter.

Consider the Possibility of Management Adjustment

In organizations where soft data are common and values are derived using imprecise methods, senior managers and administrators are sometimes offered the opportunity to review and approve the data. Because of the subjective nature of this process, management may factor (reduce) the data to make the final results more credible. In one example, senior managers at Litton Industries adjusted the value for the benefits derived from implementing self-directed teams.

Consider the Short-Term/Long-Term Issue

When data are converted to monetary values, usually one year's worth of data is included in the analysis. This is Guiding Principle #9 in Figure 4.8, which states that for short-term solutions, only the first year's benefits are used. The issue of whether a project is short-term or long-term depends on the time it takes to complete or implement the project. If one group participating in the project and working through the process take months to complete it, then it is probably not short-term. Some projects literally take years to implement even for one particular group. In general, it is appropriate to consider a project short-term when one individual takes one month or less to learn what needs to be done to make the project successful. When the lag between project implementation and the consequences is relatively brief, a short-term solution is appropriate. When a project is long-term, no time limit for data inclusion is used, but the time value should be set before the project evaluation is undertaken. Input on the time value should be secured from all stakeholders, including the sponsor, champion, implementer, designer, and evaluator. After some discussion, the estimates of the time factor should be conservative and perhaps reviewed by finance and accounting. When a project is a long-term solution, forecasting will need to be used to estimate multiple years of value. No sponsor will wait several years to see how a project turns out.

Consider an Adjustment for the Time Value of Money

Since investment in a project is made in one time period and the return is realized at a later time, some organizations adjust project benefits to reflect the time value of money using discounted cash flow techniques. The actual monetary benefits of the project are adjusted for the time period. The amount of adjustment, however, is usually small compared with the typical benefits of projects.

Although this may not be an issue for every project, it should be considered for each project, and some standard discount rate should be used. Consider the following example of how this is calculated. Assume that a project costs $100,000, and it is expected to take two years for the full value of the estimate to be realized. In other words, this is a long-term solution spanning two years. Using a discount rate of 6%, the cost for the project for the first year would be $100,000 x 106% = $106,000. For the second year it is $106,000 x 106%, or $112,360. Thus, the project cost has been adjusted for a two-year value with a 6% discount rate. This assumes that the project sponsor could have invested the money in some other project and obtained at least a 6% return on that investment.

Final Thoughts

Showing the real money requires just that – money. Business impact data that have improved as a result of a project must be converted to money. Standard values make this process easier, but easy is not always an option, and other techniques must sometimes be used. However, if a measure cannot be converted with minimum resources or with no assurance of credibility, the improvement in the measure should be reported as an intangible benefit.

After the data are converted to monetary values, the next step is collecting the project costs and calculating the ROI. We will cover these processes in the next chapter.

13

Addressing Intangibles

A physician in a provincial health system in Canada was interested in making some changes in the procedures for colon cancer surgery. He had been reading about some successes with an innovative approach from the UK regarding changes in prep and after care with some important results and wanted to give this a try. However, he knew it would be a change for the system which would require time and resources to implement it. This change had to generate enough improvements (cost saving or avoidance) that will overcome the cost of the change. In essence, he needed to show a positive ROI.

Recognizing that it's difficult to secure funds to make this change, he wanted to experiment with a trial first. A small sample would be minimal costs that could be absorbed by his particular hospital. With the help of the ROI Institute, he set up the evaluation following the ROI Methodology. He had identified impact measures that he wanted to influence: complications, infections, re-admissions, and length of stay. This new approach should have improvements on all of these measures.

A group of seventeen patients had the new procedures and their results compared with a control group of seventeen other patients properly matched with the experimental group. The control group followed the routine procedure. To make this work, the staff had to be convinced that this procedure was good for patient care and necessary to control the cost of healthcare in the providence. He also had to make sure that the staff knew how to properly take care of the prep and after care. This involved off the job training and demonstrations on the job to make it work. He had to ensure that the staff were following the new process precisely to make sure that it was being applied properly. Finally, he would monitor the impacts of the two groups.

The results were amazing. There were no complications, infections, or re-admissions in the experimental group compared to numbers that ranged from 12–24% in the control group. The length of stay was reduced by three days as well. With these dramatic results, he presented them to the senior team and asked for money for a larger sample. His thinking was that this is a small sample of seventeen and it's not statistically significant to make an inference about the rest of the population. Each year the province would have about five hundred of these surgeries.

Along with these results, there was an important measure that had to be addresses properly—the length of stay, which represented a reduction of three days. There was some debate on the value of reducing those days. Some would argue that since there is a waiting line for people to get into the healthcare system, saving a day off someone's stay doesn't actually save money. There's always someone to take the bed. The cynics would argue that the new people coming in would have some extra initial costs of testing and that for that same number of days it would probably cost more. Obviously this is short sided thinking. There would be monetary value of that measure.

Although the finance and accounting team provided costs for complications, infections, and readmissions, they said that they could actually support a value for each day saved, but there would still be some debate. Consequently, it was left as an intangible, but a very important one. The decision centered on this issue. "We don't want to debate the monetary value of saving one day on a particular stay. We know there's some value there but we will leave it as an intangible so that's our upside potential."

The good news is that this program produced a very positive ROI of more than 100%. When it was presented to the senior team, the results were so impressive that they were not only interested in funding another group, but they decided to just change the entire procedure. As the CFO said in the meeting "I see some definite cost savings that we can easily capture, particularly with re-admission and infections, and this is enough cost avoidance to cover the cost of this program and still some I can use for some other processes. And I see a valuable intangible."

This type of analysis on a very innovative new approach can make a big difference. It also shows the power of intangibles, the measures that are not converted to money but are still very powerful in making the argument.

Innovation project results include both tangible and intangible measures. Intangible measures are the benefits or detriments directly linked to a project that cannot be converted to monetary values credibly with minimum resources. By definition, and based on the guiding principles of the ROI Methodology, an intangible benefit is a measure that is not converted to money, because the conversion cannot be accomplished with minimum resources and with credibility. These measures are often monitored after the project has been completed. Although not converted to monetary values, they are nonetheless an important part of the evaluation process. In this chapter we explore the role of intangibles, how to measure them, when to measure them, and how to report them.

The range of intangible measures is almost limitless. This chapter emphasizes just a few common and desired outcomes of projects. Figure 13.1 highlights examples of these measures. Some measures make the list because of the difficulty in measuring them; others because of the difficulty in converting them to money. Others are on the list for both reasons. Being labeled as intangible does not mean that these items can never

Common Intangibles	
• Alliances	• Image
• Attention	• Intellectual capital
• Awards	• Job satisfaction
• Brand	• Leadership
• Capability	• Loyalty
• Capacity	• Mindfulness
• Clarity	• Mindset
• Collaboration	• Net promoter score
• Communication	• Networking
• Compassion	• Organizational commitment
• Compliance	• Partnering
• Conflict	• Poverty
• Corporate social responsibility	• Reputation
• Creativity	• Risk
• Culture	• Social Capital
• Customer service	• Stress
• Emotional intelligence	• Sustainability
• Employee attitudes	• Team effectiveness
• Engagement	• Timeliness
• Grit	• Trust
• Human Life	• Work/life balance

Figure 13.1 Common Intangibles.

be measured or converted to monetary values. In one study or another, each item has been monitored and quantified in financial terms. However, in typical projects, these measures are considered intangible benefits because of the difficulty in measuring them, or the difficulty in converting them to monetary values.

Why Intangibles are Important

Although intangible measures are not new, they are becoming increasingly important. Intangibles drive funding for innovation projects. They drive the economy, and organizations are built on them. In every direction we look, intangibles are becoming not only increasingly important, but also critical to organizations. Here's a recap of why they have become so important.

Intangibles are the Invisible Advantage

When examining the reasons behind the success of many well-known organizations, intangibles are often found. A highly innovative company continues to develop new and improved products. A government agency reinvents itself. A company with highly involved and engaged employees attracts and keeps talent. An organization shares knowledge with employees, providing a competitive advantage. Still another organization is able to develop strategic partners and alliances. These intangibles do not often appear in cost statements and other record keeping, but they are there, and they make a huge difference.

Sometimes at work, we measure everything except what counts. Numbers are comforting – income, expenditure, productivity, engagement, staff turnover – and create an illusion of control. But when we're confronted by spectacular success or failure, everyone from the CEO to the janitor points in the same direction: the culture. Beyond measure and sometimes apparently beyond comprehension, culture has become the secret sauce of organizational life: the thing that makes the difference but for which no one has the recipe. [1]

According to Heffernan, the paradox of organizational culture lies in the fact that, while it makes a big difference, it is comprised of small actions, habits, and choices. The accumulation of these behaviors – coming from everywhere, from the top and the bottom of the hierarchy, from inside and outside the company itself – creates an organization's culture. It feels chaotic and yet, at the same time, is susceptible to everything anyone does.

This represents both a curse and a blessing. For leaders, the curse lies in the sense that culture emerges of its own volition – not just beyond measure but also beyond their control. We may not be able to measure culture but we can measure the high rate of failure for programs aiming at culture change; that stands at around 70 percent. So the idea emerges that culture is elusive, hard to manage, impossible to command.

Trying to identify, measure, and react to intangibles may be difficult, but the ability to do so exists. Intangibles transform the way organizations work, the way employees are managed, the way products are designed, the way services are sold, and the way customers are treated. The implications are profound, and an organization's strategy must address them. Although invisible, the presence of intangibles is felt and the results are concrete.

We are Entering the Intangible Economy

The intangible economy has evolved from basic changes that date to the Iron Age, which evolved into the Agricultural Age. In the late nineteenth century and during the early twentieth century, the world moved into the Industrial Age. From the 1950s forward, the world has moved into the Technology and Knowledge Age, and these moves translate into intangibles. During this time, a natural evolution of technology has occurred. During the Industrial Age, companies and individuals invested in tangible assets like plants and equipment. In the Technology and Knowledge Age, companies invest in intangible assets, like brands, systems, collaboration, culture, and image. The future holds more of the same, as intangibles continue to evolve into an important part of the overall economic system.

More Intangibles are Converted to Tangibles

The good news is that more data once regarded as intangible are now being converted into monetary values. Because of this, classic intangibles are now accepted as tangible measures, and their value is more easily understood. Consider, for example, customer satisfaction. Just a decade ago, few organizations had a clue as to the monetary value of customer satisfaction. Now more firms have taken the extra step to link customer satisfaction directly to revenues, profits, and other measures.

Over a decade ago, Jackson made progress to place a value on reputation. [2] Tracy and Morin attempted to connect trust to the bottom line. Trust, they say, is the lubricant of society and the glue that holds societies together. When trust is present, when goals are relatively congruent, there is room for honest disagreement – an essential ingredient for innovation and growth. On the other hand, when trust is absent, innovation suffers and costs rise exponentially. Think of the games played with time logs, insurance claims, and expense accounts. No wonder economists are concerned about trust. It finds its way into all their calculations – whether the Gross National Product or the economics of the firm. [3] More recently, Worline and Dutton concluded that compassion connects to the bottom line, fuels strategic advantage, motivates innovation, and drives service quality. [4]

Companies are seeing the tremendous value that can be derived from intangibles. As this chapter will illustrate, more data are being accumulated to show monetary values, moving some intangible measures into the tangible category.

Intangibles Drive Innovation Projects

Some projects are implemented because of the intangibles. For example, the need to have greater collaboration, partnering, branding, reputation, image communication, teamwork, or customer service will drive projects. In the public sector, the need to reduce poverty, improve healthcare, lower national debt, employ disadvantaged citizens, and save lives often drives innovation projects. From the outset, the intangibles are the important drivers and become the most important measures. Consequently, more executives include a string of intangibles on their scorecards, key operating reports, key performance indicators, dashboards, and other routine reporting systems. In some cases, the intangibles represent nearly half of all measures that are monitored.

The Magnitude of the Investment

As a general rule, only 15% of the value of a contemporary organization can be tied to such tangible assets as buildings and equipment. Intangible assets have become the dominant investment in businesses. [5] They are a growing force in the economy, and measuring their values poses challenges to managers and investors. They can no longer be ignored. They must be properly identified, selected, measured, reported, and in some cases, converted to monetary values.

Measuring and Analyzing Intangibles

In some projects, intangibles are more important than monetary measures. Consequently, these measures should be monitored and reported as part of the project evaluation. In practice, every project, regardless of its nature, scope, and content, will produce intangible measures. The challenge is to identify them effectively and report them appropriately.

Measuring the Intangibles

From time to time, it is necessary to explore the issue of measuring the difficult to measure. Responses to this exploration usually occur in the form of comments instead of questions. "You can't measure it," is a typical response. This cannot be true, because anything can be measured. What the frustrated observer suggests by the comment is that the intangible is not something you can count, examine, or see in quantities, like items produced or products sold. In reality, a quantitative value can be assigned to or developed for any intangible. If it exists, it can be measured. Consider human intelligence for example. Although human intelligence is vastly complex and abstract with myriad facets and qualities, IQ scores are assigned to most people and most people seem to accept them. The software engineering institute of Carnegie-Mellon University assigns software organizations a score of 1 to 5 to represent their maturity in software engineering. This score has enormous implications for the organizations' business development capabilities, yet the measure goes practically unchallenged.

Several approaches are available for measuring intangibles. Intangibles that can be counted include customer complaints, employee complaints, and conflicts. These can be recorded easily, and constitute one of the most acceptable types of measures. Unfortunately, many intangibles are based on attitudes and perceptions that must be measured. The key is in the development of the instrument of measure. The instruments are usually developed around scales of 3, 5, and even 10 points to represent levels of perception. The instruments to measure intangibles consist of three basic varieties.

The first lists the intangible items, and asks respondents to agree or disagree on a 5-point scale (where the midpoint represents a neutral opinion). Other instruments define various qualities of the intangible, such as its reputation. A 5-point scale can easily be developed to describe degrees of reputation, ranging from the worst rating – a horrible reputation – to the best rating – an excellent reputation. Still other ratings are expressed as an assessment on a scale of 1 to 10, after respondents review a description of the intangible [6]. *Emotional Intelligence* uses these surveys routinely.

Another instrument to measure the intangible connects it, when possible, to a measure that is easier to measure or easier to value. One of the

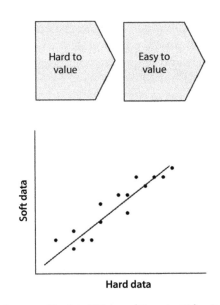

Figure 13.2 The Link between Hard-to-Value and Easy-to-Value Items.

most measured intangibles is engagement. Employee engagement often connects to sales, productivity, retention, quality, and safety. [7] As shown in Figure 13.2, most hard-to-measure items are linked to an easy-to-measure item. In the classic situation, a soft measure (typically the intangible) is connected to a hard measure (typically the tangible). Although this link can be developed through logical deductions and conclusions, having some empirical evidence through a correlation analysis (as shown in the figure) and developing a significant correlation between the items is the best approach. However, a detailed analysis would have to be conducted to ensure that a causal relationship exists. In other words, just because a correlation is apparent, does not mean that one caused the other. Consequently, additional analysis, other empirical evidence, and supporting data could pinpoint the actual causal effect.

A final instrument for measuring the intangible is the development of an index of different values. These could be a combination of both hard and soft data items that make up a particular index value. An index is a single score representing some complex factor that is constructed by aggregating the values of several different measures. Measures making up the index are sometimes weighted based on their importance to the abstract factor being measured. Some index measures are based strictly on hard data items. For example, the US poverty level is based on a family income amount equal to three times the money needed to feed a family as determined by the US Department of Agriculture, adjusted for inflation using the consumer price

Superior performance	Distinctive impact	Lasting endurance
Emotional response of audience; increase in number of standing ovations	Cleveland's style of programming increasingly copied; becoming more influential	Excellence sustained across generations of conductors—from George Szellthrough Pierre Boulez, Christoph von Dohnanyi, and Franz Wilser-Most
Wide technical range; can play any piece with excellence, no matter how difficult— from soothing and familiar classical pieces to difficult and unfamiliar modern pieces	A key point of civic pride; cab drivers say, "We're really proud of our orchestra."	Supporters donate time and money; invest in long-term success of orchestra; endowment triples
Increased demand for tickets; demand for more complex, imaginative programs in Cleveland, New York, and Europe	Orchestra leaders increasingly sought for leadership roles and perspectives in elite industry groups and gatherings	
Invited to Salzburg Festival (first time in 25 years), signifying elite status among top European orchestras		

Figure 13.3 Measuring Greatness at the Cleveland Orchestra.

Adapted from *Good to Great and the Social Sectors* by Jim Collins.

index. Sometimes an index is completely intangible, such as the customer satisfaction index developed by the University of Michigan.

Intangibles are often combined with a variety of tangibles to reflect the performance of a business unit, function, or project. Intangibles are also often associated with nonprofit, nongovernment, and public sector organizations. Figure 13.3 shows the performance measures reflecting greatness at the Cleveland Orchestra. For the Cleveland Orchestra, intangibles include such items as comments from cab drivers; tangibles include ticket sales. Collectively and regardless of how difficult they are to obtain, these data sets reflect the overall performance of the orchestra. [8]

Converting to Money

Converting the hard to measure to monetary values is challenging, to say the least. Examples in this chapter show various attempts to convert these hard-to-value measures to monetary values. When working with intangibles, the interest in the monetary contribution expands considerably. Three major groups have an interest in the monetary value. First are the sponsors who fund a particular project. They almost always seek monetary values among the measures. Second, the public is involved in some way with many intangibles. Even private sector organizations are trying to improve their image and reputation, and public confidence. These days, the public is interested in the financial impacts of these organizations. They are no longer willing to accept the notion that the intangibles are enough to fund projects, particularly if they are funded by tax dollars. Third, the individuals who are actively involved with and support the project often need, and sometimes demand, that the monetary value be developed.

The approaches to convert to monetary values were detailed in Chapter 12. The specific methods used in that chapter all represent approaches that may be used to convert the intangibles to monetary values. Although these methods will not be repeated here, showing the path most commonly used to capture values for the intangibles is helpful. Figure 13.4 shows the typical path of converting intangibles to monetary values, building on the methods in Chapter 12.

The first challenge is to locate existing data or measure the intangible item in some way, making sure the data are accurate and reliable. Next, an expert may be able to place a monetary value on the item based on experience, knowledge, credentials, and track record. Stakeholders may provide their input, although it should be factored for bias. Some stakeholders are biased in one way or the other – they want the value to be smaller or

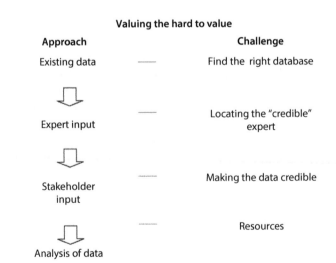

Figure 13.4 Valuing the Hard to Value.

larger depending on their particular motives. These inputs may have to be adjusted or thrown out altogether. Finally, the data are converted using the conservative processes described in Chapter 12, often adjusting for the error in the process. Unfortunately, no specific rule exists for converting each intangible to monetary value. By definition, an intangible is a measure that is not converted to money. If the conversion cannot be accomplished with minimum resources and with credibility, it is left as an intangible.

Identifying and Collecting Intangibles

Intangible measures can be taken from different sources and at different times during the project life cycle, as depicted in Figure 13.5. They can be uncovered early in the process, during alignment and needs assessment, and their collection can be planned for as part of the overall data collection strategy. For example, one technology project has several hard data measures linked to it. Job stress, an intangible measure, is also identified and monitored with no plans to convert it to a monetary value. From the beginning, this measure is destined to be a nonmonetary, intangible benefit reported with the ROI results.

A second opportunity to identify intangible benefits is in the planning process, when clients or sponsors of the project agree on an evaluation plan. Key stakeholders can usually identify the intangible measures they expect to be influenced by the project. For example, a change management project in a large multinational company was conducted, and an ROI analysis was

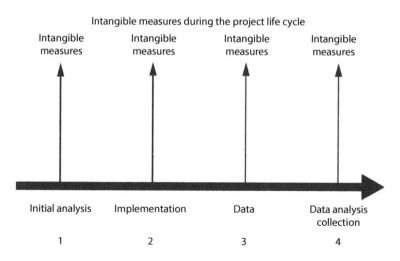

Figure 13.5   Identifying Intangible Measures during the Project Life Cycle.

planned. Project leaders, participants, participants' managers, and experts identified potential intangible measures that were perceived to be influenced by the project, including collaboration, communication, and teamwork.

A third opportunity to collect intangible measures presents itself during data collection. Although the measure may not be anticipated in the initial project design, it may surface on a questionnaire, in an interview, or during a focus group. Questions are often asked about other improvements linked to a project, and participants usually provide several intangible measures for which no plans are available to assign a value. For example, in the evaluation of a quality project, participants were asked what specifically had improved about their work area and relationships with customers as a result of the project. Participants provided more than a dozen intangible measures that managers attributed to the project.

The fourth opportunity to identify intangible measures is during data analysis and reporting, while attempting to convert data to monetary values. If the conversion loses credibility, the measure should be reported as an intangible benefit. For example, in one sales improvement project, customer satisfaction was identified early in the process as a measure of project success. A conversion to monetary values was attempted, but it lacked accuracy and credibility. Consequently, customer satisfaction was reported as an intangible benefit.

Analyzing Intangibles

For each intangible measure identified, some evidence of its connection to the innovation project must be shown. However, in many cases, no specific analysis is planned beyond tabulation of responses. Early attempts to quantify intangible data sometimes resulted in aborting the entire process, with no further data analysis being conducted. In some cases, isolating the effects of the project may be undertaken using one or more of the methods outlined in Chapter 12. This step is necessary when project leaders need to know the specific amount of change in the intangible measure that is linked to the project. Intangible data often reflect improvement. However, neither the precise amount of improvement nor the amount of improvement directly related to a project is always identified. Because the value of these data is not included in the ROI calculation, intangible measures are not normally used to justify another project, or to justify continuing an existing project. A detailed analysis is not necessary. Intangible benefits are often viewed as additional evidence of the project's success, and are presented as supportive qualitative data.

Final Thoughts

Intangible measures are crucial to reflecting the success of an innovation project. Although they may not carry the weight of measures expressed in monetary terms, they are nevertheless an important part of the overall evaluation. Intangible measures should be identified, explored, examined, and monitored for changes linked to projects. Collectively, they add a unique dimension to the project report because most, if not all, projects involve intangible variables. The range of intangible measures is practically limitless.

Now that we've identified intangible measures, we must capture the overall project costs and calculate the ROI. We'll discuss these two steps in the next chapter.

14

Measuring ROI

A publically owned electrical utility serving several states in the USA was very interested in controlling costs for its twelve power generating locations, ranging from coal fired to nuclear power. Top executives realize that the creative spirit often lies with the employees who know where improvements can be made and can see innovative opportunities to reduce costs. They wanted to tap the creativity of the team and pay them for the ideas.

The approach taken is a classic suggestion system based on cost savings which has been implemented by many organizations, often with good success. Benchmarking data suggest that, if implemented properly, about 10% of the workforce would actually make suggestions. The General Manager had requested an evaluation of the program at the ROI level.

As the Organization Effectiveness (OE) team implemented the system, they were very well aware of what's necessary to achieve this success. Using the ROI Methodology, they started with the end in mind and that's direct cost reduction or cost avoidance as the impact. There would also be some other impacts involving efficiency, effectiveness, and some intangibles such as commitment, engagement, satisfaction, and teamwork.

They knew that the reaction would be easy to measure. For learning, it's important for the employees to know how to make a suggestion, how it's evaluated, when it's evaluated, who evaluates it, when they will be notified, and when they receive the money. These knowledge points are necessary for employees to see the value of the system and plan to make suggestions. In meetings with all employees, the system was described with examples and, at the end of the meeting, reaction data were collected and learning data captured with an anonymous non-threatening true/false quiz to make sure they know how it works. At level 3, Application, employees are making the suggestions using an objective of 10%.

Since the OE team perceived this system to be operational for several years, the value stream for monetary benefits was set for two years. This time period was agreed to at the very beginning of the project, before implementation. This meant that two years of operating data would be captured and compared to the total cost of the program. Incidentally, the OE team had the luxury of waiting for this period of time. If there was pressure to see value sooner the cost savings from projects are accumulating earlier, and be projected for a two-year period assuming the same rate of idea submission and implementation.

From the beginning, the General Manager was concerned about the cost of the program. Anticipating much activity, the system project manager staffed up for the new system, placing a full-time Suggestion System Administrator (SSA) in each of their twelve facilities and four in the corporate office. These costs are significant and the GM was anxiously awaiting an ROI study after two years of operation.

When a person made a suggestion for cost savings and it's implemented, the anticipated life of that idea is established. Some would have a long life because a process is changed that will continue for a long time. Others would simply be a one time adjustment. That life value was established following some conservative financial principles and the payout is based on the life of the suggestion, not waiting until the cost savings has actually materialized. This approach is motivational for the employees because they can submit ideas that could have a five year stream, and those employees will be paid for the total amount when their suggestions were implemented. Figure 14.1 explains how the chain of impact works with the results at different levels.

The monetary savings generated for the program over a two year period were a total of $1.52 million, an impressive number. Had the evaluation stopped at that point, the group would be celebrating this milestone. However, the GM wanted to see comparison with the total cost, including the administrative cost, the salaries of the staff, their operating expenses, the actual payouts to employees, and any upfront development costs associated with the system. When the costs were tallied, the number was $2.1 million.

Employee suggestion system				
Type of data	**Data collection method**	**Data source**	**Timing**	**Results**
Reaction (Level 1)	Survey	Employees	At the end of the announcement meeting	4.3 out of 5 rating on motivational, satisfaction, and engaging
Learning (Level 2)	Quiz	Employees	At the end of the announcement meeting	7.5 out of 10 on the procedures, case documentation, award determination, and notification
Application and Implementation (Level 3)	Monitor Records	Employee Suggestion System	Routinely	10.4% participation rate
Business Impact (Level 4)	Monitor Business Performance	Employee Suggestion System	Routinely	$1.52 million in 2 years
Cost	Monitor Records	Cost Statements	Annually	$2.1 million cost in 2 years
ROI(Level 5)	—	—	—	-28%
Intangibles	Questionnaire	Sample of Employees	Annually	Increased cooperation, commitment to the organization, engagement, employee satisfaction, and teamwork

Figure 14.1 Types and Levels of Data.

The ROI is a negative value because the total operational costs ($2.1 million) exceed the monetary benefits during the same two-year period. ROI presents the ultimate accountability as the monetary benefits ($1.52 million) are compared to the cost ($2.1 million):

$$\text{ROI} = \frac{\$1.52 \text{ million} - \$2.1 \text{ million}}{\$2.1 \text{ million}} \times 100 = -28\% \text{ ROI}$$

With these negative results, the team was very disappointed and suggested that perhaps it should be continued because of important intangibles of teamwork, commitment, engagement, and satisfaction. While that logic may be feasible in some programs, the GM emphasized that it would not work here. Because the nature of this initiative is based on providing cost savings, it would not be suitable to spend more money on a cost saving system than it is providing in cost reduction or cost avoidance. The GM asked, "How will this look in the newspaper? Because we're government and we're transparent with our innovation projects, it will probably be in the newspaper." Incidentally, he reminded the team that they had an objective for a positive ROI, "Although we didn't set a precise objective, we wanted us to have more savings than its costing."

The good news is that the adjustment to make it positive was very obvious to the OE team. There were too many staff members. During data collection for the study, it appeared that the staff was only about 25% utilized in the operating plants. One person perhaps could cover two or more plants and that would not necessarily lower the outcomes.

Eight jobs were eliminated and the employees in those jobs were placed in open jobs so that no one actually lost their job, but went to an open position. This is important because without this action there's really no cost reduction for operations. Going forward with this reduction, a very positive ROI is generated.

This study shows two important issues about ROI analysis. First, you don't see the ultimate accountability until you push the evaluation to the ROI level. Second, because the program is not working doesn't mean that it is discontinued. In fact, it's rare that that's the case. The project is adjusted to deliver the value that it should be delivering.

This chapter explores the costs of innovation projects and the ROI calculation. Specific costs that should be captured are identified, along with economical ways in which they can be developed. One of the primary challenges addressed in this chapter is deciding which costs should be captured or estimated. For major projects, some costs are hidden and rarely counted. The conservative philosophy presented here is to account for all costs, direct and indirect. Several checklists and guidelines are included. The monetary values for the benefits of a project are combined with project cost data to calculate the return on investment. In this chapter we explain the various techniques, processes, and issues involved in calculating and interpreting the ROI.

Why Monitor Costs and Measure ROI?

One of the main reasons for monitoring costs is to create budgets for projects. The initial costs of most projects are usually estimated during the proposal process, and are often based on previous projects. The only way to have a clear understanding of costs so that they can be used to determine future projects and future budgets is to track them using different categories, as explained later in this chapter.

Costs should be monitored in an ongoing effort to control expenditures, and keep the project within budget. Monitoring cost activities not only reveals the status of expenditures but also gives visibility to expenditures, and encourages the entire project team to spend wisely. And, of course, monitoring costs in an ongoing fashion is much easier, more accurate, and more efficient than trying to reconstruct events to capture costs retrospectively. Developing accurate costs by category builds a database for understanding and predicting costs in the future.

Monitoring project costs is an essential step in developing the ROI calculation because it represents the denominator in the ROI formula. ROI has become a critical measure demanded by many stakeholders, including clients and senior executives. It is the ultimate level of evaluation, showing the actual payoff of the project, expressed as a percentage and based on the same formula as the evaluation for other types of capital investment.

Fundamental Cost Issues

The first step in monitoring costs is to define and address issues relating to cost control. Several rules apply to tabulating costs. Consistency and standardization are necessary. A few guidelines follow:

- Monitor all costs, even if they are not needed.
- Costs must be realistic and reasonable.
- Costs will not be precise; estimates are okay.
- Disclose all costs.

Other key issues are detailed later in this section.

Fully Loaded Costs

During the Obama administration, investigators recovered a record-breaking $4.1 billion in healthcare fraud money during 2011, a reflection of the Obama administration's increased focus on fighting fraud. At the time, USA Today noted that the federal government collected $7.20 for every dollar spent on fighting fraud according to the department of Health and Human Services (HHS) inspector general. [1] This ratio translates to an ROI calculation of 620 percent, representing an impressive return on investment of expenditures in tackling healthcare fraud. The officials attributed much of the progress to nine enforcement action teams in cities such as Chicago and Miami. The government increased funding to Senior Medicare Patrol teams from $9 million in 2010 to $18 million in 2011 in the form of Administration on Aging grants in fraud-heavy states such as California and Michigan.

With this impressive ROI came much scrutiny. Some of the critics of this program asked for an account of the benefits to see whether conservative assumptions were made in the analysis. The critics wanted to under-stand whether all of the costs to capture the fraud were included, including costs with justice systems' time and direct expenses. Sometimes these factors are underestimated in calculations. Finally, they wanted to know whether other factors outside of these patrol teams could have reduced the expenditures. At the last count, the Justice Department and HHS had not provided clear answers to these questions.

This story points out the importance of having credible analysis when the project culminates with an actual ROI calculation. ROI data are likely to be scrutinized. ROI is the one measure that is often emotional; if the measure is too high it becomes unbelievable, if the measure is too low or negative, top executives want to place blame and use the information as punitive, rather than as a process improvement tool.

Because a conservative approach is used to calculate the ROI, costs should be fully loaded, which is Guiding Principle #10 (see Chapter 4). With this approach, all costs (direct and indirect) that can be identified and linked to a particular project are included. The philosophy is simple: for the denominator, "when in doubt, put it in" (i.e., if there is any question as to whether a cost should be included, include it, even if the cost guidelines for the organization do not require it). When an ROI is calculated and reported to target audiences, the process should withstand even the closest scrutiny, when necessary, to ensure its credibility. The only way to meet this test is to include all costs. Of course, from a realistic viewpoint, if the controller or chief financial officer insists on not using certain costs, then leaving them out or reporting them in an alternative way is suggested.

Costs Reported without Benefits

A top administrator in the Ministry of Innovation asked about the success of all the design thinking workshops that had been conducted in organizations in this Southeast Asian country. The project team responded with the number of workshops, number of participants, and the total costs of the project. The Minister was disappointed and asked for the outcomes.

Because costs can easily be collected, they are presented to management in many ingenious ways, such as in terms of the total cost of the project, cost per day, and cost per participant. While these may be helpful for efficiency comparisons, presenting them without identifying the corresponding benefits may be problematic. When most executives review project costs, a logical question is raised: what benefit was received from the project? This is a typical management reaction, particularly when costs are perceived to be very high.

Unfortunately, many organizations have fallen into this trap. For example, in one organization, all the costs associated with a major transformation project were tabulated and reported to the senior management team. From an executive perspective, the total figure exceeded the perceived value of the project, and the executive group's immediate reaction was to request a summary of (monetary and nonmonetary) benefits derived from the overall transformation. The conclusion was that few, if any, economic benefits were achieved from the project. Consequently, budgets for similar projects were drastically reduced in the future. While this may be an extreme example, it shows the danger of presenting only half the equation. Because of this, some organizations have developed a policy of not communicating cost data unless the benefits can be captured and presented along with the costs, even if the benefits are subjective and intangible. This helps maintain a balance between the two components.

Develop and Use Cost Guidelines

When multiple projects are being evaluated, it may be helpful to detail the philosophy and policy on costs in the form of guidelines for the evaluators or others who monitor and report costs. Cost guidelines detail specifically which cost categories are included with projects, and how the data are captured, analyzed, and reported. Standards, unit cost guiding principles, and generally accepted values are included in the guidelines. Cost guidelines can range from a one-page brief to a 100-page document in a large, complex organization. The simpler approach is better. When fully developed, cost guidelines should be reviewed and approved by the finance and accounting staff. The final document serves as the guiding force in collecting, monitoring, and reporting costs. When the ROI is calculated and reported, costs are included in summary or table form, and the cost guidelines are usually referenced in a footnote or attached as an appendix.

Source of costs	Cost reporting issues
Project team fees and expenses	• Costs are usually accurate • Variable expenses are usually underestimated
Vendor/suppliers fees and expenses	• Costs are usually accurate • Variable expenses are usually underestimated
Client expenses, direct and indirect	• Direct expenses are usually not fully loaded • Indirect expenses are rarely included in costs • Sometimes understated
Equipment, services, and other expenses	• May lack accountability

Figure 14.2 Sources of innovation project costs.

Sources of Costs

It is sometimes helpful to first consider the sources of innovation project costs. Four major categories of sources are illustrated in Figure 14.2. The charges and expenses from the project team represent the major segment of costs, and are usually transferred directly to the client for payment. These are often placed in subcategories under fees and expenses. A second major cost category relates to the vendors or suppliers who assist with the project. A variety of expenses, such as consulting or advisory fees, may fall in this category. A third major cost category is those expenses borne by the client organization, both direct and indirect. In many projects, these costs are not identified but nevertheless are part of the costs of the project. The final cost category involves expenses not covered in the other three categories. These include payments for equipment and services needed for the project. Finance and accounting records should track and reflect the costs from these different sources, and the process presented in this chapter can also help track these costs.

Prorated versus Direct Costs

Usually all costs related to a project are captured and expensed to that project. However, some costs are prorated over a longer period. Equipment purchases, software development and acquisitions, and the construction of facilities are all significant costs with a useful life that may extend beyond the project. Consequently, a portion of these costs should be prorated to the project. Under a conservative approach, the expected life of the project is fixed. Some organizations will assume a period of one year of operation for a simple project. Others may consider three to five years as appropriate. If a question is raised about the specific time period to be used in this calculation, the finance and accounting staff should be consulted, or appropriate guidelines should be developed and followed.

Employee Benefits Factor

Employee time is valuable, and when time is required for a project, the costs for that time must be fully loaded, representing total compensation including employee benefits. This means that the employee benefits factor should be included. This number is usually well known in the organization and is used in other costing formulas. It represents the cost of all employee benefits expressed as a percentage of payroll. In some organizations, this value is as high as 50–60%. In others, it may be as low as 25–30%. The average in the United States is 38% [2].

Specific Costs to Include

Figure 14.3 shows the recommended cost categories for a fully loaded, conservative approach to estimating project costs. Consistency in capturing all

Cost Item	Prorated	Expensed
Initial analysis and assessment	✓	
Development of solutions	✓	
Acquisition of solutions	✓	
Implementation and application		
Salaries/benefits for project team time		✓
Salaries/benefits for coordination time		✓
Salaries/benefits for participant time		✓
Project materials		✓
Hardware/software	✓	
Travel/lodging/meals		✓
Use of facilities		✓
Capital expenditures	✓	
Maintenance and monitoring		✓
Administrative support and overhead	✓	
Evaluation and reporting		✓

Figure 14.3 Project Cost Categories

these costs is essential, and standardization adds credibility. Each category is described in this section.

Initial Analysis and Assessment

One of the most underestimated items is the cost of conducting the initial analysis and assessment that leads to the need for the project. In a comprehensive innovation project, this involves data collection, problem solving, assessment, and analysis. In some projects, this cost is near zero because the project is implemented without an initial assessment of need. However, as more project sponsors place attention on needs assessment and analysis in the future, this item will become a significant cost.

Development of Project Solutions

Also significant are the costs of designing and developing the project. These costs include time spent in both the design and development, and the purchase of supplies, technology, and other materials directly related to the solution. As with needs assessment costs, design and development costs are usually charged to the project. However, if the solution can be used in other projects, the major expenditures can be prorated.

Acquisition Costs

In lieu of development costs, some project leaders use acquisition costs connected to the purchasing of solutions from other sources, to use directly or in a modified format. The costs for these solutions include the purchase price, support materials, and licensing agreements. Some projects have both acquisition costs and solution development costs. Acquisition costs can be prorated if the acquired solutions can be used in other projects.

Implementation Costs

The largest cost segment in a project is associated with implementation and delivery. The time (salaries and benefits), travel, and other expenses of those involved in the project in any way should be included. These costs can be estimated using average or midpoint salary values for corresponding job classifications. When a project is targeted for an ROI calculation, participants can provide their salaries directly in a confidential manner. Project materials, such as field journals, instructions, reference guides, case studies, surveys, and participant workbooks, should be included in the implementation costs, along with license fees, user fees, and royalty payments. Supporting hardware, software, and videos should also be included.

The cost for the use of facilities needed for the project should be included. For external meetings, this is the direct charge for the conference center, hotel, or motel. If the meetings are conducted in-house, the conference room represents a cost for the organization, and the cost should be estimated and incorporated, even if it is uncommon to include facilities costs in other cost reporting. If a facility or building is constructed or purchased for the project, it is included as a capital expenditure, but is prorated. The same is true for the purchase of major hardware and software when they are considered capital expenditures.

Maintenance and Monitoring

Maintenance and monitoring involve routine expenses necessary to maintain and operate the project. These are ongoing expenses that allow the new project solution to continue. They may involve staff members and additional expenses, and they may be significant for some projects.

Support and Overhead

The cost of support and overhead includes the additional costs not directly charged to the project – any project cost not considered in the above calculations. Typical items are the cost of administrative and clerical support, telecommunication expenses, office expenses, salaries of client managers, and other fixed costs. Usually, this is provided in the form of an estimate allocated in some convenient way.

Evaluation and Reporting

The total evaluation cost completes the fully loaded costs. Activities under evaluation costs include developing the evaluation strategy, designing instruments, collecting data, analyzing data, preparing a report, and communicating the results. Cost categories include time, materials, purchased instruments, surveys, and any consulting fees.

The ROI Calculation

The term return on investment for projects and programs is occasionally misused, sometimes intentionally. In this misuse, we find a very broad definition for ROI is given that includes any benefit from the project. ROI becomes a vague concept in which even subjective data linked to a program are included.

In this book, the return on investment is defined more precisely and represents an actual value determined by comparing project costs to benefits. The two most common measures are the benefits/costs ratio (BCR) and the ROI formula. Both are presented, along with other approaches to calculate the return or payback.

The formulas presented in this chapter use annualized values so that the first-year impact of the investment can be calculated for short-term projects. Using annualized values is becoming an accepted practice for developing the ROI in many organizations. This approach is a conservative way to develop the ROI, since many short-term projects have added value in the second or third year. For long-term projects, longer time frames should be used. For example, in an ROI analysis of a project involving major software purchases, a five-year time frame was used. However, for short-term projects that take only a few weeks to implement (such as a leadership development program), first-year values are appropriate.

In selecting the approach to measure ROI, the formula used and the assumptions made in arriving at the decision to use this formula should be communicated to the target audience. This helps prevent misunderstandings and confusion surrounding how the ROI value was developed. Although several approaches are described in this chapter, two stand out as preferred methods: the benefits/costs ratio and the basic ROI formula. These two approaches are described next.

Benefits/Costs Ratio

One of the original methods for evaluating projects was the benefits/costs ratio. This method compares the benefits of the project with the costs, using a simple ratio. In formula form:

$$BCR = \frac{\text{Project Benefits}}{\text{Project Costs}}$$

In simple terms, the BCR compares the annual economic benefits of the project with the costs of the project. A BCR of 1 means that the benefits equal the costs. A BCR of 2, usually written as 2:1, indicates that for each dollar spent on the project, two dollars were returned in benefits.

The following example illustrates the use of the BCR. An innovation project was implemented at an electric and gas utility. In a follow-up evaluation, action planning and business performance monitoring were used to capture the benefits. The first-year payoff for the program was $1,077,750. The total, fully loaded implementation costs were $215,500. Thus, the ratio was:

$$BCR = \frac{\$1,077,750}{\$215,500} = 5:1$$

For every dollar invested in the project, five dollars in benefits were realized.

ROI Formula

Perhaps the most appropriate formula for evaluating project investments is net program benefits divided by costs. This is the traditional financial ROI, and is directly related to the BCR. The ROI ratio is usually expressed as a percentage where the fractional values are multiplied by 100. In formula form:

$$ROI(\%) = \frac{\text{Net project benefits}}{\text{Projects costs}} \times 100$$

Net project benefits are project benefits minus costs. Another way to calculate ROI is to subtract 1 from the BCR and multiply by 100 to get the ROI percentage. For example, a BCR of 2.45 is the same as an ROI value of 145% (1.45 x 100%). This formula is essentially the same as the ROI for capital investments. For example, when a firm builds a new plant, the ROI is developed by dividing annual earnings by the investment. The annual earnings are comparable to net benefits (annual benefits minus the cost). The investment is comparable to the fully loaded project costs.

An ROI of 50% means that the costs were recovered, and an additional 50% of the costs were returned. A project ROI of 150% indicates that the costs have been recovered, and an additional 1.5 times the costs are returned.

An example illustrates the ROI calculation. Public and private sector groups concerned about literacy have developed a variety of projects to address the issue. Magnavox Electronics Systems Company was involved in one unique literacy project that focused on language and math skills for entry-level electrical and mechanical assemblers. The results of the project were impressive. Productivity and quality alone yielded an annual value of $321,600.

The total, fully loaded costs for the project were just $38,233. Thus, the return on investment was:

$$\text{ROI} = \frac{\left(\$321,600 - \$38,233\right)}{\$38,233} \times 100$$

For each dollar invested, Magnavox received $7.41 in return after the costs of the project were recovered.

Investments in plants, equipment, subsidiaries, or other major items are not usually evaluated using the benefits/costs method. Using the ROI formula to calculate the return on project investments essentially places these investments on a level playing field with other investments whose valuation uses the same formula and similar concepts. The ROI calculation is easily understood by key management and financial executives who regularly work with investments and their ROIs.

Profits can be generated through increased sales or cost savings. Typically in practice, there are more opportunities for cost savings than for profits. Cost savings can be realized when improvements in productivity, quality, efficiency, cycle time, or actual cost reduction occur. In a review of almost 500 studies, the vast majority of them were based on cost savings. Approximately 85% of the studies used a payoff based on cost savings from output, quality, efficiency, time, or a variety of soft data measures. The others used a payoff based on sales increases, where the earnings were derived from the profit margin. Cost savings are important for nonprofits and public-sector organizations, where opportunities for profit are often unavailable. Most projects or programs are connected directly to cost savings; ROIs can still be developed in such settings.

The formula provided above should be used consistently throughout an organization. Deviations from or misuse of the formula can create confusion, not only among users but also among finance and accounting staff. The chief financial officer (CFO) and the finance and accounting staff should become partners in the implementation of the ROI Methodology. The project staff must use the same financial terms as those used and expected by the CFO. Without the support, involvement, and commitment of these individuals, the wide-scale use of ROI will be unlikely.

Figure 14.4 shows some financial terms that are misused in literature. Terms such as return on ideas (or innovation), abbreviated as ROI, do nothing but confuse the CFO, who assumes that ROI refers to the return on investment described above. Sometimes return on expectations (ROE), return on anticipation (ROA), and return on client expectations (ROCE) are used, also confusing the CFO, who assumes the abbreviations refer to return on equity, return on assets, and return on capital employed,

Term	Misuse	CFO Definition
ROI	Return on ideas	Return on investment
	Return of impact	
	Return of information	
	Return on Innovation	
	Return on inspiration	
	Return of intelligence	
ROE	Return on expectation	Return on equity
	Return on events	
ROA	Return on anticipation	Return on assets
ROCE	Return on client expectation	Return on capital employed
ROP	Return on people	?
ROR	Return on resources	?
ROT	Return on technology	?
ROW	Return on web	?
ROM	Return on marketing	?
ROO	Return on objectives	?
ROQ	Return on quality	?
ROC	Return on character	?

Figure 14.4 Misused Financial Terms.

respectively. The use of these terms in the payback calculation of a project will also confuse and perhaps lose the support of the finance and accounting staff. Other terms such as return on people, return on resources, return on technology, and return on web are often used with almost no consistency in terms of financial calculations. The bottom line: don't confuse the CFO. Consider this person an ally, and use the same terminology, processes, and concepts when applying financial returns for projects.

ROI Objective

Specific expectations for ROI should be developed before an evaluation study is undertaken. Although no generally accepted standards exist, four strategies have been used to establish a minimum expected requirement, or hurdle rate, for the ROI of a project or program.

The first approach is to set the ROI using the same values used for investing in capital expenditures, such as equipment, facilities, and new companies. For North America, Western Europe, and most of the Asia-Pacific area, including Australia and New Zealand, the cost of capital is quite low, and the internal hurdle rate for ROI is usually in the 15–20% range. Thus, using this strategy, organizations would set the expected ROI for a project at the same value expected from other investments.

A second strategy is to use an ROI minimum target value that is above the percentage expected for other types of investments. The rationale is that the ROI process for projects and programs is still relatively new and often involves subjective input, including estimations. Because of this, a higher standard is required or suggested.

A third strategy is to set the ROI value at a breakeven point. A 0% ROI represents breakeven; this is equivalent to a BCR of 1. This approach is used when the goal is to recapture the cost of the project only. This is the ROI objective for many public-sector organizations, where most or all of the value and benefit from the program come through the intangible measures, which are not converted to monetary values. Thus, an organization will use a breakeven point for the ROI based on the reasoning that it is not attempting to make a profit from a particular project.

A fourth and often the recommended strategy is to let the client or program sponsor set the minimum acceptable ROI value. In this scenario, the individual who initiates, approves, sponsors, or supports the project establishes the acceptable ROI. Almost every project has a major sponsor, and that person may be willing to specify an acceptable value. This links the expectations for financial return directly to the expectations of the sponsor.

Other ROI Measures

In addition to the traditional ROI formula, several other measures are occasionally used under the general heading of return on investment. These measures are designed primarily for evaluating other financial measures but sometimes work their way into project evaluations.

Payback Period (Breakeven Analysis)

The payback period is commonly used for evaluating capital expenditures. With this approach, the annual cash proceeds (savings) produced by an investment are compared against the original cash outlay for the investment to determine the multiple of cash proceeds that is equal to the original investment. Measurement is usually in terms of years and months. For example, if the cost savings generated from a project are constant each year, the payback period is determined by dividing the original cash investment (including development costs, expenses, etc.) by the expected or actual annual savings. The net savings are found by subtracting the project expenses.

To illustrate this calculation, assume that the initial cost of a project is $100,000, and the project has a three-year useful life. Annual net savings from the project are expected to be $40,000. Thus, the payback period is:

$$\text{Payback period}=\frac{\text{Total investments}}{\text{Annual savings}}=\frac{\$100,000}{\$40,000}=2.5\text{years}$$

In this case, the project will "pay back" the original investment in 2.5 years.

The payback period method is simple to use but has the limitation of ignoring the time value of money.

Discounted Cash Flow

Discounted cash flow is a method of evaluating investment opportunities in which certain values are assigned to the timing of the proceeds from the investment. The assumption behind this approach is that a dollar earned today is more valuable than a dollar earned a year from now, based on the accrued interest possible from investing the dollar.

There are several ways of using the discounted cash flow concept to evaluate a project investment. The most common approach uses the net present value of an investment. The savings each year are compared with the outflow of cash required by the investment. The expected annual savings are discounted based on a selected interest rate, and the outflow of cash is discounted by the same interest rate. If the present value of the savings exceeds the present value of the outlays after the two have been discounted by the common interest rate, the investment is usually considered acceptable by management. The discounted cash flow method has the advantage of ranking investments, but it requires calculations that can become difficult. Also, for the most part, it is subjective.

Internal Rate of Return

The internal rate of return (IRR) method determines the interest rate necessary to make the present value of the cash flow equal zero. This represents the maximum rate of interest that could be paid if all project funds were borrowed, and the organization was required to break even on the project. The IRR considers the time value of money, and is unaffected by the scale of the project. It can be used to rank alternatives, and to accept or reject decisions when a minimum rate of return is specified. A major weakness of the IRR method is that it assumes all returns are reinvested at the same internal rate of return. This can make an investment alternative with a high rate of return look even better than it really is, and make a project with a low rate of return look even worse. In practice, the IRR is rarely used to evaluate project investments.

Final Thoughts

ROI, the final evaluation level, compares costs with benefits. Costs are important, and should be fully loaded in the ROI calculation. From a practical standpoint, some costs may be optional, and depend on the organization's guidelines and philosophy. However, because of the scrutiny ROI calculations typically receive, all costs should be included, even if this goes beyond the requirements of the organization's policy. After the benefits are collected and converted to monetary values and the innovation project costs are tabulated, the ROI calculation itself is easy. Plugging the values into the appropriate formula is the final step. We presented the two basic approaches for calculating return: the ROI formula and the benefits/costs ratio in this chapter. Each has its advantages and disadvantages. We also briefly discussed alternatives to the standard ROI determination.

Now that we have fully detailed the process, our next chapter details how to forecast the value of a project, including its ROI.

15

Forecasting Value, Including ROI

Lars Rienhold, CEO, is proud of the accomplishments of Family Mutual Health and Life Insurance Company (FMI), which has enjoyed a rich history of serving families throughout North America for almost 80 years. With a focus on health and life insurance products, FMI is regarded as a very innovative and low-cost health insurance provider. Top executives are proud of their cost control efforts and the low prices they can offer. Company advertisements regularly highlight their low-cost approach, quality of service and ethical practices. [1]

Lars is a man of considerable and contagious personality, continually trying to offer affordable health and life insurance policies, provide excellent customer service, and be a responsible citizen. As part of this effort, Lars wanted to ensure that FMI was doing all it could to help the environment. While FMI's carbon footprint is relatively low compared to manufacturing companies, its headquarters was located in a congested area where employees had high commute times. This is having an impact on the environment.

During a recent trip to Calgary, Canada, he saw a television report about a local company that had implemented a work-at-home program. The report presented the actual amount of carbon emissions that had been

273

prevented with this project. Lars thought that FMI should be able to implement a similar program, with the possibility of employees working from home. He brought this idea to Melissa Lufkin, executive vice president of human resources. The message was short. "I want us to make a difference. I think this is the way to do it. But we can't just let people work from home. We have to make the office at home look, feel, and function like the office at headquarters." Lars added that this is major change in policy and can be quite expensive. He added, "Let's consider this for a few job groups but forecast the ROI before we proceed. This must add business value."

Melissa began her investigation by discussing the issue with the operations chief. Although there was some resistance, John Speegle, executive vice president of operations, was interested in exploring the idea. John was concerned about the lack of a productivity increase in the past three years with the largest segment of employees, the claims processors and the claims examiners. That should be the target. About 950 employees are involved in processing or examining claims submitted by customers or healthcare providers. Claims examiners reviewed claims that were disputed or when an audit sparked a review of a particular claim. These job groups had grown to the point that the office space they occupied in Building 2 was overflowing, impeding productivity. Given the company's continued growth, it was likely that a new building space or perhaps a new facility was needed to manage the growth.

John was very interested in lowering the real estate cost of new office space, which averaged about $17,000 per person per year and improving productivity, which was at a rate of 33.2 claims processed and 20.7 claims examined per day.

Melissa discussed the issue with Linda Green, the vice president of claims, to hear her concerns about processors and examiners working at home. Linda was supportive but raised some concerns. "Some of our managers want to keep tabs on what is going on and they think employees need to be in the building to see that everyone is working and busy. I'm afraid it is a matter of control, which they may have a hard time giving up if people work remotely." Linda added, "I realize that the right approach might make their jobs easier, but right now they may not be at that point."

Next, Melissa met with the IT department and discussed how they could equip workstations at home with the latest technology. She found a supportive audience in Tim Holleman, senior vice president and chief information officer, who thought that employees could be setup with adequate security and technology to work at home in the same manner as they were working onsite. Tim added, "They can have full access to all databases and they could be using high-speed processes. It would cost FMI a substantial amount the first year, but may not represent a very significant cost in the long run."

Melissa then contacted Anne Burson, executive vice president of sales and marketing, to uncover any customer service issues that might arise. Anne was in favor of the move as long as customer service would not suffer. The claims examiners were in direct contact with the customers and she wanted to make sure that acceptable customer service was maintained. Also, many of the processors had to make routine direct telephone or email contact with healthcare suppliers, as well as patients, and they wanted to maintain these contacts at an acceptable level.

Lastly, Melissa met with the chief financial officer, Rodrick Harper, to discuss the project and the plan to measure its success. Melissa was eager to show the value of the innovation project and had challenged her staff to measure success, even using ROI. Rod's interest really piqued. He said, "Let's make sure this is very credible analysis and that it is very conservative. Frankly, I think we want to be involved when you discuss ROI. I think it's proper that we use a standard approach to analysis and we would like to be involved in this every step of the way, if you don't mind." Melissa was pleased with the support, but somewhat anxious about working with the Finance and Accounting Team to evaluate a project that she ultimately would own.

Melissa and her staff explored the anticipated reaction of the employees to determine how they would perceive a work-at-home program. She was not sure how many would take advantage of the opportunity. The staff conservatively estimated that at least a third would opt to participate in the program. For many in this group, working at home would be a huge motivator and would make a difference in retaining them at FMI. Current annualized turnover of the two groups is 22.3%.

With the approval of the key team, Melissa and her team got busy developing the forecast. The first step is to pinpoint the objectives. Figure 15.1 shows the objectives for the project by different levels, ranging from reaction to ROI. Melissa secured agreement on the objectives from those stakeholders involved.

With a clear understanding of the proposed project and the connection to the business impact measures, a forecast was now possible.

The first important input to the forecast was the expected number of employees who would participate. The HR Team thought that about one-third of employees would sign up for this program. One-third of 950 is 317, so the forecast is based on 317 participating employees. Based on the percentage makeup of the two groups, this translates into 237 and 80, respectively, for processors and examiners.

After implementing this project:
Reaction
• Employees should see the work-at-home project as satisfying, important, rewarding, and motivational. • Managers must see this project as necessary, appropriate, and important to FMI.
Learning
• Employees must know the realities of working at home, the conditions, roles, and regulations. • Employees must have the discipline and tenacity to work at home. • Managers must be able to explain company policy and regulations for working at home. • Managers must be able to manage remotely.
Application
• Managers should conduct a meeting with direct reports to discuss policy, expected behavior, and next steps. • At least 30% of eligible employees should volunteer for at-home assignments within one month. • At-home offices are built and should be properly equipped. • Work-at-home employees should work effectively at home. • The at-home workplace should be free from distractions and conflicting demands. • Managers should properly administer the company's policy. • Managers should manage the remote employees effectively.
Impact
For those involved in the program: • Commute time should be reduced to an average of 15 minutes per day. • Office expense per person should reduce by 20% in six months. • Productivity should increase by 5% in six months. • Employee turnover should reduce to 12% in six months. • Unplanned absenteeism should be reduced. • Stress should be reduced. • Carbon emissions should be reduced. • The company's image as a green company should be enhanced. • Employee engagement should improve.
ROI
• The company should achieve a 25% return on investment.

Figure 15.1 Detailed Objectives.

Figure 15.2 shows the development of the monetary forecast, following estimated improvement in business measures. The estimated business impact was obtained directly from the chief of operations and the vice president of claims. The monetary value of a claim also was obtained by these stakeholders, estimated to be $10 cost for processing a claim and $12 for review of a claim. The office expenses were estimated to be $17,000 and the cost of a turnover taken directly from a similar study (where the cost of turnover was pegged as a percent of annual pay) was provided at $25,400. With this in mind, the calculations are listed below:

Anticipated Participation
• Target Group: 950
• Predicted Enrollment: 1/3
• 950 x 33 1/3% = 317
• Allocation: 237 processors
80 examiners

Estimated Impact
• Productivity: 1 additional claim processed
1 additional claim examined
• Office expense: 20% reduction
$17,000 x 20% = $3,400
• Turnover reduction   22.3% to 12% = 10.3% improvement

Converting Productivity to Money
• Value of one claim = $10.00
• Value of one disputed claim = $12.00
• Daily improvement = 1 claim per day
• Daily improvement = 1 examined claim per day
• Annual value = 237 x 220 work days x 1 x 10.00 = $521,400
• Annual value = 80 x 220 days x 1 x 12.00 = $211,200

Office Expense Reduction
• Office expenses in company office: $17,000 annually per person
• Office expenses at home office: $13,600 first year per person
• Net improvement: $3,400, first year
• Total annual value = 317 x 3,400 = $1,077,800

Converting Turnover Reduction to Money
• Value of one turnover statistic = $25,400
• Annual improvement related to program = 10.3%
• Turnover prevention: 317 x 10.3% = 33 turnovers prevented
• Annual value = $25,400 x 33 = $838,200

Figure 15.2 Forecast of Monetary Benefits.

The costs of the project were estimated to be about $1 million. This estimate is the total cost including the amount of the initial analysis to determine whether this was the proper solution and the development of that solution. The majority of the charges were in the IT support and maintenance, administrative and coordination categories. When the monetary benefits are combined with the cost, the ROI forecast is developed, as shown in Figure 15.3.

Although this number is quite impressive, in her presentation to the senior executives, Melissa stressed that there were significant intangibles, such as the contribution to the environment, which is not included in this calculation. Other factors such as job satisfaction, job engagement, stress reduction and image were huge intangibles that should be directly

Total Forecasted Monetary Benefits		
Benefits =	$521,400 211,200 1,077,800 838,200 $2,648,600	Processor Productivity Examiner Productivity Office Costs Turnover Reduction
Costs =	$1,000,000	Conservative Estimate
BCR =	$2,648,600 $1,000,000	2.65
ROI =	$2,648,600 – 1,000,000 $1,000,000	165%

Figure 15.3 Forecasted ROI.

influenced from this. However, because these projects need to be based on good business decisions, the ROI forecast is credible and conservative and based on only one year of value. Much more value will be realized after the first year, because most of the office setup expenses will occur in the first year. The top executives felt comfortable with the analysis and gave the go ahead for the project.

This case study reveals the need to forecast ROI before the project is implemented. It also underscores the power of analysis for developing the forecast. Although critical for the go/no-go decision, the forecast also makes it a better project.

Confusion sometimes exists about when to develop the ROI. The traditional approach, which we described in previous chapters, is to base ROI calculations on business impact obtained after the project or program is implemented, using business performance measures converted to monetary values. With this chapter we illustrate that ROI can be calculated at earlier stages – even before the project or program is initiated.

Why Forecast ROI?

Although ROI calculations based on postproject data are the most accurate, sometimes it is important to know the forecast before the innovation project is initiated, or before final results are tabulated. Certain critical issues drive the need for a forecast before the project is completed, or even pursued.

Expensive Projects

In addition to reducing uncertainty, forecasting may be appropriate for costly projects. In these cases, implementation is not practical until the project has been analyzed to determine the potential ROI. For example, if the project involves a significant amount of effort in design, development, and implementation, a client may not want to expend the resources, not even for a pilot test, unless some assurance of a positive ROI can be given. In another example, an expensive equipment purchase may be necessary to launch a process or system. An ROI may be necessary before purchase, to ensure that the monetary value of the process outcomes outweigh the cost of equipment and implementation. While there may be trade-offs in deploying a lower-profile, lower-cost pilot, the preproject ROI is still important and may prompt some clients to stand firm until an ROI forecast is produced.

High Risks and Uncertainty

Sponsors want to remove as much uncertainty as possible from the innovation project, and act on the best data available. This concern sometimes pushes the project to a forecast ROI, even before any resources are expended to design and implement it. Some projects are high-risk opportunities or solutions. In addition to being expensive, they may represent critical initiatives that can make or break an organization. Or the situation may be one where failure would be disastrous, and where there is only one chance to get it right. In these cases, the decision maker must have the best data possible, and the best data possible often include a forecast ROI.

For example, one fine dining restaurant chain decided to eliminate the waiters. Customers were handed a tablet when they arrived. They perused the menu and wine list, made their order, and the food and wine was delivered by the kitchen. Ad the end of the meal, the bill was settled. Because of the project's high stakes and critical nature, company executives requested a forecast before pursuing the project. They needed to know not only whether this innovation would be worthwhile financially, but also what specifically would change, and how specifically the project would unfold. This required a comprehensive forecast involving various levels of data, up to and including the ROI.

Postproject Comparison

An important reason for forecasting ROI is to see how well the forecast holds up under the scrutiny of postproject analysis. Whenever a plan is in place to collect data on a project's success, comparing actual results to pre-project expectations is helpful. In an ideal world, a forecast ROI would have a defined relationship with the actual ROI – or at least one would lead to the other, after adjustments. The forecast is often an inexpensive process because it involves estimates and assumptions. If the forecast becomes a reliable pre-dictor of the postproject analysis, then the forecast ROI might substitute for the actual ROI. This could save money on the use of postproject analysis.

Compliance

More than ever, organizations are requiring a forecast ROI before they undertake major projects. For example, one organization requires any project with a budget exceeding $500,000 to have a forecast ROI before it grants project approval. Some units of government have enacted legislation that requires project forecasts. With increasing frequency, formal policy and legal structures are reasons to develop ROI forecasts.

Collectively, these reasons are leading more organizations to develop ROI forecasts so their sponsors will have an estimate of projects' expected payoff.

The Trade-offs of Forecasting

The ROI can be developed at different times and with different levels of data. Unfortunately, the ease, convenience, and costs involved in capturing a forecast ROI create trade-offs in accuracy and credibility. As shown in Figure 15.4, there are five distinct time intervals during an innovation

ROI with	Data collection timing (Relative to project)	Credibility	Accuracy	Cost to develop	Difficulty
1. Pre-project data	Before project	Not very credible	Not very accurate	Inexpensive	Not difficult
2. Reaction data	During project				
3. Learning data	During project				
4. Application data	After project	↓	↓	↓	↓
5. Business impact data	After project	Very credible	Very accurate	Expensive	Very difficult

Figure 15.4 Time Intervals When ROI Can Be Developed.

project when the ROI can be developed. The relationship between the timing of the ROI and the factors of credibility, accuracy, cost, and difficulty is also shown in this table.

- A preproject forecast can be developed using estimates of the impact of the project. This approach lacks credibility and accuracy, but is the least expensive and least difficult to calculate. Because of the interest in preproject forecasting, this scenario is expanded in the next section of this chapter.
- Reaction data can be extended to develop an anticipated impact, including the ROI. In this case, participants anticipate the chain of impact as a project is implemented and drives specific business measures. This is done after the project has begun. While accuracy and credibility increase from the preproject basis, this approach lacks the credibility and accuracy desired in many situations. However, it is easily accomplished and is a low-cost option.
- In projects where there is a substantial learning component, learning data can be used to forecast the ROI. This approach is applicable only when formal testing shows a relationship between test scores and subsequent business performance. When this correlation is available (it is usually developed to validate the test), test data can be used to forecast subsequent performance. The performance can then be converted to monetary impact, and the ROI can be developed. This has less potential as a forecasting tool and is not discussed in more detail.
- When frequency of skills or knowledge use is critical, the application and implementation of those skills or knowledge can be converted to a value using a concept called utility analysis. While this is particularly helpful in situations where competencies are being developed and values are placed on improving competencies, it has limited applications in most projects and is not discussed in more detail.
- Finally, the ROI can be developed from business impact data converted directly to monetary values, and compared to the cost of the program. This is not a forecast, but is a postproject evaluation, and the basis for other ROI calculations in this book. It is the preferred approach, but because of the pressures outlined above, examining ROI calculations at other times and with other levels is sometimes necessary.

Following sections in this chapter review in detail preproject ROI fore-casting, and ROI forecasting based on reactions. In less detail, ROI fore-casts developed from learning and application data are also discussed.

Preproject ROI Forecasting

Perhaps one of the most useful ways to convince a sponsor that a project is beneficial is to forecast the ROI for the project. The process is similar to the postproject analysis, except that the extent of the impact must be estimated along with the project costs.

Basic Model

Figure 15.5 shows the basic model for capturing the data necessary for a preproject forecast. This is a modified version of the postprogram ROI pro-cess model presented in Chapter 4. In the preproject forecast, the project outcomes are estimated, rather than being collected after project imple-mentation. Data collection is kept simple, and relies on interviews, focus groups, or surveys of experts. Tapping into benchmarking studies or locat-ing previous studies may also be helpful.[1]

Beginning at the reaction level, anticipated or estimated reactions are captured. Next, the anticipated learning that must occur is developed, fol-lowed by the anticipated application and implementation data. Here, the estimates focus on what must be accomplished for the project to be suc-cessful. These items may be based on the objectives at each of these lev-els. Finally, the impact data are estimated by experts. These experts may include subject matter experts, the supplier, or potential participants in the project. In this model, the levels build on each other. Having data estimated

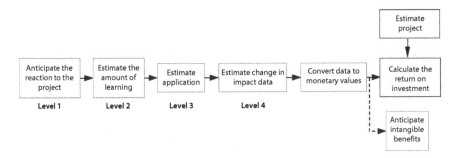

Figure 15.5 Pre-Project Forecasting Model.

at Levels 1, 2, and 3 enhances the quality of the estimated data at Level 4 (impact), which is needed for the analysis.

The model shows that there is no need to isolate the effects of a project as in the postproject model. The individual providing the data is asked the following question: "How much will the business impact measure change as a result of the project?" This question ties the change in the measure directly to the project; thus, isolation is not needed. This approach makes this process easier than the postevaluation model, where isolating project impact is always required.

Converting data to money is straightforward using a limited number of techniques. Locating a standard value or finding an expert to make the estimate is the logical choice. Analyzing records and databases as the numerator, and the estimated cost of the project is inserted as the denominator. The projected cost-benefit analysis can be developed along with the ROI. The specific steps to develop the forecast are detailed next.

Basic Steps to Forecast ROI

Eighteen detailed steps are necessary to develop a credible preproject ROI forecast using expert input:

1. *Understand the situation.* Individuals providing input to the forecast and conducting the forecast must have a good understanding of the present situation. This is typically a requirement for selecting the experts.
2. *Predict the present.* The project is sometimes initiated because a particular business impact measure is not doing well. However, such measures often lag the present situation; they may be based on data that are several months old. Also, these measures are based on dynamic influences that may change dramatically and quickly. It may be beneficial to estimate where the measure is now, based on assumptions and current trends. Although this appears to be a lot of work, it does not constitute a new responsibility for most of the experts, who are often concerned about the present situation. Market share data, for example, are often several months old. Trending market share data and examining other influences driving market share can help organizations understand the current situation.

3. *Observe warnings.* Closely tied to predicting the present is making sure that warning signs are observed. Red flags signal that something is going against the measure in question, causing it to go in an undesired direction or otherwise not move as it should. These often raise concerns that lead to projects. These are early warnings that things may get worse; they must be factored into the situation as forecasts are made.

4. *Describe the new process, project, program, or solution.* The project must be completely and clearly described to the experts so they fully understand the mechanics of what is to be implemented. The description should include the project scope, the individuals involved, time factors, and whatever else is necessary to express the magnitude of the project and the profile of the solution.

5. *Develop specific objectives.* These objectives should mirror the levels of evaluation, and should include reaction objectives, learning objectives, application objectives, and impact objectives. Although these may be difficult to develop, they are developed as part of the up-front analysis described in Chapter 5. Objectives provide clear direction toward the project's end. The cascading levels represent the anticipated chain of impact that will occur as the project is implemented.

6. *Estimate what participants will think about the project.* In this step, the experts are trying to understand participants' reaction. Will they support the project? How will they support it? What may cause participants to become unsupportive? The response is important because a negative reaction can cause a project to fail.

7. *Estimate what the participants will learn.* To some extent, every project will involve learning, and the experts will estimate what learning will occur. Using the learning objectives, the experts will define what the participants will learn as they enter the project, identifying specific knowledge, skills, and information the participants must acquire or enhance during the project.

8. *Anticipate what participants should accomplish in the project.* Building on the application objectives, the experts will identify what will be accomplished as the project is implemented

successfully. This step details specific actions, tasks, and processes that will be taken by the individuals. Steps 6, 7, and 8 – based on reaction, learning, and application – provide important information that serves as the basis for the next step, estimating improvement in business impact data.

9. *Estimate the improvement in business impact data.* This is a critical step in that the data generated are needed for the financial forecast. The experts will provide the estimate, in either absolute numbers or percentages, of the monetary change in the business impact measure (ΔP). While accuracy is important, it is also important to remember that a forecast is no more than an estimate based on the best data available at a given point. This is why the next step is included.

10. *Apply the confidence estimate.* Because the estimate attained in the previous step is not very accurate, an error adjustment is needed. This is developed by deriving a confidence estimate on the value identified in Step #9. The experts are asked to indicate the confidence they have in the previous data. The confidence level is expressed as a percentage, with 0% indicating "no confidence" and 100% indicating "certainty." This becomes a discount factor in the analysis.

11. *Convert the business impact data to monetary values.* Using one or more methods described in Chapter 12, the data are converted to money. If the impact measure is a desired improvement such as productivity, the value represents the gain obtained by having one more unit of the measure. If it is a measure that the organization is trying to reduce – like downtime, mistakes, or complaints – the value is the cost that the organization incurs as a result of one incident. For example, the cost of product returns may be 5% of sales. This value is noted with the letter V.

12. *Develop the estimated annual impact of each measure.* The estimated annual impact is the first-year improvement directly related to the project. In formula form, this is expressed as $\Delta I = \Delta P \times V \times 12$ (where ΔI = annual change in monetary value, ΔP = annual change in performance of the measure, and V = the value of that measure). If the measure is weekly or monthly, it must be converted to an annual amount. For example, if three lost-time accidents will be prevented each month, the time saved represents a total of 36.

13. *Factor additional years into the analysis for projects that will have a significant useful life beyond the first year.* For these projects, the factor should reflect the diminished benefit of subsequent years. The client or sponsor of the project should provide some indication of the amount of the reduction, and the values developed for the second, third, and successive years. It is important to be conservative by using the smallest numbers possible.

14. *Estimate the fully loaded project costs.* In this step, use all the cost categories described in Chapter 14, and denote the value as C when including it in the ROI equation. Include all direct and indirect costs in the calculation.

15. *Calculate the forecast ROI.* Using the total projected benefits and the estimated costs in the standard ROI formula. Calculate the forecast ROI as follows:

$$\mathrm{ROI}(\%) = \frac{\Delta I - C}{C} \times 100$$

16. *Use sensitivity analysis to develop several potential ROI values with different levels of improvement (ΔP).* When more than one measure is changing, the analysis may take the form of a spreadsheet showing various output scenarios and the subsequent ROI forecasts. The breakeven point will be identified.

17. *Identify potential intangible benefits.* Anticipate intangible benefits using input from those most knowledgeable about the situation, on the basis of assumptions from their experience with similar projects. Remember, the intangible benefits are those benefits not converted to monetary values, but possessing value nonetheless.

18. *Communicate the ROI projection and anticipated intangibles with caution.* The target audience must clearly understand that the forecast is based on several assumptions (clearly defined), and that although the values are the best possible estimates, they may include a degree of error.

Following these 18 steps will enable an individual to forecast the ROI.

Sources of Expert Input

Everyone would benefit from seeing further into the future, whether buying new technology, crafting policy, launching a new product, or simply planning a customer event. Good forecasting doesn't require powerful computers or arcane methods. It involves gathering evidence from a variety of sources, thinking probabilistically, working in teams, keeping score, and being willing to admit error and change course. [2]

Several sources of expert input are available for estimating improvement in impact data when the innovation project is implemented. Ideally, experience with similar projects in the organization will help form the basis of the estimates the experts make. The experts may include:

- Clients and/or sponsors
- Members of project team
- Prospective participants
- Subject matter experts
- External experts
- Advocates (who can champion the project)
- Finance and accounting staff
- Analysts (if one is involved with the project)
- Executives and/or managers
- Customers

Collectively, these sources provide an appropriate array of possibilities for helping estimate the value of an improvement. Because errors may develop, ask for a confidence measure when using estimates from any source.

Securing Input

With the experts clearly identified, three major steps must be addressed before developing the ROI. First, data must be collected from the individuals listed as experts. If the number of individuals is small (for example, one person from each of the expert groups involved), a short interview may suffice. During interviews, it is critical to avoid bias and to ask clear, succinct questions that are not leading. Questions should be framed in a balanced way to capture what may occur as well as what may not. If groups are involved, using focus groups may be suitable. For large numbers, surveys or questionnaires may be appropriate.

When the groups are diverse and scattered, the Delphi technique may be appropriate. This technique, originally developed by the Rand Corporation in the 1950s, has been used in forecasting and decision making in a variety of disciplines. The Delphi technique was originally devised to help experts achieve better forecasts than they might obtain through traditional group meetings, by allowing access to the group without in-person contact. Necessary features of a Delphi procedure are anonymity, continuous iteration, controlled feedback to participants, and a physical summary of responses. Anonymity is achieved by means of a questionnaire that allows group members to express their opinions and judgments privately. Between all iterations of the questionnaire, the facilitator informs the participants of the opinions of their anonymous colleagues. Typically this feedback is presented as a simple statistical summary using a mean or median value. The facilitator takes the group judgment as the statistical average in the final round.

In some cases, benchmarking data may be available and can be considered as a source of input for this process. The success of previous studies may provide input essential to the project as well. It may include an extensive search of databases using a variety of search engines. The important point is to understand, as much as possible, what may occur as a result of the project.

Conversion to Money

The measures forecast by the experts must be converted to monetary values for one, two, three, or more years depending on the nature and scope of the project. Standard values are available for many of these measures. Considering the importance of these measures, someone has probably placed monetary values on them. If not, experts are often available to convert the data to monetary values. Otherwise, existing records or databases may be appropriate sources. Another option is to ask stakeholders, perhaps some of the experts listed above, to provide these values for the forecast. This step is the only means of showing the money made from the project. Chapter 12 covered these techniques in more detail.

Estimate Project Costs

Innovation project cost estimates are based on the most reliable information available, and include the typical categories outlined in Table 16.2. The estimates can be based on previous projects. Although the costs are unknown, this task is often relatively easy to accomplish because of its similarity to budgeting, a process with usually routine procedures and policies in place. Dividing costs into categories representing the functional processes of the project provides additional insight into project costs. Areas often not given enough attention include analysis, assessment, evaluation, and reporting. If these elements are not properly addressed, much of the value of the project may be missed. With these costs and monetary benefits, the forecast can be made using the calculations presented in Chapter 14.

Case Study

Global Financial Services (GFS) wanted an innovative approach to enable its sales relationship managers to track routine correspondence and communication with customers. A needs assessment and initial analysis determined that customer content management software was needed. The project would involve further detailing software requirements, selecting an appropriate software package, and implementing the software with appropriate job aids, support tools, and training. However, before pursuing the project and purchasing the software, a forecast ROI was needed. Following the steps previously outlined, it was determined that four business impact measures would be influenced by implementation of this project:

1. Increase in sales to existing customers
2. Reduction in customer complaints caused by missed deadlines, late responses, and failure to complete transactions
3. Reduction in response time for customer inquiries and requests
4. Increase in the customer satisfaction composite survey index

Several individuals provided input in examining the potential problem. With comprehensive customer contact management software in place, relationship managers should benefit from quick and effective customer communication, and have easy access to customer databases. The software should also provide the functionality to develop calendars and to-do lists. Relationship managers should further benefit from features such as built-in contact management, calendar sharing, and the fact that the software is Internet-ready. To determine the extent to which the four measures would change, input was collected from six sources:

1. Internal software developers with expertise in various software applications provided input on expected changes in each of the measures.

Expert	Potential sales increase	Basis	Potential complaint reduction (Monthly Reduction)	Basis	Expected ROI	Credibility rating (5 = highest 1 = lowest)
Relationship mgr.	3.5%	Sales opportunity	3	Lower response time	60%	3
District mgr.	4%	Customer satisfaction	4	Lower response time	90%	4
Marketing analyst	3%	Missed opportunity	5	Quicker response	120%	4
Project sponsor	5%	Customer services	4	Quicker response	77%	4
Vendor	10%	Customer loyalty	12	Higher priority	180%	2
IT Analyst	2%	Customer relationships	3	Faster response	12%	2

Figure 15.6 Expected ROI values for different outputs.

2. Marketing analysts supplied information on sales cycles, customer needs, and customer care issues.
3. Relationship managers provided input on expected changes in the variables if the software was used regularly.
4. The analyst who confirmed the initial need for the software provided supplemental data.
5. The sponsor provided input on what could be expected from the project.
6. The proposed vendor provided input based on previous experience.

When input is based on estimates, the actual results will usually differ significantly. However, GFS was interested in a forecast based on analysis that, although very limited, would be strengthened with the best easily available expert opinion. Input was adjusted on the basis of the estimates and other information to assess its credibility. After discussing the availability of data and examining the techniques to convert it to monetary values, the following conclusions were reached:

- The increase in sales could easily be converted to a monetary value, as the average margin for sales increase is applied directly.
- The cost of a customer complaint could be based on an internal value currently in use, providing a generally accepted cost.
- Customer response time was not tracked accurately, and the value of this measure was not readily available, making it an intangible benefit.
- No generally accepted value for increasing customer satisfaction was available, so customer satisfaction impact data would be listed as an intangible benefit.

The forecast ROI calculation was developed from combined input based on the variety of estimates. The increase in sales was easily converted to monetary values using the margin rates, and the reduction in customer complaints was easily converted using the discounted value of a customer complaint. The costs for the project could easily be estimated based on input from those who briefly examined the situation. The total costs included development costs, materials, software, equipment, facilitators, facilities, and lost time for learning activities, coordination, and evaluation. This fully loaded projected cost, compared to the benefits, yielded a range of expected ROI values. Figure 15.6 shows possible scenarios based on payoffs of the two measures, as assessed by six experts. The ROI values range from a low of 12% to a high of 180%. The breakeven point could be developed with different scenarios. With these values in hand, the decision to move forward was easy: even the worst-case scenarios were positive, and the best case was expected to yield more than 10 times the ROI of the worst. As this example illustrates, the process must be simple, and must use the most credible resources available to quickly arrive at estimates.

Forecasting with a Pilot Program

Because of inaccuracies inherent in a preproject forecast, a better approach is to develop a small-scale pilot project, with the ROI based on postprogram data. This involves the following steps:

1. As in the previous process, develop Level 1, 2, 3, and 4 objectives.
2. Implement the project on a small-scale sample as a pilot project, excluding all the bells and whistles. (This keeps the project costs low without sacrificing project integrity.)
3. Fully implement the project with one or more of the groups who can benefit from the initiative.
4. Develop the ROI using the ROI process model for postproject analysis as outlined in previous chapters.
5. Based on the results of the pilot project, decide whether to implement the project throughout the organization. Data can be developed using all six of the measures outlined in this book: reaction, learning, application, impact, ROI, and intangibles.

Evaluating a pilot project and withholding full implementation until its results can be developed provides less risk than developing an ROI forecast. Wal-Mart uses this method to evaluate pilot programs before implementing them throughout its chain of several thousand US stores. Using pilot groups of 18–30 stores called "flights", the decision to implement a project throughout the system is based on six types of postprogram data (reaction, learning, application, impact, ROI, and intangibles).

Forecasting with Reaction Data

To forecast ROI at this level, participants are asked at the beginning of a project to state specifically how they plan to use the project, and what results they expect to achieve. They are asked to convert their planned accomplishments into monetary values, and show the basis for developing the values. Participants can adjust their responses with a confidence factor to make the data more credible. Next, estimates are adjusted for confidence level. When tabulating data, participants multiply the confidence levels by annual monetary values. This produces a conservative estimate for use in data analysis. For example, if a participant estimated the monetary impact of the project at $10,000 but was only 50% confident in his or her estimate, a $5,000 value would be used in the ROI forecast calculations.

To develop a summary of the expected benefits, discard any data that are incomplete, unusable, extreme, or unrealistic. Then total the individual data items. Finally, as an optional exercise, adjust the total value again by a factor that reflects the unknowns in the process, and the possibility that participants will not achieve the results they anticipate. This adjustment factor can be estimated by the project team. In one organization, the benefits are divided by two to develop a number to use in the calculation. Finally, calculate the forecast ROI using the net benefits from the project divided by the project costs.

Case Study: Forecasting ROI from Reaction Data

This process can best be described using an actual case. Global Engineering and Construction Company (GEC) designs and builds large commercial facilities like plants, paper mills, and municipal water systems. Safety is always a critical matter at GEC, and commands much management attention. To improve safety performance, a safety improvement project was initiated for project engineers and construction superintendents. The project solution involved policy changes, audits, and training. The project focused on safety leadership, safety planning, safety inspections, safety meetings, accident investigation, safety policies and procedures, safety standards, and workers' compensation. Safety engineers and superintendents (the participants) were expected to improve the safety performance of their individual construction projects.

A dozen safety performance measures used in the company were discussed and analyzed at the beginning of the project. At that time, participants completed a feedback questionnaire that probed specific action items planned as a result of the safety project, and provided estimated monetary values of the planned actions. In addition, participants explained the basis for estimates and placed a confidence level on their estimates. Figure 15.7 presents data provided by the participants. Only 19 of the 25 participants supplied data. (Experience has shown that approximately 50–90% of participants will provide usable data on this series of questions.) The estimated cost of the project, including participants' salaries for the time devoted to the project, was $358,900.

The monetary values of the planned improvements were extremely high, reflecting the participants' optimism and enthusiasm at the beginning of an impressive project, from which specific actions were planned. As a first step in the analysis, extreme data items were omitted (one of the guiding principles of the ROI Methodology). Data such as "millions," "unlimited," and "$4 million" were discarded, and each remaining value was multiplied by the confidence value and totaled. This adjustment is one way of reducing highly subjective estimates. The resulting tabulations yielded a total improvement of $990,125 (rounded to $990,000). The projected ROI, which was based on the feedback questionnaire at the beginning of the project, is:

$$\text{ROI} = \frac{\left(\$990,000 - \$358,900\right)}{\$358,900} \times 100 = 176\%$$

Although these projected values are subjective, the results were generated by project participants who should be aware of what they could accomplish. A follow-up study would determine the true results delivered by the group.

Use of the Data

Caution is required when using a forecast ROI. The calculations are highly subjective, and may not reflect the extent to which participants will achieve results. A variety of influences in the work environment and project setting can enhance or inhibit the attainment of performance goals. Having high expectations at the beginning of a project is no guarantee that those expectations will be met. Project disappointments are documented regularly.

Although the process is subjective and possibly unreliable, it does have some usefulness.

1. If the evaluation must stop at this point, this analysis provides more insight into the value of the project than data from typical reaction input, which report attitudes and feelings about a project. Sponsors and managers usually

Participant no.	Estimated value	Basis	Confidence level	Adjusted
1	$80,000	Reduction in lost-time accidents	90%	$72,000
2	91,200	OSHA Reportable injuries	80%	72,960
3	55,000	Accident reduction	90%	49,500
4	10,000	First-aid visits/visits to doctor	70%	7,000
5	150,000	Reduction in lost-time injuries	95%	142,500
6	Millions	Total accident cost	100%	—
7	74,800	Worker's compensation	80%	59,840
8	7,500	OSHA citations	75%	5,625
9	50,000	Reduction in accidents	75%	37,500
10	36,000	Worker's compensation	80%	28,800
11	150,000	Reduction in total accident costs	90%	135,000
12	22,000	OSHA Fines/citations	70%	15,400
13	140,000	Accident reductions	80%	112,000
14	4 million	Total cost of safety	95%	—
15	65,000	Total worker's compensation	50%	32,500
16	Unlimited	Accidents	100%	—
17	20,000	Visits to doctor	95%	19,000
18	45,000	Injuries	90%	40,500
29	200,000	Lost-time injuries	80%	160,000
				Total $990,125

Figure 15.7 Level 1 data for ROI forecast calculations.

find this information more useful than a report stating that "40% of project team participants rated the project above average."

2. These data can form a basis for comparing different projects of the same type (e.g., safety projects). If one project forecast results in an ROI of 300% and a similar project forecast results in a 30% ROI, it would appear that one project may be more effective. The participants in the first project have more confidence in the planned implementation of the project.

3. Collecting these types of data focuses increased attention on project outcomes. Participants will understand that specific action is expected, which produces results for the project. The data collection helps participants plan the implementation of what they are learning. This issue becomes clear to participants as they anticipate results and convert them to monetary values. Even if the forecast is ignored, the exercise is productive because of the important message it sends to participants.

4. The data can be used to secure support for a follow-up evaluation. A skeptical manager may challenge the data, and this challenge can be converted into support for a follow-up to see whether the forecast holds true. The only way to know whether these results will materialize is to conduct a post-project evaluation.

5. If a follow-up evaluation of the project is planned, the postproject results can be compared to the ROI forecast. Comparisons of forecast and follow-up data are helpful. If there is a defined relationship between the two, the less expensive forecast can be substituted for the more expensive follow-up. Also, when a follow-up evaluation is planned, participants are usually more conservative with their projected estimates.

The use of ROI forecasting with reaction data is increasing, and some organizations have based many of their ROI forecast calculations on this type of data. For example, Wells Fargo Bank routinely develops ROI forecasts with reaction data. Although they may be subjective, the calculations do add value, particularly if they are part of a comprehensive evaluation system.

Forecasting Guidelines

The enterprise of the future, based on empiricism and analytical decision making, will indeed be considerably different from today's enterprise. In the future, even more than today, businesses will be expected to possess the talent, tools, processes, and capabilities to enable their organizations to implement and utilize continuous analysis of past business performance and events to gain forward-looking insight to drive business decisions and actions. [3]

With the four different forecasting time frames outlined in this chapter, it may help to follow a few guidelines known to drive the forecasting possibilities within an organization. These guidelines are based on our experiences in forecasting in a variety of projects and programs [4].

1. *If you must forecast, forecast frequently.* Forecasting is an art and a science. Users can build comfort, experience, and history with the process by using it frequently.

2. *Make forecasting an essential part of the evaluation mix.* This chapter began with a list of essential reasons for forecasting. The use of forecasting is increasingly being demanded by many organizations. It can be an effective and useful tool when used properly and in conjunction with other types of evaluation data. Some organizations have targets for the use of forecasting (e.g., if a project exceeds a certain cost, it will always require a preproject forecast). Others will target a certain number of projects for a forecast based on reaction data, and use those data in the manner described. It is important to plan for the forecast and let it be a part of the evaluation mix, using it regularly.

3. *Forecast different types of data.* Although most of this chapter focuses on how to develop a forecast ROI using the standard ROI formula, forecasting the value of the other types of data is important as well. A useable, helpful forecast will include predictions about reaction and perceived value, the extent of learning, and the extent of application and implementation. These types of data are very important in anticipating movements and shifts, based on the project that is planned. It assists in developing the overall forecast, and helps the project team understand the project's total anticipated impact.

4. *Secure input from those who know the process best.* As forecasts are developed, it is essential to secure input from individuals who understand the dynamics of the workplace and the measures being influenced by the project. Go to the experts. This will increase not only the accuracy of the forecast, but also the credibility of the results. In other situations,

it may be the analysts who are aware of the major influences in the workplace and the dynamics of those changes.

5. *Long-term forecasts will usually be inaccurate.* Forecasting works better when it covers a short time frame. Most short-term scenarios afford a better grasp of the influences that might drive the measures. In the long-term, a variety of new influences, unforeseen now, could enter the process and drastically change the impact measures. If a long-term forecast is needed, it should be updated regularly.

6. *Expect forecasts to be biased.* Forecasts will consist of data coming from those who have an interest in the issue. This is unavoidable. Some will want the forecast to be optimistic; others will have a pessimistic view. Almost all input is biased in one way or another. Every attempt should be made to minimize the bias, adjust for the bias, or adjust for the uncertainty in the process. Still, the audience should recognize the forecast as a biased prediction.

7. *Serious forecasting is hard work.* The value of forecasting often depends on the amount of effort put into the process. High-stake projects or programs need a serious approach, collecting all possible data, examining different scenarios, and making the best prediction available. It is in these situations that mathematical tools can be most valuable.

8. *Review the success of forecasting routinely.* As forecasts are made, it is imperative to revisit the forecast with postproject data to check its accuracy. This can aid in the continuous improvement of the processes. Sources could prove to be more or less credible, specific inputs may be more or less biased, certain analyses may be more appropriate than others. It is important to constantly improve the methods and approaches for forecasting within the organization.

9. *The assumptions are the most serious error in forecasting.* Of all the variables that can enter the process, assumptions offer the greatest opportunity for error. It is important for the assumptions to be clearly understood and communicated. When multiple inputs are given, each forecaster should use the same set of assumptions, if possible.

10. *Utility is the most important characteristic of forecasting.* The most important use of forecasting is providing information and input for the decision maker. Forecasting is a tool for those attempting to make decisions about project

implementation. It is not a process intended to maximize the output or minimize any particular variable. It is not a process undertaken to dramatically change the way a project is implemented. It is a process to provide data for decisions.

Final Thoughts

In this chapter we illustrated that ROI calculations can be developed at different times and at different evaluation levels, even though most project leaders focus only on impact data for ROI calculations. Although post-project data are desired, impact data are not yet available in many situations. ROI forecasts developed before a project begins can be useful to the sponsor, and are sometimes necessary before projects can be approved. Forecasts made during project implementation can be useful to management and participants, and can focus participants' attention on the economic impact of the project. However, using ROI estimates during the project may give a false sense of accuracy.

As expected, preproject ROI forecasts have the least credibility and accuracy, yet have the advantage of being inexpensive and relatively easy to develop. ROI calculations using impact data are more credible and accurate than forecasts, but are expensive and difficult to develop. The reality is that forecasting is an important part of the measurement mix. It should be pursued routinely and used regularly in decision making.

Whether you have complete a forecast ROI or a postanalysis ROI, the results must be reported to stakeholders. In the next chapter we detail how and when results are communicated, and to whom they are communicated.

16

Reporting Results

"I've had the opportunity to deliver a presentation to the then-CEO of Proctor & Gamble (P&G) A.G. Lafley four or five times in the decade he held that position. The first time was unforgettable. That day I learned a valuable lesson—the hard way—about how not to present to the CEO.

I'd been given 20 minutes on the agenda of the Executive Global Leadership Council meeting. This group included the CEO and a dozen or so of the top officials in the company. They met weekly in a special room on P&G's executive floor designed just for them. It was a perfectly round room with modern features, centered on a perfectly round table. Even the doors were curved so as not to stray from the round motif. My presentation was the first item on the agenda that day, so I arrived 30 minutes early to set up my computer and make sure all the audiovisual equipment worked properly. I was, after all, making my first presentation to the CEO. I wanted to make sure everything went smoothly.

The executives began filing into the room at the appointed time and taking up seats around the table. After half of them had arrived, Mr. Lafley entered the room. He walked almost completely around the table, saying hello to each of his team members and, to my horror, sat down in the seat immediately underneath the projection screen—with his back to it!

This was not good. "He'll be constantly turning around in his seat to see the presentation," I thought, "and he'll probably hurt his neck. Then he'll be in a bad mood, and he might not agree to my recommendation." But I wasn't going to tell the boss where to sit, so I started my presentation.

About five minutes in, I realized Mr. Lafley hadn't turned around even once to see the slides. I stopped being worried about his neck and started worrying that he wasn't going to understand my presentation. And if he didn't understand it, he certainly wouldn't agree to my recommendation. But again, I wasn't going to tell the CEO what to do. So I just kept going.

At ten minutes into the presentation—halfway through my allotted time—I noticed that he still hadn't turned around once to look at my slides. At that point, I stopped being worried and just got confused. He was looking right at me and was clearly engaged in the conversation. So why wasn't he looking at my slides?

When 20 minutes had expired, I was done with my presentation, and the CEO hadn't ever bothered to look at my slides. But he did agree to my recommendation. Despite the success, as I was walking back to my office, I couldn't help but feel like I'd failed somehow. I debriefed the whole event in my head, wondering what I had done wrong. Was I boring? Did I not make my points very clear? Was he distracted with some billion-dollar decision far more important than whatever I was talking about?

But then it occurred to me. He wasn't looking at my slides because he knew something that I didn't know until that moment. He knew if I had anything important to say, I would say it. It would come out of my mouth, not from that screen. He knew those slides were there more for my benefit than for his.

As CEO, Mr. Lafley probably spent most of his day reading dry memos and financial reports with detailed charts and graphs. He was probably looking forward to that meeting as a break from that tedium and as an opportunity to engage someone in dialogue—to have someone tell him what was happening on the front lines of the business, to share a brilliant idea, and to ask for his help. In short, he was hoping for someone to tell him a story. Someone like me. That was my job during those 20 minutes. I just didn't know it yet.

Looking back, I realize it was probably no accident Mr. Lafley chose the seat he did. There were certainly others he could have chosen. That position kept him from being distracted by the words on the screen and allowed him to focus on the presenter and on the discussion." [1]

—Paul Smith, author of Lead with a Story and former P & G executive

Now that we have the results in hand, what's next? Do we tell a story? If so, how should it be structured? Should we use the results to modify the innovation project, change the process, demonstrate the contribution, justify new projects, gain additional support, or build goodwill? How should the data be presented? The worst course of action is to do nothing. Achieving results without communicating them is like planting seeds and failing to fertilize and cultivate the seedlings – the yield will be less than optimal. This chapter provides useful information for presenting evaluation data to your various audiences in the form of both oral and written reports.

The Importance of Communicating Results?

Communicating results is critical to project success. The results achieved must be conveyed to stakeholders not just at project completion, but throughout the duration of the project. Continuous communication maintains the flow of information so that adjustments can be made and all stakeholders are kept up to date on the status of the project.

Mark Twain once said, "Collecting data is like collecting garbage – pretty soon we will have to do something with it." Measuring project success and gathering evaluation data mean nothing unless the findings are communicated promptly to the appropriate audiences, so that they are apprised of the results and can take action in response if necessary. Communication is important for many reasons, some of which are detailed next.

Communication is Necessary to Make Improvements

Information is collected at different points during the process, and providing feedback to involved groups enables them take action and make adjustments if needed. Thus, the quality and timeliness of communication are critical to making improvements. Even after the project is completed, communication is necessary to make sure the target audience fully understands the results achieved, and how the results may be enhanced in future projects, or in the current project if it is still operational. Communication is the key to making important adjustments at all phases of the project.

Communication is Necessary to Explain the Contribution

The overall contribution of the project, as determined from the six major types of measures, is unclear at best. The different target audiences will each need a thorough explanation of the results. The communication strategy – including techniques, media, and the overall process – will determine the extent to which each group understands the contribution. Communicating results, particularly in terms of business impact and ROI, can quickly overwhelm even the most sophisticated target audiences. Communication must be planned and implemented with the goal of making sure the respective audiences understand the full contribution.

Communication is a Politically Sensitive Issue

Communication is one of those issues that can cause major problems. Because the results of a project may be closely linked to political issues within an organization, communicating the results can upset some individuals while pleasing others. If certain individuals do not receive the information, or if it is delivered inconsistently between groups, problems can quickly surface. Not only must the information be understood, but issues relating to fairness, quality, and political correctness make it crucial that the communication be constructed and delivered effectively to all key individuals.

Different Audiences Need Different Information

With so many potential target audiences requiring communication on the success of a project, the communication must be individually tailored to their needs. A varied audience has varied needs. Planning and effort are necessary to ensure that each audience receives all the information it needs, in the proper format, at the proper time. A single report for presentation to all audiences is inappropriate. The scope, the format, and even the content of the information will vary significantly from one group to another. Thus, the target audience is the key to determining the appropriate method of communication.

Communication is a critical need for the reasons just cited, although it is often overlooked or underfunded in projects. This chapter presents a variety of techniques for accomplishing communication of all types for various target audiences.

Principles of Communicating Results

The skills one must possess to communicate results effectively are almost as sensitive and sophisticated as those necessary for obtaining results. The style of the communication is as important as the substance. Regardless of the message, audience, or medium, a few general principles apply.

Communication Must Be Timely

In general, project results should be communicated as soon as they become known. From a practical standpoint, however, it is sometimes best to delay the communication until a convenient time, such as the publication of the next client newsletter or the next general management meeting. Several questions are relevant to the timing decision. Is the audience ready for the results in view of other issues that may have developed? Is the audience expecting results? When will the delivery have the maximum impact on the audience? Do circumstances dictate a change in the timing of the communication?

Communication Should Be Targeted to Specific Audiences

As stated earlier, communication is usually more effective if it is designed for the specific group being addressed. The message should be tailored to the interests, needs, and expectations of the target audience. The results of the project should reflect outcomes at all levels, including the six types of data presented in this book. Some of the data are developed earlier in the project, and communicated during the implementation of the project. Other data are collected after project implementation and communicated in a follow-up study. The results, in their broadest sense, may incorporate early feedback in qualitative form all the way to ROI values expressed in varying quantitative terms.

Media Should Be Carefully Selected

Certain media may be more appropriate for a particular group than others. Face-to-face meetings may be preferable to special bulletins. A memo distributed exclusively to top executives may be a more effective outlet than the company newsletter. The proper format of communication can determine the effectiveness of the process.

Communication Should Be Unbiased and Modest in Tone

For communication to be effective, facts must be separated from fiction, and accurate statements distinguished from opinions. Some audiences may approach the communication with skepticism, anticipating the presence of biased opinions. Boastful statements can turn off recipients, and most of the content will be lost. Observable phenomena and credible statements carry much more weight than extreme or sensational claims. Although such claims may get an audience's attention, they often detract from the importance of the results.

Communication Must Be Consistent

The timing and content of the communication should be consistent with past practices. A special presentation at an unusual time during the course of the project may provoke suspicion. Also, if a particular group, such as top management, regularly receives communication on outcomes, it should continue receiving communication even if the results are not positive. Omitting unfavorable results leaves the impression that only positive results will be reported.

Make the Message Clear

The communication must be clear and precise. In short, it must be well written. Harold Evans, one of the greatest editors of our time, offers timeless advice for making meaning clearer: "Refresh your writing. Unravel convoluted sales talk written to deceive. See through campaigns erected on a tower of falsehoods. Billions of words come at us every day with unimaginable velocity and shriveled meaning, in social media posts, bloated marketing, incomprehensible contracts, and political language designed to make lies sound truthful. The digital era has had unfortunate effects on understanding. Ugly words and phrases are picked up by the unwary and passed on like a virus. Cryptic assertion supplants explanation and reasoned argument. Muddle and contradiction suffocate meaning." [2]

Testimonials Must Come from Respected Individuals

Opinions are strongly influenced by other people, particularly those who are respected and trusted. Testimonials about project results, when solicited from individuals who are respected within the organization, can influence the effectiveness of the message. This respect may be related to leadership ability, position, special skills, or knowledge. A testimonial from an individual who commands little respect and is regarded as a substandard performer can have a negative impact on the message.

The Audience's Bias of the Project Will Influence the Communication Strategy

Opinions are difficult to change, and a negative opinion toward a project or project team may not change with the mere presentation of facts. However, the presentation of facts alone may strengthen the opinions held by those who already support the project. Presentation of the results reinforces their position, and provides them with a defense in discussions with others. A project team with a high level of credibility and respect may have a relatively easy time communicating results. Low credibility can create problems when one is trying to be persuasive.

Storytelling is Essential

Armed with six levels of data (inputs, plus five levels of outcomes) and intangibles, the challenge is to tell a convincing story with data. Bill Tai is a career venture capitalist who has been investing in companies since 1991. Tai has seen several waves of technology in Silicon Valley and he believes that now, more than ever, the ability to communicate ideas simply and clearly and to tell compelling stories is critical to standing apart in the marketplace of ideas. Technologists and scientists no longer talk to just their peers. If they can't explain the benefits of their projects, their ideas or messages won't catch on. They must translate the language of bits and bytes into a story every person understands. Storytelling is the act of framing the message as a narrative to inform, illuminate, and inspire. [3]

These general principles are vital to the overall success of the communication effort. They should serve as a checklist for the project team planning the dissemination of project results.

The Process for Communicating Results

The communication of innovation project results must be systematic, timely, and well planned, and the process must include seven components in a precise sequence. The first step is critical and consists of an analysis of the need to communicate the results from a project. Possibly, a lack of support for the project was identified, or perhaps the need for adjusting or maintaining the funding for the project was uncovered. Instilling confidence or building credibility for the project may be necessary. It is important first of all to outline the specific reasons for communicating the results.

The second step focuses on the plan for communication. Planning should include numerous agenda items to be addressed in all communications about the project. Planning also covers the actual communication, detailing the specific types of data to be communicated, and when and to which groups the communication will be presented.

The third step involves selecting the target audiences for communication. Audiences range from top management to past participants, and each audience has its own special needs. All groups should be considered in the communication strategy. An artfully crafted, targeted delivery may be necessary to win the approval of a specific group.

The fourth step is developing a report, the written material explaining project results. This can encompass a wide variety of possibilities, from a brief summary of the results to a detailed research document on the evaluation effort. Usually, a complete report is developed, and selected parts or summaries from the report are used for different media.

Media selection is the fifth step. Some groups respond more favorably to certain methods of communication. A variety of approaches, both oral and written, are available to the project leaders.

The sixth step is to deliver the message in the form of appropriate information. The communication is delivered with the utmost care, confidence, and professionalism.

The last step, but certainly not the least significant, is analyzing reactions to the communication. Positive reactions, negative feedback, and a lack of comments are all indicators of how well the information was received and understood. An informal analysis may be appropriate for many situations. For an extensive and more involved communication effort, a formal, structured feedback process may be necessary. The nature of the reactions could trigger an adjustment to the subsequent communication of results for the same project, or provide input for adapting future project communications.

The various steps are discussed further in the following sections.

The Need for Communication

Because there may be various reasons for communicating results, a list should be tailored to the organization and adjusted as necessary. The reasons for communicating results depend on the specific project, the setting, and the unique needs of each party. Some of the most common reasons are:

- Securing approval for the project and the allocation of time and money
- Gaining support for the project and its objectives
- Securing agreement on the issues, solutions, and resources
- Enhancing the credibility of the project leader
- Reinforcing the processes used in the project
- Driving action for improvement in the project
- Preparing participants for the project
- Optimizing results throughout the project and the quality of future feedback

- Showing the complete results of the project
- Underscoring the importance of measuring results
- Explaining techniques used to measure results
- Motivating participants to become involved in the project
- Demonstrating accountability for expenditures
- Marketing future projects

There may be other reasons for communicating results, so the list should be tailored to the needs of each organization.

The Communication Plan

Any activity must be carefully planned to achieve maximum results. This is a critical part of communicating the results of the project. The actual planning of the communication is important to ensure that each audience receives the proper information at the right time, and that necessary actions are taken. Several issues are crucial in planning the communication of results:

- What will be communicated?
- When will the data be communicated?
- How will the information be communicated?
- Where will the information be communicated?
- Who will communicate the information?
- Who is the target audience?
- What are the specific actions required or desired?

The communication plan is usually developed when the project is approved. This plan details how specific information is to be developed and communicated to various groups, and the expected actions. In addition, this plan details how the overall results will be communicated, the time frame for communication, and the appropriate groups to receive the information. The project leader, key managers, and stakeholders need to agree on the degree of detail in the plan.

The Audience for Communications

The following questions should be asked about each potential audience for communication of project results:

Primary target audience	Reason for communication
Client, top executives	To secure approval for the project
Immediate managers, team leaders	To gain support for the project
Participants, team leaders	To secure agreement with the issues
Top executives	To enhance the credibility of the project leader
Immediate managers	To reinforce the processes used in the project
Project team	To drive action for improvement
Team leaders	To prepare participants for the project
Participants	To improve the results and quality of future feedback
Stakeholders	To show the complete results of the project
Client, project team	To underscore the importance of measuring results
Client, project support staff	To explain the techniques used to measure results
Team leaders	To create the desire for a participant to be involved
All employees	To demonstrate accountability for expenditures
Prospective clients	To market future projects

Figure 16.1 Common target audiences.

- Are they interested in the project?
- Do they really want to receive the information?
- Has a commitment been made to include them in the communications?
- Is the timing right for this audience?
- Are they familiar with the project?
- How do they prefer to have results communicated?
- Do they know the project leader? The project team?
- Are they likely to find the results threatening?
- Which medium will be most convincing to this group?

For each target audience, three steps are necessary. To the greatest extent possible, the project leader should get to know and understand the target audience. Also, the project leader should find out what information is needed and why. Each group will have its own required amount of information; some will want detailed information, while others will prefer a brief overview. Rely on the input from others to determine the audience's needs. Finally, the project leaders should take into account audience bias. Some audiences will immediately support the results, others may oppose them, and still others will be neutral. The staff should be empathetic and try to understand the basis for the differing views. Given this understanding, communications can be tailored to each group. This is critical when the potential exists for the audience to react negatively to the results.

Basis for Selecting the Audience

The target audiences for information on project results are varied in terms of job levels and responsibilities. Determining which groups will receive a particular item of communication requires careful thought, because problems can arise when a group receives inappropriate information or is overlooked altogether. A sound basis for audience selection is to analyze the reason for the communication, as discussed earlier. Table 16.1 identifies common target audiences and the basis for audience selection. Several audiences stand out as critical. Perhaps the most important audience is the client. This group (or individual) initiates the project, reviews data, usually selects the project leader, and weighs the final assessment of the effectiveness of the project. Another important target audience is top management. This group is responsible for allocating resources to the project and needs information to help them justify expenditures and gauge the effectiveness of the efforts.

Participants need feedback on the overall success of the effort. Some individuals may not have been as successful as others in achieving the desired results. Communicating the results creates additional pressure to implement the project effectively and improve results in the future. For those achieving excellent results, the communication will serve as reinforcement. Communication of results to project participants is often overlooked, with the assumption that once the project is completed, they do not need to be informed of its success.

Communicating with the participants' immediate managers is essential. In many cases, these managers must encourage participants to implement the project. Also, they are key in supporting and reinforcing the objectives of the project. An appropriate return on investment strengthens the commitment to projects and enhances the credibility of the project team.

The project team must receive information about project results. Whether for small projects in which team members receive a project update, or for larger projects where a complete team is involved, those who design, develop, facilitate, and implement the project require information on the project's effectiveness. Evaluation data are necessary so that adjustments can be made if the project is not as effective as it was projected to be.

Information Development: The Impact Study

The type of formal evaluation report to be issued depends on the degree of detail in the information presented to the various target audiences. Brief summaries of project results with appropriate charts may be sufficient for some communication efforts. In other situations, particularly those involving major projects requiring extensive funding, a detailed evaluation report is crucial. A complete and comprehensive impact study report is usually necessary. This report can then be used as the basis for more streamlined information aimed at specific audiences and using various media. One possible format for an impact study report is presented in Figure 16.2.

While the impact study report is an effective, professional way to present ROI data, several cautions are in order. Since this report documents the success of a project involving a large group of employees, credit for the success must go completely to the participants and their immediate leaders. Their performance generated the success. Also, it is important to avoid boasting about results. Grand claims of overwhelming success can quickly turn off an audience, and interfere with the delivery of the desired message.

The methodology should be clearly explained, along with the assumptions made in the analysis. The reader should easily see how the values were developed, and how specific steps were followed to make the process more conservative, credible, and accurate. Detailed statistical analyses should be placed in an appendix.

Media Selection

Many options are available for the dissemination of project results. In addition to the impact study report, commonly used media are meetings, interim and progress reports, organization publications, and case studies. Figure 16.3 lists a variety of options to develop the content and the message.

Meetings

If used properly, meetings are fertile ground for the communication of project results. All organizations hold a variety of meetings, and some

- General information
  - Background
  - Objectives of study
- Methodology for impact study
  - Levels of evaluation
  - ROI process
  - Collecting data
  - Isolating the effects of the project
  - Converting data to monetary values
- Data analysis issues
- Costs
- Results: General information
  - Response profile
  - Success with objectives
- Results: Reaction and perceived
  - Data sources
  - Data summary
  - Key issues
- Results: Learning and confidence
  - Data sources
  - Data summary
  - Key Issues
- Results: Application and implementation
  - Data sources
  - Data summary
  - Key issues
- Results: Impact and consequences
  - General comments
  - Linkage with business measures
  - Key issues
- Results: ROI and its meaning
- Results: Intangible measures
- Barriers and enablers
  - Barriers
  - Enablers
- Conclusions and recommendations
  - Conclusions
  - Recommendations
- Exhibits

Figure 16.2 Format for an impact study report.

Meetings	Detailed reports	Brief reports	Electronic reporting	Mass publications
Executives	Impact study	Executive summary	Website	Announcements
Management	Case study (internal)	Slide overview	E-mail	Bulletins
Stakeholders	Case study (external)	One-page summary	Blog	Newsletters
Staff	Major articles	Brochure	Video	Brief articles

Figure 16.3 Options for communicating results.

may provide the proper context to convey project results. Along the chain of command, staff meetings are held to review progress, discuss current problems, and distribute information. These meetings can be an excellent forum for discussing the results achieved in a project that relates to the group's activities. Project results can be sent to executives for use in a staff meeting, or a member of the project team can attend the meeting to make the presentation.

Regular meetings with management groups are a common practice. Typically, discussions will focus on items that might be of help to work units. The discussion of a project and its results can be integrated into the regular meeting format. A few organizations have initiated the use of periodic meetings for all key stakeholders, where the project leader reviews progress and discusses next steps. A few highlights from interim project results can be helpful in building interest, commitment, and support for the project.

Interim and Progress Reports

A highly visible way to communicate results, although usually limited to large projects, is the use of interim and routine memos and reports. Published or disseminated by e-mail on a periodic basis, they are designed to inform management about the status of the project, to communicate interim results of the project, and to spur needed changes and improvements.

A secondary reason for the interim report is to enlist additional support and commitment from the management group, and to keep the project intact. This report is produced by the project team and distributed to a select group of stakeholders in the organization. The report may vary considerably in format and scope and may include a schedule of planned steps or activities, a brief summary of reaction evaluations, initial results achieved from the project, and various spotlights recognizing team members or participants. Other topics may also be appropriate. When produced in a professional manner, the interim report can boost management support and commitment.

Routine Communication Tools

To reach a wide audience, the project leader can use internal, routine publications. Whether a newsletter, magazine, newspaper, or electronic file, these media usually reach all employees or stakeholders. The content can have a significant impact if communicated appropriately. The scope should be limited to general-interest articles, announcements, and interviews.

Results communicated through these types of media must be important enough to arouse general interest. For example, a story with the headline "Innovation Project Helps Produce Record Sales Accident" will catch the attention of many readers because it is likely they participated in the project and can appreciate the relevance of the results. Reports on the accomplishments of a group of participants may not generate interest if the audience cannot relate to the accomplishments.

For many projects, results are not achieved until weeks or even months after the project is completed. Participants need reinforcement from many sources. Communicating results to a general audience may lead to additional pressure to continue the project or introduce similar ones in the future.

Stories about participants involved in a project and the results they have achieved can help create a favorable image. Employees are made aware that the organization is investing time and money to improve performance and prepare for the future. This type of story provides information about a project that employees otherwise may be unfamiliar with, and it sometimes creates a desire in others to participate if given the opportunity.

General-audience communication can bring recognition to project participants, particularly those who excel in some aspect of the project. Public recognition of participants who deliver exceptional performance can enhance their self-esteem, and their drive to continue to excel. A project can generate many human interest stories. A rigorous project with difficult challenges can provide the basis for an interesting story on participants who made the extra effort.

E-mail and Electronic Media

Internal and external Internet pages, company-wide intranets, and e-mails are excellent vehicles for releasing results, promoting ideas, and informing employees and other target groups of project results. E-mail, in particular, provides a virtually instantaneous means of communicating results to and soliciting responses from large groups of people. For major projects, some organizations create blogs to present results and elicit reactions, feedback, and suggestions.

Project Brochures and Pamphlets

A brochure might be appropriate for a project conducted on a continuing basis, or where the audience is large and continuously changing. The brochure should be attractive and present a complete description of the project, with a major section devoted to results obtained with previous participants, if available. Measurable results and reactions from participants, or even direct quotes from individuals, can add spice to an otherwise dull brochure.

Case Studies

Case studies represent an effective way to communicate the results of a project. A typical case study describes the situation, provides appropriate background information (including the events that led to the project), presents the techniques and strategies used to develop the study, and highlights the key issues in the project. Case studies tell an interesting story of how the project was implemented and the evaluation was developed, including the problems and concerns identified along the way.

Delivering the Message

The key to delivering the message is to understand the audience and their perspective, and then show what's in it for them. Regardless of the form of communication (briefing, meeting, webinar, blog, one page summary, article, or case study), the challenge is to drive home the message and persuade the audience. Darlene Price, communications expert, provides her advice for delivering the message:

- Stop worrying about perfecting your communication and start connecting with your audience

- Organize your presentation with persuasive logic and an effective structure
- Ensure a dynamic, confident delivery every time with live presentations
- Engage and involve your audience when possible to make your message meaningful and memorable
- Use PowerPoint more effectively to reinforce your message and optimize impact
- Manage nervousness and create a great first impression in live and recorded presentations
- Cultivate a variety of image enhancers that will subtly lend power to your presentation – and much more

Being able to communicate to a group of decision makers and positively influence their thinking is a sure path to success. [4]

Routine Feedback on Project Progress

A primary reason for collecting reaction and learning data is to provide feedback, so that adjustments can be made throughout the innovation project. For most projects, data are routinely collected and quickly communicated to a variety of groups. A feedback action plan designed to provide information to several audiences using a variety of media may be an option. These feedback sessions may point out specific actions that need to be taken. This process becomes complex and must be managed in a very proactive manner. The following steps are recommended for providing feedback and managing the overall process. Some of the steps and concepts are based on the recommendations of Peter Block in his successful book *Flawless Consulting* [5].

- *Communicate quickly.* Whether the news is good news or bad, it should be passed on to individuals involved in the project as soon as possible. The recommended time for providing feedback is usually a matter of days, and certainly no longer than a week or two after the results become known.
- *Simplify the data.* Condense the data into an easily understandable, concise presentation. This is not the appropriate situation for detailed explanations and analysis.
- *Examine the role of the project team and the client in the feedback process.* The project leader is often the judge, jury,

prosecutor, defendant, and/or witness. On the other hand, sometimes the client fills these roles. These respective functions must be examined in terms of reactions to the data and the actions that are called for.

- *Use negative data in a constructive way.* Some of the data will show that things are not going so well, and the fault may rest with the project leader or the client. In this case, the story basically changes from "Let's look at the success we've achieved" to "Now we know which areas to change."

- *Use positive data in a cautious way.* Positive data can be misleading, and if they are communicated too enthusiastically, they may create expectations that exceed what finally materializes. Positive data should be presented in a cautious way – almost in a discounting manner.

- *Choose the language of the meeting and the communication carefully.* The language used should be descriptive, focused, specific, short, and simple. Language that is too judgmental, macro, stereotypical, lengthy, or complex should be avoided.

- *Ask the client for reactions to the data.* After all, the client is the number one customer, and it is most important that the client be pleased with the project.

- *Ask the client for recommendations.* The client may have some good suggestions for what needs to be changed to keep a project on track, or to put it back on track should it derail.

- *Use support and confrontation carefully.* These two actions are not mutually exclusive. At times, support and confrontation are both needed for a particular group. The client may need support and yet be confronted for lack of improvement or sponsorship. The project team may be confronted regarding the problem areas that have developed, but may need support as well.

- *React to and act on the data.* The different alternatives and possibilities should be weighed carefully to arrive at the adjustments that will be necessary.

- *Secure agreement from all key stakeholders.* It is essential to ensure that everyone is willing to make any changes that may be necessary.

- *Keep the feedback process short.* Allowing the process to become bogged down in long, drawn-out meetings or lengthy documents is a bad idea. If this occurs, stakeholders will avoid the process instead of being willing participants.

Following these steps will help move the project forward and generate useful feedback, often ensuring that adjustments are supported and can be executed.

Storytelling

Numbers cannot tell the whole story and that other means of communication are required to define and articulate the results. Stories are uniquely useful in their ability to bring people onto the same page and to organize information and present it in an efficient and accessible manner.

Stories foster empathy and connectedness, as they prioritize information and objectives. They provide a clear beginning, middle, and end. The narrative structure of a story is a teaching tool that can make complex data or relationships more easily accessible to an audience. Because the import-ant ideas are set in a metaphor that people can easily understand, both storytellers and listeners can move past arcane details and focus on the problem at hand. The immediacy of the story helps people track the important relationships while empathizing with the subject. This allows for a richer experience and fosters greater insight into the nature of the program, its place in the organization, and how the choices of the participants contribute to its success. [6]

Why tell stories? The simple reason is that they work. Here are eight of Paul Smith's ten most compelling reasons to tell stories, and he has much evidence to back them up:

1. Storytelling is simple.
2. Storytelling is timeless.
3. Stories are contagious.
4. Stories are easier to remember.
5. Stories inspire.
6. Stories appeal to all types of audiences.
7. Stories fit in the workplace where most of the work happens.
8. Telling stories shows respect for the audience. [7]

A logical structure is helpful to develop stories. Although the structure can vary, Figure 16.4 presents an efficient checklist appropriate for most stories from a story-telling expert.

Finally, some input from another storytelling expert. Here are ten of Carmine Gallo's secrets: [8]

1. Make stories at least 65 percent of your presentation.
2. Use simple words and analogies to hide complexity.

Hook
- Why should I listen to this story?

Content
- Where and when did it happen?
- Who is the hero? (Are they relatable?)
- What do they want? (Is that worthy?)

Challenge
- What is the problem/opportunity? (Relevant?)

Conflict
- What did the hero do about it? (Honest struggle?)

Resolution
- How did it turn out in the end?

Lesson
- What did you learn?

Recommended Action
- What do you want me to do?

Figure 16.4 Story Structure Checklist.

3. Enrich your story with specific and relevant details.
4. Deliver serious topics with a side of humor.
5. Tell authentic and personal stories tailored to your audience.
6. Be succinct; use a few well-chosen words.
7. Use pictures to illustrate your story.
8. Wrap data in stories to make a personal connection.
9. Take every opportunity to hone your presentation skills.
10. Don't make your story good; make it great.

Presentation of Results to Senior Management

Perhaps one of the most challenging and stressful types of communication is presenting an impact study to the senior management team, which also serves as the client for a project. The challenge is convincing this highly skeptical and critical group that outstanding results have been achieved (assuming they have) in a very reasonable time frame, addressing the salient points, and making sure the managers understand the process. Two potential reactions can create problems. First, if the results are very impressive, making the managers accept the data may be difficult. On the other extreme, if the data are negative, ensuring that managers don't overreact to the results and look for someone to blame is important. Several guidelines can help ensure that this process is planned and executed properly.

Arrange a face-to-face meeting with senior team members to review the results. If they are unfamiliar with the ROI Methodology, this meeting is necessary to make sure they understand the process. The good news is that they will probably attend the meeting because they have never seen ROI data developed for this type of project. The bad news is that it takes precious executive time, usually about an hour, for this presentation. After the meeting with a couple of presentations, an executive summary may suffice. At this point, the senior members will understand the process, so a shortened version may be appropriate. When a particular audience is familiar with the process, a brief version may be developed, including a one to two page summary with charts and graphs showing the six types of measures.

The results should not be disseminated before the initial presentation or even during the session, but should be saved until the end of the session. This will allow enough time to present the process and collect reactions to it before the target audience sees the ROI calculation. Present the ROI Methodology step by step, showing how the data were collected, when they were collected, who provided them, how the effect of the project was isolated from other influences, and how data were converted to monetary values. The various assumptions, adjustments, and conservative approaches are presented along with the total cost of the project, so that the target audience will begin to buy into the process of developing the ROI.

When the data are actually presented, the results are given one level at a time, starting with Level 1, moving through Level 5, and ending with the intangibles. This allows the audience to observe the reaction, learning, application and implementation, business impact, and ROI procedures. After some discussion of the meaning of the ROI, the intangible measures are presented. Allocate time for each level as appropriate for the audience. This helps to defuse potential emotional reactions to a very positive or negative ROI.

Show the consequences of additional accuracy if this is an issue. The trade-off for more accuracy and validity often is more expense. Address this issue when necessary, agreeing to add more data if they are required. Collect concerns, reactions, and issues involving the process and make adjustments accordingly for the next presentation.

Collectively, these steps will help in the preparation and presentation of one of the most important meetings in the ROI Methodology. Figure 16.5 shows the recommended approach to an important meeting with the sponsor.

Reactions to Communication

The best indicator of how effectively the results of a project have been communicated is the level of commitment and support from the managers, executives, and sponsors. The allocation of requested resources and voiced commitment from top management are strong evidence of management's positive perception of the results. In addition to this macro-level reaction, a few techniques can also be helpful in measuring the effectiveness of the communication effort.

When results are communicated, the reactions of the target audiences can be monitored. These reactions may include nonverbal gestures, oral remarks, written comments, or indirect actions that reveal how the communication was received. Usually, when results are presented in a meeting, the presenter will have some indication of how they were received by the group. Usually, the interest and attitudes of the audience can be quickly evaluated. Comments about the results, formal or informal, should be noted and tabulated.

Project team meetings are an excellent arena for discussing the reaction to communicated results. Comments can come from many sources depending on the particular target audience. When major project results are communicated, a feedback questionnaire may be administered to the entire audience or a sample of the audience. The purpose of the questionnaire is to determine the extent to which the audience understood and/or believed the information presented. This is practical only when the effectiveness of the communication will have a significant impact on future actions by the project team.

Final Thoughts

The final step in the ROI Methodology, communicating results, is a crucial step in the overall evaluation process. If this step is not executed adequately, the full impact of the results will not be recognized, and the study may amount to a waste of time. We began the chapter with general principles and steps for communicating project results; these can serve as a guide for any significant communication effort. We then discussed the various target audiences, with emphasis on the executive group because of its importance. We also suggested a format for a detailed evaluation report. Additionally, in this chapter, we presented the most commonly used media for communicating project results, including meetings, client publications, and electronic media.

17

Implementing and Sustaining ROI

In 2012, *Fortune* magazine featured Reed Hastings, Netflix founder and CEO, as its business person of the year. Founded in 1999, Netflix is now the world's largest online DVD rental service and video streaming firm, with more than 100,000 titles in its library, 60 million subscribers, and annual revenues of more than $4 billion. In 2002, the year Netflix went public, prime competitor Blockbuster had revenues of $5.5 billion, 40 million customers, and 6,000 stores. Yet only eight years later, on September 23, 2010, Blockbuster filed for bankruptcy. Netflix was added to the S&P 500 shortly after.[1]

When Netflix went public in 2002, a Blockbuster spokesperson said that it was "serving a niche market. We don't believe that there is enough demand for mail order – it's not a sustainable business model."[2] In 2005, as Netflix began moving into the streaming of videos over the Internet, the chief financial officer of Blockbuster said, "We don't think the economics [of streaming] works well right now."[3]

But before these public dismissals, there was a private one. In 2000, Reed Hastings flew to Dallas to meet with the senior executives at Blockbuster. He proposed that they purchase a 49% stake in Netflix, which would then become the online service provider for Blockbuster.com. Blockbuster wasn't interested. Blockbuster didn't have to buy Netflix—though it could have—to rent videos by mail. It had all the resources needed to crush a freshman firm that had revenues of only $270,000 and was a fraction of Blockbuster's size when it went public. But by the time Blockbuster got around to renting videos by mail in 2004, it was too late.[4]

This story is about the failure to change and see changes in the market. Blockbuster saw themselves as a DVD rental business. Netflix was an online movie service. Even though their mail-in rentals caught on first, they've been focused from day one on how to be a broadband delivery company. "It was why we originally named the company Netflix, not DVD-by-mail." The Netflix strategy emphasizes value, convenience, and selection. To deliver on these, they have been willing to cut prices and invest aggressively in new technologies ($50 million in 2006–2007 in video on demand). More important, they have been willing to cannibalize their old business to succeed in the new.[5]

While change and change management is needed for an organization's approach to innovation, change management is also needed for implementing a new measurement system to know, prove, and show the value of innovation. Even the best-designed process, model, or technique is worthless unless it is effectively and efficiently integrated into the organization.

Resistance to the ROI process arises from various stakeholders. Some of this resistance is based on fear and misunderstanding. Some is real, based on actual barriers and obstacles. Although the ROI methodology presented in this book is a step-by-step, methodical, and simplistic procedure, it can fail if it is not integrated properly, fully accepted, and supported by those who must make it work with innovation in the organization. This chapter focuses on some of the most effective ways of overcoming resistance to implementing the ROI process in an organization.

Why is this Important?

Six Sigma (6σ) is a set of techniques and tools for process improvement. It was introduced by engineers Bill Smith and Mikel J. Harry while working at Motorola in 1986. It seeks to improve the quality of the output of a process by identifying and removing the causes of defects and minimizing variability in manufacturing and business processes. It uses a set of quality management methods, mainly empirical, statistical methods, and creates a special infrastructure of people within the organization who are experts in these methods. Each Six Sigma project carried out within an organization follows a defined sequence of steps and has specific value targets, for example: reduce process cycle time, reduce pollution, reduce costs, increase customer satisfaction, and increase profits. The term Six Sigma was registered as a Motorola trademark on December 28, 1993.

Jake Welch made Six Sigma central to his business strategy at General Electric in 1995. Welch used Six Sigma to focus transformation efforts not just on efficiency, but also on growth. It served as a foundation for innovation throughout the organization, from manufacturing and product development to sales and service delivery functions. At GE, under Welch's leadership and determination, Six Sigma took on several key roles for its successful implementation:

- Executive Leadership included the CEO and other members of top management. They were responsible for setting up a vision for Six Sigma implementation. They also empowered the other role holders with the freedom and resources to explore new ideas for breakthrough improvements by transcending departmental barriers and overcoming inherent resistance to change.
- Champions took responsibility for Six Sigma implementation across the organization in an integrated manner. The Champions also acted as mentors to Black Belts.
- Master Black Belts, identified by Champions, acted as in-house coaches on Six Sigma, devoting 100% of their time to Six Sigma. They assisted Champions and guide Black Belts and Green Belts.
- Black Belts operated under Master Black Belts to apply Six Sigma methodology to specific projects. They devoted 100% of their valued time to Six Sigma.
- Green Belts were the employees who took up Six Sigma implementation along with their other job responsibilities, operating under the guidance of Black Belts.[6]

This top leadership focus made Six Sigma work in GE, and Jack Welch credited much of the success of GE to Six Sigma during his tenure. Although the process was created at Motorola, GE made it work and put Six Sigma on the map. Top executive leadership will be needed for a new measurement system for innovation to be successful.

To implement ROI and sustain it as an important accountability tool, the resistance must be minimized or removed. Successful implementation essentially equates to overcoming resistance. Here are five key reasons to have a detailed plan in place to overcome resistance.

Resistance is Always Present

Resistance to change is a constant. Sometimes, there are good reasons for resistance, but often it exists for the wrong reasons. The important point is to sort out both kinds of resistance and try to dispel the myths. When legitimate barriers are the basis for resistance, minimizing, or removing them altogether is the challenge.

Implementation is the Key to Success

As with any process, effective implementation is the key to its success. This occurs when the new technique, tool, or process is integrated into the routine framework for innovation. Without effective implementation, even the best process will fail. A process that is never removed from the shelf will never be understood, supported, or improved. Systematic steps must be in place for designing a comprehensive implementation process that will overcome resistance.

Consistency is Needed

Consistency is an important consideration as the ROI process is implemented. With consistency come accuracy and reliability . . . and accountability. The only way to make sure consistency is achieved is to follow clearly defined processes, procedures, and standards each time the ROI methodology is used. Proper effective implementation will ensure that this occurs.

Efficiency

Cost control and efficiency will be significant considerations in any major undertaking, and the ROI methodology is no exception. During implementation, tasks must be completed efficiently and effectively. Doing so will help ensure that process costs are kept to a minimum, time is used economically, and the process remains affordable.

Value is Maximized

Making ROI work through a systematic effort will maximize the value of innovation projects. It helps the organization to design for results from these projects. Funding is based on hard evidence or credible analysis instead of vague hopes and promises. The innovation budget can be maintained or enhanced in the future.

Implementing the Process: Overcoming Resistance

Resistance shows up in varied ways: in the form of comments, actions, or behaviors. Table 17.1 lists representative comments that indicate open resistance to the ROI process. Each comment signals an issue that must be resolved or addressed in some way. A few are based on realistic barriers, whereas others are based on myths that must be dispelled. Sometimes, resistance to the process reflects underlying concerns. For example, the individuals involved may fear losing control of their processes, and others may feel vulnerable to whatever action may follow if the process is not successful. Still others may be concerned about any process that brings change or requires the additional effort of learning.

Project team members may resist the ROI process and openly make comments similar to those listed in the table. It may take heavy persuasion and evidence of tangible benefits to convince team members that it is in their best interest to make the project a success. Although most team members do want to see the results of innovation, they may have concerns about the information they are asked to provide and about whether their personal performance is being judged while the project is undergoing evaluation.

The challenge is to implement the methodology systematically and consistently so that it becomes a normal course of action and a routine and standard process built into projects. The implementation necessary to overcome resistance covers a variety of areas. Figure 17.1 shows actions

Table 17.1 Typical Objections to Use of ROI Methodology.

Open Resistance
1. This will kill innovation.
2. This takes too much time.
3. Who is asking for this?
4. This is not my jobdescription.
5. I did not have input on this process.
6. I do not understand this process.
7. What happens when the results are negative?
8. How can we be consistent with this?
9. ROI looks too subjective.
10. Our managers will not support this.
11. ROI is too narrowly focused.
12. This is not practical.

Figure 17.1 Building Blocks to Overcome Resistance.

outlined in this chapter presented as building blocks to overcoming resistance. They are all necessary to build the proper framework to dispel myths and remove or minimize barriers. The remainder of this chapter presents specific strategies and techniques devoted to each of these building blocks.

Review Current Results

As a first step toward implementation, some organizations assess the current climate for achieving results. One way to do this is to develop a survey to determine current practices with the elements of the ROI Methodology. This compares the types of outcome data currently collected and used, the process to collect, analyze, and report data, and the standards used to guide the process. This may involve interviews with key stakeholders to determine their willingness to follow the project through to ROI. With an awareness of the current status, the project leaders can plan for significant changes and pinpoint particular issues that need support as the ROI process is implemented.

Developing Roles and Responsibilities

Defining and detailing specific roles and responsibilities for different groups and individuals addresses many of the resistance factors and helps pave a smooth path for implementation.

Identifying a Champion

As an early step in the process, one or more individual(s) should be designated as the internal leader or champion for the ROI methodology. As in most change efforts, someone must take responsibility for ensuring that the process is implemented successfully. This leader serves as a champion for ROI and is usually the one who understands the process best and sees vast potential for its contribution. More important, this leader is willing to teach others and will work to sustain sponsorship.

Developing the ROI Leader

The ROI leader is a member of the R&D team or innovation function who has the responsibility for evaluation. This person holds a full-time position in larger project teams or a part-time position in smaller teams. All functions in an organization (such as engineers, manufacturing, logistics, or supply chain) may also have an ROI leader who pursues the ROI methodology from the function's perspective. The typical job title for a full-time ROI leader is Manager of Measurement and Evaluation. Some organizations assign this responsibility to a team and empower it to lead the ROI effort.

In preparation for this assignment, individuals usually receive special training to build specific skills and knowledge of the ROI process. The role of the implementation leader is quite broad and serves a variety of specialized duties. In some organizations, the implementation leader can take on many roles, ranging from problem solver to communicator to ROI expert. Leading the ROI process can be a difficult and challenging assignment that requires unique skill. Fortunately, programs are available that teach these skills. For example, one such program is designed to certify individuals who will be assuming leadership roles in the implementation of the ROI methodology. For more detail, visit www.roiinstitute.net. This certification is built around 10 specific skill sets linked to successful ROI implementation, focusing on the critical areas of data collection, isolating the effects of the innovation project, converting data to monetary value, presenting evaluation data, and building capability. This process is quite comprehensive but may be necessary to build the skills necessary for taking on this challenging assignment.

Establishing a Task Force

Making the ROI methodology work well may require the use of a task force. A task force usually comprises a group of individuals from different parts of the function or department who are willing to develop the ROI methodology and implement it in the organization. The selection of the task force may involve volunteers, or participation may be mandatory depending on specific job responsibilities. The task force should represent the cross section necessary for accomplishing goals. Task forces have the additional advantage of bringing more people into the process and developing more ownership of and support for the ROI methodology. The task force must be large enough to cover the key areas but not so large that it becomes too cumbersome to function. Six to twelve members is a good size.

Assigning Responsibilities

Determining specific responsibilities is critical because confusion can arise when individuals are unclear about their specific assignments in the use of the ROI methodology. Responsibilities apply to two areas. The first is the measurement and evaluation responsibility of the entire project team. Everyone involved in innovation projects must have some responsibility for measurement and evaluation. These responsibilities include providing input on designing instruments, planning specific evaluations, analyzing data, and interpreting the results. Typical responsibilities include

- Ensuring that the initial analysis for the project includes specific business impact measures
- Developing specific application and business impact objectives for the project
- Keeping participants focused on application and impact objectives
- Communicating rationale and reasons for evaluation
- Assisting in follow-up activities to capture application and business impact data
- Providing assistance for data collection, data analysis, and reporting

Although involving each member of the project team in all these activities may not be appropriate, each individual should have at least one responsibility as part of his or her routine job duties. This assignment of responsibility keeps the ROI methodology from being disjointed and separated during projects. More important, it brings accountability to those directly involved in project implementation.

Another issue involves technical support. Depending on the size of the project team, establishing an individual or a group of technical experts to provide assistance with the ROI methodology may be helpful. When the group is established, the project team must understand that the experts have been assigned not for the purpose of relieving the team of its evaluation responsibilities, but to supplement its ROI efforts with technical expertise. These technical experts are typically the individuals who participated in the certification and training process to build special skills. Responsibilities of the technical support group involve six key areas:

1. Designing data collection instruments
2. Providing assistance for developing an evaluation strategy
3. Analyzing data, including specialized statistical analyses
4. Interpreting results and making specific recommendations
5. Developing an evaluation report or case study to communicate overall results
6. Providing technical support in all phases of the ROI methodology

The assignment of responsibilities for evaluation requires attention throughout the evaluation process. Although the project team must be assigned specific responsibilities during an evaluation, requiring others to serve in support functions to help with data collection is not unusual. These responsibilities are defined when a particular evaluation strategy plan is developed and approved.

Establishing Goals and Plans

Establishing goals, targets, and objectives is critical to the implementation, particularly when several projects are planned. The establishment of goals can include detailed planning documents for the overall process and for individual ROI projects. The next sections discuss aspects of the establishment of goals and plans.

Setting Evaluation Targets

Establishing specific targets for evaluation levels is an important way to make progress with measurement and evaluation. As emphasized throughout this book, not every project should be evaluated to ROI. Knowing in advance to which level the project will be evaluated helps in planning which measures will be needed and how detailed the evaluation must be at each level. Table 17.2 presents examples of targets set for

Table 17.2 Evaluation Targets in a Large Organization with Many Innovation Projects.

Level	Target
Level 1, Reaction	100%
Level 2, Learning	80%
Level 3, Application and Implementation	60%
Level 4, Business Impact	40%
Level 5, ROI	20%

evaluation at each level when there are many different types of projects. The setting of targets should be completed early in the process with the full support of the entire project team. If practical and feasible, the targets should also have the approval of key managers—particularly the senior management team.

Developing a Plan for Implementation

An important part of implementation is establishing a timetable for the complete implementation of the ROI methodology. This document becomes a master plan for completion of the different elements presented earlier. Beginning with forming a team and concluding with meeting the targets previously described, this schedule is a project plan for transitioning from the present situation to the desired future situation. Items on the schedule include developing specific ROI projects, building staff skills, developing policy, and teaching managers the process. Figure 17.2 is an example of an implementation plan. The more detailed the document, the more useful it becomes. The project plan is a living, long-range document that should be reviewed frequently and adjusted as necessary. More important, those engaged in work on the ROI methodology should always be familiar with the implementation plan.

Revising or Developing Policies and Guidelines

Another part of planning is revising or developing the organization's policy on project measurement and evaluation. The policy statement contains information developed specifically for the measurement and evaluation process. It is developed with input from the project team and key managers or stakeholders. Sometimes, policy issues are addressed during internal workshops designed to build measurement and evaluation skills. The policy statement addresses critical matters that will influence the effectiveness

	J	F	M	A	M	J	J	A	S	O	N	D	J	F	M	A	M	J	J	A	S	O	N
Team formed	▓																						
Responsibilities defined	▓																						
Policy developed			▓	▓	▓																		
Targets set	▓	▓																					
Workshops developed				▓	▓	▓																	
ROI Project (A)				▓	▓	▓	▓	▓	▓														
ROI Project (B)							▓	▓	▓	▓	▓	▓											
ROI Project (C)									▓	▓	▓	▓	▓	▓									
ROI Project (D)												▓	▓	▓	▓	▓	▓	▓	▓				
Project teams trained								▓	▓	▓	▓	▓	▓										
Managers trained																▓	▓	▓	▓	▓			
Support tools developed				▓	▓																		
Guidelines developed			▓	▓	▓	▓	▓																

Figure 17.2 Implementation Plan for a Large Organization with Many Innovation Projects.

of the measurement and evaluation process. These may include adopting the framework presented in this book, requiring objectives at all levels for some or all projects, and defining responsibilities for the project team.

Policy statements are important because they provide guidance and direction for the staff and others who work closely with the ROI methodology. These individuals keep the process clearly focused, and enable the group to establish goals for evaluation. Policy statements also provide an opportunity to communicate basic requirements and fundamentals of performance and accountability. More than anything else, they serve as learning tools to teach others, especially when they are developed in a collaborative way. If policy statements are developed in isolation, staff and management will be denied the sense of their ownership, making them neither effective nor useful.

Guidelines for measurement and evaluation are important for showing how to use the tools and techniques, guide the design process, provide consistency in the ROI process, ensure that appropriate methods are used, and place the proper emphasis on each of the areas. The guidelines are more technical than policy statements and often include detailed procedures showing how the process is undertaken and developed. They often include specific forms, instruments, and tools necessary to facilitate the process.

Preparing the Project Team

Project team members may resist the ROI methodology. They often see evaluation as an unnecessary intrusion into their responsibilities that absorbs precious time and stifles creative freedom. The cartoon character Pogo perhaps characterized it best when he said, "We have met the enemy, and he is us." Several issues must be addressed when preparing the project team for ROI implementation.

Involving the Project Team

For each key issue or major decision involving ROI implementation, the project team should be involved in the process. As policy statements are prepared and evaluation guidelines developed, team input is essential. Resistance is more difficult if the team helped design and develop the ROI process. Convene meetings, brainstorming sessions, and task forces to involve the team in every phase of developing the framework and supporting documents for ROI.

Using ROI as a Learning and Project Improvement Tool

One reason the project team may resist the ROI process is that the project's effectiveness will be fully exposed, putting the reputation of the team on the line. They may have a fear of failure. To overcome this, the ROI methodology should be clearly positioned as a tool for learning, not a tool for evaluating project team performance (at least not during the early years of use). Team members will not be interested in developing a process that may reflect unfavorably on their performance.

Evaluators can learn as much from failures as from success. If the project is not working, it is best to find out quickly so that issues can be understood firsthand, not from others. If a project is ineffective and not producing the desired results, the failure will eventually be known to clients and the management group (if they are not aware of it already). A lack of results will make managers less supportive of immediate and future projects. If the project's weaknesses are identified and adjustments quickly made, not only can more effective projects be developed, but the credibility of and respect for project implementation will be enhanced.

Teaching the Team

The project team and project evaluator usually have inadequate skills in measurement and evaluation, and will need to develop some expertise.

Measurement and evaluation are not always a formal part of the team's or evaluator's job preparation. Consequently, the project team leader must learn ROI methodology and its systematic steps, and the evaluator must learn to develop an evaluation strategy and specific plan, to collect and analyze data from the evaluation, and to interpret results from data analysis. A one- to two-day workshop can help build the skills and knowledge needed to understand the process and appreciate what it can do for project success and for the client organization. Such a teach-the-team workshop can be a valuable tool in ensuring successful implementation of ROI methodology.

Initiating ROI Studies

The first tangible evidence of the value of using the ROI methodology may be seen at the initiation of the first project for which an ROI calculation is planned. The next sections discuss aspects of identifying appropriate projects and keeping them on track.

Selecting the Initial Project

It is critical that appropriate projects be selected for ROI analysis. Only certain types of projects qualify for comprehensive, detailed analysis. Characteristic of projects that are suitable for analysis are those that: (1) are important to strategic objectives; (2) involve large groups of participants; (3) will be linked to major operational problems and opportunities upon completion; (4) are expensive; (5) are time-consuming; (6) have high visibility; and (7) have the interest of management in performing their evaluation. Using these or similar criteria, the project leader must select the appropriate projects to consider for ROI evaluation. Ideally, sponsors should agree with or approve the criteria.

Developing the Planning Documents

Perhaps the two most useful ROI documents are the data collection plan and the ROI analysis plan. The data collection plan shows what data will be collected, the methods used, the sources, the timing, and the assignment of responsibilities. The ROI analysis plan shows how specific analyses will be conducted, including how to isolate the effects of the project and how to convert data to monetary values. Each evaluator should know how to develop these plans. These documents were discussed in detail in various chapters in this book.

Reporting Progress

As the projects are developed and the ROI implementation gets under way, status meetings should be conducted to report progress and discuss critical issues with appropriate team members. These meetings keep the project team focused on the critical issues, generate the best ideas for addressing problems and barriers, and build a knowledge base for better implementation evaluation of future projects. Sometimes, these meetings are facilitated by an external consultant, perhaps an expert in the ROI process. In other cases, the project leader may facilitate. In essence, the meetings serve three major purposes: reporting progress, learning, and planning.

Establishing Discussion Groups

Because the ROI methodology is considered difficult to understand and apply, establishing discussion groups to teach the process may be helpful. These groups can supplement formal workshops and other learning activities and are often very flexible in format. Groups are usually facilitated by an external ROI consultant or the project leader. In each session, a new topic is presented for a thorough discussion that should extend to how the topic applies to the organization. The process can be adjusted for different topics as new group needs arise, driving the issues. Ideally, participants in group discussions will have an opportunity to apply, explore, or research the topics between sessions. Group assignments such as reviewing a case study or reading an article are appropriate between sessions to further the development of knowledge and skills associated with the process.

Preparing the Sponsors and Management Team

Perhaps no group is more important to the use of the ROI methodology than the management team that must allocate resources for the project and support its implementation. In addition, the management team often provides input to and assistance for the ROI methodology. Preparing, training, and developing the management team should be carefully planned and executed.

One effective approach for preparing executives and managers for ROI is to conduct a briefing. Varying in duration from one hour to half a day, a practical briefing such as this can provide critical information and enhance support for ROI use. Managers leave these briefings with greater appreciation of the use of ROI and its potential impact on projects, and with a clearer understanding of their role in the ROI process. More important, they often renew their commitment to react to and use the data collected by the ROI methodology.

A strong, dynamic relationship between the project team and key managers is essential for successful implementation of the ROI methodology. A productive partnership is needed that requires each party to understand the concerns, problems, and opportunities of the other. The development of such a beneficial relationship is a long-term process that must be deliberately planned for and initiated by key project team members. The decision to commit resources and support to a project may be based on the effectiveness of this relationship.

Removing Obstacles

As the ROI methodology is implemented, there will inevitably be obstacles to its progress. The obstacles are based on concerns discussed in this chapter, some of which may be valid, others of which may be based on unrealistic fears or misunderstandings.

Dispelling Myths

As part of the implementation, attempts should be made to dispel the myths and remove or minimize the barriers or obstacles. Much of the controversy regarding ROI stems from misunderstandings about what the process can and cannot do and how it can or should be implemented in an organization. After years of experience with ROI, and having noted reactions during hundreds of projects and workshops, we have recognized many misunderstandings about ROI. These misunderstandings are listed below as myths about the ROI methodology:

- ROI is too complex for most users.
- ROI is expensive and consumes too many critical resources.
- If senior management does not require ROI, there is no need to pursue it.
- ROI is a passing fad.
- ROI is only one type of data.
- ROI is not future-oriented; it only reflects past performance.
- ROI is rarely used by organizations.
- The ROI methodology cannot be easily replicated.
- ROI is not a credible process; it is too subjective.
- ROI cannot be used with soft conceptual projects.

- Isolating the influence of other factors is not always possible.
- ROI is appropriate only for large organizations.
- No standards exist for the ROI methodology.

For more information on these myths see www.roiinstitute.net.

Delivering Bad News

One of the obstacles perhaps most difficult to overcome is receiving inadequate, insufficient, or disappointing news. Addressing a bad-news situation is an issue for most project leaders and other stakeholders involved in a project. Table 17.3 presents the guidelines to follow when addressing bad news. As the table makes clear, the time to think about bad news is early in the process, but without ever losing sight of the value of the bad news. In essence, bad news means that things can change and need to change and that the situation can improve. The team and others need to be convinced that good news can be found in a bad-news situation.

Using the Data

It is unfortunately too often the case that projects are evaluated and significant data are collected, but nothing is done with the data. Failure to use data is a tremendous obstacle because once the project has concluded, the team has a tendency to move on to the next project or issue and get on with

Table 17.3 How to Address Bad News.

Delivering Bad News
• Never fail to recognize the power to learn from and improve with a negative study.
• Look for red flags along the way.
• Lower outcome expectations with key stakeholders along the way.
• Look for data everywhere.
• Never alter the standards.
• Remain objective throughout the process.
• Prepare the team for the bad news.
• Consider different scenarios.
• Find out what went wrong.
• Adjust the story line to "Now we have data that show how to make this project more successful." In an odd way, this puts a positive spin on data that are less than positive.
• Drive improvement.

Table 17.4 How Data Should Be Used.

Use of evaluation data	Appropriate level of data				
	1	2	3	4	5
Adjust project design	✓	✓			
Improve implementation			✓	✓	
Influence application and impact			✓	✓	
Improve management support for the project			✓	✓	
Improve stakeholder satisfaction			✓	✓	✓
Recognize and reward participants		✓	✓	✓	
Justify or enhance budget				✓	✓
Reduce costs		✓	✓	✓	✓
Market projects in the future	✓		✓	✓	✓

other priorities. Table 17.4 shows how the different levels of data can be used to improve projects. It is critical that the data be used—the data were essentially the justification for undertaking the project evaluation in the first place. Failure to use the data may mean that the entire evaluation was a waste. As the table illustrates, many reasons exist for collecting the data and using them after collection. These can become action items for the team to ensure that changes and adjustments are made. Also, the client or sponsor must act to ensure that the uses of data are appropriately addressed.

Monitoring Progress

A final element of the implementation process is monitoring the overall progress made and communicating that progress. Although often over-looked, an effective progress report can help keep the implementation on target and can let others know what the ROI methodology is accomplishing for project leaders and the client.

The initial schedule for implementation of ROI is based on key events or milestones. Routine progress reports should be developed to communicate the status of these events or milestones. Reports are usually developed at six-month intervals but may be more frequent for short-term projects. Two target audiences—the project team and senior managers—are critical for progress reporting. All project team members should be kept informed of the progress, and senior managers should know the extent to which ROI is being implemented and how it is working within the organization.

Final Thoughts

Even the best model or process will die if it is not used and sustained. This chapter explored the implementation of the ROI process and ways to sustain its use. If not approached in a systematic, logical, and planned way, the ROI process will not be an integral part of project evaluation, and project accountability will consequently suffer. This chapter presented the different elements that must be considered and issues that must be addressed to ensure that implementation is smooth and uneventful. Smooth implementation is the most effective means of overcoming resistance to ROI. The result provides a complete integration of ROI as a mainstream component of major projects.

This book makes the case for a new measurement system for innovation, to know, prove, and show what works to measure impact and ROI. This helps to plan and evaluate a given project and determine if and how to replicate.

ROI is the ultimate measure of economic success. It is *the* indicator of a given project's viability and value for some executives. But there is perhaps more value in the other data sets and the actual process. Some believe that ROI can't be measured for certain innovation projects, given their uncertainty and complexity. Others believe that ROI will kill innovation. The innovation project may be the cure for a major disease, in which case the value is many times the investment if it works, or negative value if it doesn't. While these claims can be valid to a certain extent in extreme cases, this should not stand in this way of implementing a process.

The benefit of evaluating innovation goes way beyond the possibility of an accounting measure, such as ROI or something else. The ROI Methodology is a means to design, plan, and communicate, as well as to measure in the more traditional sense. This has been an ongoing theme of this book.

The ROI Methodology approach is sophisticated in its systematic logical framework, more than its technical requirements. The capabilities required to use the Methodology are not overwhelming. It requires logical thinking, project management, attention to detail, and the desire to solve problems, and make adjustments before and during a project, as opposed to reliance on *post facto* traditional accounting analysis. It requires communication and explanations to build organizational consensus and engagement.

When it comes to knowing, proving, and showing the value of innovation:

- Hope is not a strategy
- Luck is not a factor
- Doing nothing is not an option

You are now armed with a compelling rationale, an understanding of how, and confidence in your capabilities to get the job done. Don't let perfection get in the way of progress. Remember, change is inevitable, progress is optional. Learn, improve, and gain efficiency. And let us know if we can help. You may reach us at info@roiinstitute.net and at

PO Box 380637, Birmingham, Al 35238-0637.

References

FM

1. Keely, Larry, Ryan Pikkel, Brian Quinn, and Helen Walters. *Ten Types of Innovation: The Discipline of Building Breakthroughs*. Hoboken, NJ: Wiley, 2013.

Chapter 1

1. "Ideas Know No Borders." *Fortune*. August 2017. 10.
2. P. Drucker. *Innovation and Entrepreneurship: Practice and Principles*. Waltham, MA: Butterworth Heineman. 1985.
3. C.A. O'Reilly and M.L. Tushman. *Lead and Disrupt: How to Solve the Innovator's Dilemma*. Stanford, CA: Stanford Business Press. 2016.
4. "The Global 500." *Fortune*. August 2017. 57.
5. "Briefing." *Fortune*. July 2017.
6. G. Satell. *Mapping Innovation: A Playbook for Navigating a Disruptive Age*. New York, NY: McGraw-Hill. 2017.
7. D. Robertson and K. Linebeck. *The Power of Little Ideas: A Third Way to Innovate for Market Success*. Boston, MA: Harvard Business Review Press. 2017.

8. D.C. Robertson and B. Breen. *Brick by Brick: How LEGO Rewrote the Rules of Innovation and Conquered the Global Toy Industry*. New York, NY: Crown Business. 2013.

9. L. Keeley and H. Walters. *Ten Types of Innovation: The Discipline of Building Breakthroughs*. Hoboken, NJ: Wiley. 2013.

10. V. Govindarajan and C. Trimble. *Beyond the Idea: How to Execute Innovation in Any Organization*. New York, NY: St. Martins Press. 2013.

11. G. Satell. *Mapping Innovation: A Playbook for Navigating a Disruptive Age*. New York, NY: McGraw-Hill. 2017.

12. A.M. Knott. *How Innovation Really Works: Using the Trillion-Dollar R&D Fix to Drive Growth*. New York, NY: McGraw-Hill. 2017.

13. H. Chesbrough. *Open Innovation: The New Imperative for Creating and Profiting from Technology*. Boston, MA: Harvard Business Review Press. 2003.

14. R. Zirkelbach. "The Cost of Innovation." *The Catalyst*, PhRMA. November 2014. http://catalyst.phrma.org/the-cost-of-innovation.

15. "What Does Innovation Cost? Not Always A Lot." *Destination Innovation*. http://www.destination-innovation.com/what-does-innovation-cost-not-always-a-lot/.

16. L.A. Hill, G. Brandeau, E. Truelove, and K. Linebeck. *Collective Genius: The Art and Practice of Leading Innovation*. Boston, MA: Harvard Business Review Press. 2014.

17. G. Bradt. "Why You Should Eliminate Your Chief Innovation Officer." *Forbes*. May 16, 2016.

18. M. McKeown. *The Innovation Book: How to Manage Ideas and Execution for Outstanding Results*. Harlow, UK: Pearson. 2014.

19. A. Imber. *The Innovation Formula: The 14 Science-Based Keys for Creating a Culture Where Innovation Thrives*. Hoboken, NJ: Wiley. 2016.

20. E. Griffith. "On Message, Off Target: The World is Eager to Dock Start-up Style Business Practices, but What If They're Wrong." *Fortune*. July 2017.

21. T. Kelley. *The Ten Faces of Innovation: IDEO's Strategies for Beating the Devil's Advocate and Driving Creativity Throughout Your Organization*. New York, NY: Currency, Doubleday. 2005.

22. J.P. Andrew and H.L. Sirkin. *Payback: Reaping the Rewards of Innovation*. Boston, MA: Harvard Business Review Press. 2006.

23. D. Nichols. *Return on Ideas: A Practical Guide to Making Innovation Pay*. Chichester, UK: John Wiley & Sons, Ltd. 2008.

24. M. Ramanujam and G. Tacke. *Monetizing Innovation: How Smart Companies Design the Product Around the Price*. Hoboken, NJ: Wiley. 2016.

Chapter 2

1. M. McKeon. *The Innovation Book: How to Manage Ideas and Execution for Outstanding Results*. Harlow, UK: Pearson Harlow. 2014.

2. "Designing Global Businesses for Innovation and Growth." The Conference Board. 2014.
3. M. McKeon. *The Innovation Book: How to Manage Ideas and Execution for Outstanding Results.* Harlow, UK: Pearson Harlow. 2014.
4. M. McKeon. *The Innovation Book: How to Manage Ideas and Execution for Outstanding Results.* Harlow, UK: Pearson Harlow. 2014.
5. E. Ries. *The Lean Startup: How Today's Entrepreneurs Use Continuous Innovation to Create Radically Successful Businesses.* New York, NY: Crown Business Books. 2011.
6. C. Seelos and J. Mair. *Innovation and Scaling for Impact: How Effective Social Enterprises Do It.* Stanford, CA: Stanford University Press. 2017.
7. A. Griffin, R. Price, and B.A. Vojak. *Serial Innovators: How Individuals Create and Deliver Breakthrough Innovations in Mature Firms.* Stanford, CA: Stanford University Press. 2012.
8. Global Innovation Index. 2015.
9. "Comparative Analysis of Innovation Performance." European Innovation Scorecard. 2009.
10. Global Creativity Index (constructed by Martin Prosperity Institute). 2015.
11. Global Entrepreneurship Index (constructed by the Global Entrepreneurship and Development Institute). 2016.
12. Portfolio Innovation Index. 2016.
13. H. Hollanders. "Measuring Services Innovation: Service Sector Innovation Index." Six Countries Programme (6CP) Workshop. October 2008.
14. "Measuring Sectoral Innovation Capability in Nine Areas of the UK Economy." NESTA. Report for Innovation Index project. 2009.
15. "Productive Innovation Index of the Pharmaceutical Industry." IDEA Pharma. 2016.
16. "Productive Innovation Index of the Financial Services." Innotribe. 2015.
17. "McKinsey Global Survey Results: Assessing Innovation Methods." McKinsey. 2010.
18. "Measuring Innovation 2006." Boston Consulting Group. 2006.
19. "Technology Innovation Survey." KPMG. 2013.
20. J.X. Hao, B. van Ark, and A. Ozyildirim. "Signposts of Innovation: A Review of Innovation Metrics." The Conference Board. 2017.
21. "McKinsey Global Survey Results: Assessing Innovation Methods." McKinsey. 2008.
22. R. Cordero. "The Measurement of Innovation Performance in the Firm: An Overview." *Research Policy*, vol. 19. 185 – 192.
23. L. Morris. "Innovation Metrics: The Innovation Process and How to Measure It." Innovation Labs. 2008.
24. S. Jefferson. "The Cultural Barrier." *Chief Innovation Officer*, issue 6. 2015.
25. J. Tidd, J. Bessant, and K. Bavitt. *Managing Innovation: Integrating Technological Market and Organizational Change.* Chichester, UK: Wiley & Sons. 2005.
26. M.T. Hansen and J. Birkinshaw. *The Innovation Value Chain.* Boston, MA: Harvard Business Review. 2007.

27. L. Morris. "Innovation Metrics: The Innovation Process and How to Measure It." *Innovation Labs*. 2008.
28. J.X. Hao, B. van Ark, and A. Ozyildirim. "Signposts of Innovation: A Review of Innovation Metrics." The Conference Board. 2017.

Chapter 3

1. "The World's Most Innovative Companies." *Forbes*. September 5, 2017.
2. A.M. Knott. *How Innovation Really Works: Using the Trillion-Dollar R&D Fix to Drive Growth*. New York, NY: McGraw-Hill. 2017.
3. T. Brown. *Change By Design: How Design Thinking Transforms Organizations and Inspires Innovation*. New York, NY: Harper Business. 2009.
4. I. Mootee. *Design Thinking for Strategic Innovation: What They Can't Teach You at Business or Design School*. Hoboken, NJ: Wiley. 2013
5. J.J. Phillips and P.P. Phillips. *The Business Case for Learning: Using Design Thinking to Deliver Business Results and Increase the Investment in Talent Development*. Alexandria, VA: HRDQ and ATD Press. 2017.
6. R.S. Kaplan and D.P. Norton. *The Balanced Scorecard: Translating Strategy into Action*. Boston, MA: Harvard Business Review Press. 1996.

Chapter 4

1. H. Wolfson. "Program Reduces Blood Infections in Alabama Hospitals." The Birmingham News. October 25, 2011.
2. J.J. Phillips and P.P. Phillips. *Show Me the Money: How to Determine ROI in People, Projects, and Programs*. San Francisco, CA: Barrett-Koehler Publishers, Inc. 2007.

Chapter 5

1. *Fortune*. August 1, 2017.
2. J.M. Jakicic, K.K. Davis, and R.J. Rogers. "Effects of Wearable Technology Combined with a Lifestyle Intervention on Long-Term Weight Loss." *JAMA*. 2016.
3. J.J. Phillips and P.P. Phillips. *Value for Money: Measuring the Return on Non-Capital Investments*. Birmingham, AL: BWE Press. 2018.

Chapter 6

1. A.J. Rucci, S.P. Kim, and R.T. Quinn. "The Employee-Customer Profit Chain at Sears." Harvard Business Review. January – February 1998. 82 – 97.

Chapter 7

1. Gram Vikas. http://www.gramvikas.org/
2. C. Seelos and J. Mair. *Innovation and Scaling for Impact: How Effective Social Enterprises Do It.* Stanford, CA: Stanford University Press. 2017.
3. R. Safion. "Trust Your Feelings, Now More Than Ever." *FastCompany.com.* 2017.

Chapter 8

1. S. Mautz. *Make It Matter: How Managers Can Motivate by Creating Meaning.* New York, NY: AMACOM. 2015.
2. V.V. Buzchero, J.J. Phillips, P.P. Phillips, and Z.L. Phillips. *Measuring ROI in Healthcare: Tools and Techniques to Measure the Impact and ROI in Healthcare Improvement Projects and Programs.* New York, NY: McGraw-Hill. 2013.
3. W. Miller. "Building the Ultimate Resource: Today's Competitive Edge Comes from Intellectual Capital." *Management Review.* January 1999. 42 – 44.
4. P. Senge. *The Fifth Discipline: The Art and Practice of the Learning Organization.* New York, NY: Random House. 1990.
5. K.E. Watkins and V.J. Marsick, editors., J. Phillips, series editor. *Creating the Learning Organization.* Alexandria, VA: ASTD Press. 1996.
6. L.D. Antionette and R. Lepsinger. *The Art and Science of Competency Models: Pinpointing Critical Success Factors in Organizations.* San Francisco, CA: Jossey-Bass/Pfeiffer. 1999.
7. V. Govindarajan and C. Trimble. *Beyond the Idea: How to Execute Innovation in Any Organization.* New York, NY: St. Martins Press. 2013.
8. J.J. Phillips and P.P. Phillips. *The Business Case for Learning: Using Design Thinking to Deliver Business Results and Increase the Investment in Talent Development.* Alexandria, VA: HRDQ and ATD Press. 2017.
9. J.J. Phillips and P.P. Phillips. *Handbook of Training Evaluation and Measurement Methods.* Abingdon, UK: Routledge. 2016.

Chapter 9

1. P.P. Phillips, J.J. Phillips, and R. Ray. *Measuring the Success of Leadership Development: A Step-by-Step Guide for Measuring Impact and Calculating ROI.* Alexandria, VA: ATD Press. 2015.
2. V.V. Buzchero, J.J. Phillips, P.P. Phillips, and Z.L. Phillips. *Measuring ROI in Healthcare: Tools and Techniques to Measure the Impact and ROI in Healthcare Improvement Projects and Programs.* New York, NY: McGraw-Hill. 2013.
3. J.J. Phillips and P.P. Phillips. *Handbook of Training Evaluation and Measurement Methods.* Abingdon, UK: Routledge. 2016.

Chapter 10

1. P.P. Phillips. *Measuring ROI in Learning and Development: Case Studies from Global Organizations*. Alexandria, VA: ASTD Press. 2012.
2. S. Kerr. "On the Folly of Rewarding A, While Hoping for B." *Academy of Management Journal*, vol. 18. 1995. 769 – 783. / A. Mayo. *Measuring Human Capital*. London: The Institute of Chartered Accountants. June 2003.
3. H.R. Nalbantian, R.A. Guzzo, D. Keiffer, and J. Doherty. *Play to Your Strengths: Managing Your Internal Labor Markets for Lasting Competitive Advantage*. New York, NY: McGraw-Hill. 2004.

Chapter 11

1. S.D. Levitt and S.J. Dubner. *Freakonomics: A Rogue Economist Explores the Hidden Side of Everything*. New York, NY: William Morrow. 2005.
2. P.P. Phillips and J.J. Phillips. *Value for Money: Measuring the Return on Non-Capital Investments*. Birmingham, AL: ROI Institute, Inc. 2018.
3. J. Surowieki. *The Wisdom of Crowds: Why the Many Are Smarter Than the Few and How Collective Wisdom Shapes Businesses, Economics, Societies and Nations*. New York, NY: Doubleday. 2004.

Chapter 12

4. P.W. Farris, N.T. Bendle, P.E. Pfeifer, and D.J. Robstein. *Marketing Metrics: 50+ Metrics Every Executive Should Master*. Upper Saddle River, NJ: Wharton School Publishing. 2006.
5. C. Fishman. *The Wal-Mart Effect: How the World's Most Powerful Company Really Works – and How It's Transforming the American Economy*. New York, NY: Penguin. 2006.
6. P.W. Farris, N.T. Bendle, P.E. Pfeifer, and D.J. Robstein. *Marketing Metrics: 50+ Metrics Every Executive Should Master*. Upper Saddle River, NJ: Wharton School Publishing. 2006.
7. J. Campanella, editor. *Principles of Quality Costs*, 3rd edition. Milwaukee, WI: American Society for Quality. 1999.
8. D. Ulrich, editor. *Delivering Results*. Boston, MA: Harvard Business School Press. 1998.
9. M. Graham, K. Bishop, and R. Birdsong. "Self-Directed Work Teams" in *Action: Measuring Return on Investment*, vol. 1. J.J. Phillips, editor. Alexandria, VA: ASTD Press. 1994. 105 – 122.

Chapter 13

1. M. Heffernan. Beyond Measure: The Big Impact of Small Changes. New York, NY: TED Books, Simon & Schuster. 2015.
2. R.E.S. Boulton, B.D. Libert, and S.M. Samek. *Cracking the Value Code*. New York, NY: Harper Business. 2000.
3. K.T. Jackson. Building Reputational Capital: Strategies for Integrity and Fair Play that Improve the Bottom Line. Oxford, UK: Oxford University Press. 2004.
4. D. Tracy and W.J. Morin. Truth, Trust, and the Bottom Line: 7 Steps to Trust-Based Management. Chicago, IL: Dearborn Trade. 2001.
5. M.C. Worline and J.E. Dutton. Awakening Compassion at Work: The Quiet Power That Elevates People and Organizations. San Francisco, CA: Barrett-Koehler Publishers, Inc. 2017.
6. The Federal Reserve. https://www.federalreserve.gov/
7. J. Alden. "Measuring the 'Unmeasureable.'" *Performance Improvement*. May/June 2006. 7.
8. T. Bradberry and J. Greaves. "Emotional Intelligence 2.0." San Diego, CA: TalentSmart. 2009.
9. P.P. Phillips, J.J. Phillips, and R. Ray. *Measuring the Success of Employee Engagement: A Step-by-Step Guide for Measuring Impact and Calculating ROI.* Alexandria, VA: ATD Press. 2016.
10. J. Collins. Good to Great and the Social Sectors. New York, NY: Harper Collins. 2005.

Chapter 14

1. K. Kennedy. "Fight Against Health Care Fraud Recovers $4.1B." *USA Today*. February 14, 2012. https://usatoday30.usatoday.com/news/washington/story/2012-02-14/sebelius-holder-announce-health-care-fraud-money/53097474/1
2. "Annual Employee Benefits Report." *Nation's Business*. January 2006.

Chapter 15

1. P.P. Phillips and J.J. Phillips. *Value for Money: Measuring the Return on Non-Capital Investments*. Birmingham, AL: ROI Institute, Inc. 2018.
2. J.J. Phillips and P.P. Phillips. *The Consultant's Guide to Results-Driven Business Proposals: How to Write Proposals That Forecast Impact and ROI*. New York, NY: McGraw Hill. 2010.
3. P.E. Tetlock and D. Gerdner. *Superforecasting: The Art and Science of Prediction*. New York, NY: Crown Publishers. 2016.

4. S.J. Armstrong. *Principles of Forecasting: A Handbook for Researchers and Practitioners.* Boston, MA: Kluwer Academic Publishers. 2001.
5. L.S. Maisel and G. Cokins. *Predictive Business Analytics: Forward-Looking Capabilities to Improve Business Performance.* Hoboken, NJ: Wiley. 2014.
6. D.A. Bowers. *Forecasting for Control and Profit.* Menlo Park, CA: Crisp Publications. 1997.

Chapter 16

1. P. Smith. *Lead with a Story: A Guide to Crafting Business Narratives That Captivate, Convince, and Inspire.* New York, NY: AMACOM, 2012.
2. H. Evans. *Do I Make Myself Clear? Why Writing Well Matters.* New York, NY: Little, Brown and Company. 2017.
3. D. Price. *Well Said! Presentations and Conversations that Get Results.* New York, NY: AMACOM. 2012.
4. P. Block. *Flawless Consulting,* 3rd edition. San Diego, CA: Pfeiffer. 2011.
5. I. Mootee. *Design Thinking for Strategic Innovation: What They Can't Teach You at Business or Design School.* Hoboken, NJ: Wiley. 2013
6. P. Smith. *Lead with a Story: A Guide to Crafting Business Narratives That Captivate, Convince, and Inspire.* New York, NY: AMACOM, 2012.
7. C. Gallo. *The Storyteller's Secret: From TED Speakers to Business Legends, Why Some Ideas Catch On and Others Don't.* New York, NY: St. Martin's Press. 2016.

Chapter 17

1. C.A. O'Reilly and M.L. Tushman. *Lead and Disrupt: How to Solve the Innovator's Dilemma.* Stanford, CA: Stanford Business Press. 2016.
2. HBS Case 9-607-138. "Netflix." Boston, MA: Harvard Business Publishing. May 2007.
3. K. Frieswick. "The Turning Point." *CFO Magazine.* April 2005. 48.
4. C.A. O'Reilly and M.L. Tushman. *Lead and Disrupt: How to Solve the Innovator's Dilemma.* Stanford, CA: Stanford Business Press. 2016.
5. Stanford GSB Case CG-19. "Equity on Demand: The Netflix Approach to Compensation." Stanford, CA: Stanford Graduate School of Business. January 2010.
6. Wikipedia. https://en.wikipedia.org/wiki/Six_Sigma.

Index

CPSIA information can be obtained
at www.ICGtesting.com
Printed in the USA
LVHW01*2222220218
567625LV00001B/1/P